Leviticus and Its Reception in the Dead Sea Scrolls from Qumran

Leviticus and Its Reception in the Dead Sea Scrolls from Qumran

Baesick Choi

PICKWICK *Publications* · Eugene, Oregon

LEVITICUS AND ITS RECEPTION IN THE DEAD SEA SCROLLS FROM QUMRAN

Pickwick Publications
An Imprint of Wipf and Stock Publishers
199 W. 8th Ave., Suite 3
Eugene, OR 97401

www.wipfandstock.com

PAPERBACK ISBN: 978-1-5326-9222-2
HARDCOVER ISBN: 978-1-5326-9223-9
EBOOK ISBN: 978-1-5326-9224-6

Cataloguing-in-Publication data:

Names: Choi, Baesick, author.

Title: Leviticus and its reception in the Dead Sea Scrolls from Qumran / Baesick Choi.

Description: Eugene, OR: Pickwick Publications, 2020. | Includes bibliographical references and index.

Identifiers: ISBN 978-1-5326-9222-2 (paperback). | ISBN 978-1-5326-9223-9 (hardcover). | ISBN 978-1-5326-9224-6 (ebook).

Subjects: LCSH: Bible.—Leviticus—Criticism, interpretation, etc. | Bible.—Leviticus—Hebrew Versions. | Bible.—Leviticus—Aramaic—Versions. | Dead Sea Scrolls. | Book of Jubilees—Criticism, textual.

Classification: BS1255.52 C27 2020 (print). | BS1255.52 (ebook).

Manufactured in the U.S.A. OCTOBER 12, 2020

Unless otherwise stated, biblical quotations in English are from *The Holy Bible: New Revised Standard Version, Anglicized* (New York: Division of Christian Education of the National Council of the Churches of Christ in the United States of America, 1995).

All Hebrew Bible quotations are from *Biblica Hebraica Stuttgartensia* (Stuttgart: Deutsche Bibelgesellschaft), 1990.

Unless otherwise stated, all Hebrew texts of the Dead Sea Scrolls are taken from the Hebrew texts in Accordance Bible Software module "QUMRAN." See Martin G. Abegg, "Qumran Text and Grammatical Tags," Version 12.0.6 in Accordance (Altamonte Springs, Florida: OakTree Software), 2017.

Contents

Acknowledgments

I AM SO THANKFUL for the opportunity to study the Scriptures at the University of Manchester for my doctoral dissertation. Though challenging, it was a very enjoyable academic journey. However, this work could not have been completed without the kind support and help of several people to whom I wish to express my thanks.

First of all, I am deeply grateful to my supervisor, Prof. George J. Brooke, for his immeasurable time, clear guidance, insightful instruction, and careful reading of my manuscript. Words cannot express the depth of my gratitude for Prof. Brooke. In addition, I wish to thank Dr. Renate Smithuis for her careful reading of my text and her comments. Also, I would like to give special thanks to Dr. Matthew Collins, Prof. Peter Oakes, and Prof. Dirk Büchner for their many insightful academic suggestions and wise counsel that truly increased the value of this dissertation.

Next, I would like to express thanks to my parish at West Franklin Charge (Bethany & Maple Grove United Methodist Churches) in Ferrum, Virginia. Their endless love, support, and generosity always encouraged me to continue my studies at Manchester, giving me great comfort and joy. I cannot find adequate words to convey the love in my humble heart toward them. My sincere thanks also goes to many of my colleagues in the Virginia Annual Conference—Bishop Sharma D. Lewis, Bishop Young Jin Cho, Rev. Myung J. Kim, Rev. Anthony Layman, Rev. Janine Howard, Rev. David J. Rochford, Rev. Walter B. Failes, Rev. Sung Hak Jung, and Sandra Fulcher, not only as colleagues but also as friends. I am also grateful to Dr. Joyce Quiring Erickson, Dr. Marvin L. Miller, Dr. Jarod Jacobs, and Joyce D. Scott for the many hours they spent editing and clarifying my writing.

There are many more whom I could name; I will remember each of them in my heart as I continue my life journey in gratitude to them.

Last but not least, I would like to thank my families, especially my mother Ok Seon Lee, brother-in-law Won Hyuk Kim, and my daughter Joyce Choi, for their patience, encouragement, and endless support during the years of my academic journey. I am very thankful for the grace of God who led me to this point with all of the blessings that I have received.

Abbreviations

Abbreviations used follow *The SBL Handbook of Style,* 2nd ed, Billie Jean Collins, project director; Bob Buller, publishing director; John F. Kutsko, executive director (Atlanta: SBL Press 2014).

I

Introduction

THE CHOICE OF TOPIC

IN 2012, DURING THE writing of my thesis[1] for the Master of Arts in Biblical Studies programme at Trinity Western University in Canada, I worked on Leviticus and its structure, contents, and ideology, all of which intrigued me very much. Throughout my MA studies, I noticed that many scrolls from Qumran referred to Leviticus; I realized that the extensive presence of Leviticus among the scrolls and its widespread use in several other compositions required further investigation.

Given the large amount of Leviticus material among the scrolls, there is surprisingly little secondary scholarly analysis of the role of Leviticus in the scrolls' corpus. The book of Leviticus survives in several manuscripts; it also features in quotations and allusions and seems to be a foundational basic source for the ideology behind the composition of some of the non-scriptural texts.

1. Choi, "The Exegetical Interpretation of Leviticus 19:1–18 and the Restoration of the Jewish Community in the Post-Exilic Period."

METHODOLOGICAL ISSUES AND APPROACHES

Preliminary Comments on Methods

Textual Criticism

As is well known, the Dead Sea Scrolls have changed the landscape of textual criticism of the Hebrew Bible/Old Testament. Those changes are most apparent in the ways that Emanuel Tov has incorporated many of the features of the so-called biblical scrolls within the discipline of textual criticism.[2] It is not necessary to rehearse all that he and other scholars have accomplished, though it is important to note two things. First, all the new information from the scriptural scrolls has revealed that scribes in the Second Temple period were seldom mere copyists. Second, more often than not they participated actively in the transmission of the texts that they were reproducing. For Tov, that realization has resulted in his paying increasing attention to the overlap between literary criticism and textual criticism. Such an approach is summarized neatly by Martin Jan Mulder in his comments on the transmission of the biblical text. Mulder states, "The process of multiplication and transmission of the text through copying has begun. In this stage of the development of the biblical text, the Ancient Versions are beginning to exert their influence. Text-forms come into being that differ from the present canonical text in many details, and sometimes also in major points."[3]

Adaptations, alterations, and revisions were inevitable during the transmission of the text.[4] Many of the examples in Chapter II show that texts of Leviticus occur in different text forms; however, it is also possible to notice the emergence of a standardized form of Leviticus in the late Second Temple period.[5]

In Chapter II many of the insights of those who have produced editions of the manuscripts of Leviticus found in the Qumran Caves and elsewhere will be assumed. The concern of Chapter II is to build on earlier insights and to ask some further questions about the functions of the manuscripts of Leviticus, particularly as those functions might be discernable in the various features of the manuscripts themselves, both materially and textually.

2. Tov, *Textual Criticism of the Hebrew Bible.*
3. Mulder, "The Transmission of the Biblical Text," esp. 87.
4. Mulder, "Transmission," 87–125.
5. Mulder, "Transmission," 87–125, esp. 132.

Literary Criticism and the Use of Scripture

Beyond Chapter II, in which I have built on the insights of textual criticism, most of the rest of my volume is concerned with the literary analysis of compositions from the Qumran Caves. The major feature of such literary analysis is a focus on the rich and varied ways in which new compositions depend upon and engage with earlier authoritative scriptural sources, particularly the book of Leviticus. This book is present in several compositions in both major and minor ways: in major ways as an influence on the literary structure of a composition, in minor ways as a resource for conveying the new compositions' ideologies.

As with the use of textual criticism in Chapter II, in the remaining chapters of this volume I am also dependent on the insights of previous scholars, especially those of the last generation who have been able to take into account the new evidence of the multiple uses of scripture now attested in the scrolls from the Qumran Caves.[6] Three approaches underpin much of the discussion in Chapters III–VII: inner-biblical interpretation, explicit pre-canonical scriptural interpretation, and scriptural rewriting.

First, for inner-biblical interpretation many scholarly insights depend upon and engage with the landmark work of Michael Fishbane, who discusses extensively how scripture is used within scripture in early Jewish scribal communities. The Hebrew Bible is "a thick texture of traditions received and produced over many generations" that needs to be considered in two ways: as a body of scripture and as a corpus of interpretations.[7] While the collective biblical texts were passed from generation to generation orally and later in written form, there was freedom to edit the texts. Fishbane further asserts:

> The canonical corpus contains a vast range of annotations, adaptations, and comments on earlier traditions. We call this 'inner-Biblical Exegesis.' With the close of the canon one could not add or subtract to these examples within Scripture itself.[8]

There are two types of inner-biblical interpretation: First, the introduction of comments, glosses, expansions, etc.; second, the use of other traditions, generally authoritative ones, to make comments and create

6. As survey examples of the multiple usages of scripture in the scrolls, see Fishbane, "Use, Authority and Interpretation of Mikra at Qumran"; and García Martínez, "Ancient Interpretations of Jewish Scriptures in Light of Dead Sea Scrolls."

7. Fishbane, *Biblical Interpretation in Ancient Israel*, 458–99; Fishbane, *The Garments of Torah*, 3–18; Fishbane, "Inner-Biblical Exegesis," esp. 34.

8. Fishbane, "Inner-Biblical Exegesis," esp. 35.

harmonisations or cross-references. It is the latter with which Fishbane is particularly concerned. He discusses how scripture is used within scripture in early reception[9] and introduces the concept that scripture has interpreted scripture, most commonly through "theme-words," as scribes or interpreters depended upon other texts that were also of emerging authority. Fishbane defines "theme-word"[10] as a word whose stem may recur differently in other places. "Such repetition, where it occurs, gives a text special texture; and it also serves to highlight major and minor features of content."[11] I will engage with inner-biblical interpretation especially in Chapter VI in which detailed attention is paid to how allusions to Leviticus are combined with other authoritative texts to create adjusted legal prescriptions.

Second, for explicit pre-canonical scriptural interpretation, there are multiple studies. Among the most well-known is the series of volumes edited by Craig Evans, commonly in association with other scholars, notably James Sanders.[12] Many of those volumes juxtapose the use of scripture in various New Testament books with its use in other early Jewish sources. The production of such volumes has been stimulated by the rich and varied use of scripture visible in the Dead Sea Scrolls, especially the sectarian compositions. The essays in these volumes concern numerous topics of interest, especially a concern to identify the ways in which the scriptures are handled. Chapter V in this dissertation is a discussion of the use of Leviticus in the Damascus Document; much of that discussion is concerned with verbal overlaps with Leviticus together with many implicit allusions to the book. The insights of those who have discussed pre-canonical biblical interpretation have also been important in the investigation and analysis of *Miqṣat Maʿaśe Ha-Torah* (MMT) in Chapter VI, where the juxtaposition of implicit and explicit interpretation is also readily apparent.

Third, scriptural rewriting has become an important field of study in its own right, especially since the foundational work of Geza Vermes.[13] Two approaches have been articulated in recent scholarship. On the one hand several scholars have wished to continue the work of Vermes by

9. Fishbane, "Inner-Biblical Exegesis," 37.

10. Fishbane, *Text and Texture*, xii.

11. Fishbane, *Text and Texture*, xii.

12. Evans, *Noncanonical Writings and New Testament Interpretation*, 46; Charlesworth and Evans, eds., *The Pseudepigrapha and Early Biblical Interpretation*; Evans and Sanders, eds., *Early Christian Interpretation of the Scriptures of Israel*; Evans and Sanders, *The Function of Scripture in Early Jewish and Christian Tradition*; Evans, ed., *Of Scribes and Sages: Early Jewish Interpretation and Transmission of Scripture*, vol. 1, *Ancient Versions and Traditions*; Sanders, *Torah and Canon*, 2nd ed., xxiv.

13. Vermes, *Scripture and Tradition in Judaism*, 67–96.

considering Rewritten Bible as a literary genre primarily based on the adaptation of scriptural narratives. Chief among the proponents of this approach are Moshe Bernstein and Molly Zahn.[14] Bernstein has worked mostly with narrative compositions such as the Genesis Apocryphon. Zahn has engaged principally with the so-called Reworked Pentateuch manuscripts.

On the other hand, some scholars have preferred to understand scriptural rewriting not as a genre but as a process applied to many genres. A significant study in this respect is that by Anders Klostergaard Petersen in which he reviews the methods and approaches of other scholars to draw a distinction between those who see Rewritten Bible as a genre and those who are more concerned with the process of scriptural rewriting.[15] Among other scholars who have paid attention to rewriting as a process is George Brooke.[16]

Attention to rewritten scripture is especially important in Chapters III and IV of this dissertation. Both Jubilees and the Temple Scroll have often been described as Rewritten Bible; that is, they have been understood as thoroughly engaged with authoritative scriptural sources through implicit interpretation. Although this volume does not attempt to judge between those who take Rewritten Bible to be a genre and those who see it as a process, the argument of Chapters III and IV will expound both literary features and processes of production for the two compositions concerned, highlighting the ways in which implicit interpretation is taking place.

The Process of Investigation

The process of investigation will involve three stages. Chapter II presents all the manuscripts that are thought to contain complete or partial copies of the book of Leviticus. Evidence for this chapter has relied upon the standard editions of the various manuscripts, especially in the Discoveries in the

14. Bernstein, "The Employment and Interpretation of Scripture in 4QMMT," esp. 46; Zahn, "Genre and Rewritten Scripture"; Bernstein, *Reading and Re-Reading Scripture at Qumran*, 1:39–62.

15. Petersen, "Rewritten Bible as a Borderline Phenomenon."

16. Brooke, "The Explicit Presentation of Scripture in 4QMMT"; Brooke, "Biblical Interpretation in the Qumran Scrolls and the New Testament." The term "rewritten" refers to retelling the biblical passages or stories with "omissions, supplements and loose paraphrases." Based upon Brooke's notes, "rewritten compositions from the Second Temple period are a major indicator of the emergence of an authoritative body of Jewish literature after the exile." See Brooke, "The Rewritten Law, Prophets and Psalms," esp. 31; Heger, "Qumran Exgesis, 'Rewritten Torah' or Interpretation?"; Brooke, "Biblical Interpretation at Qumran," esp. 301; Crawford, "The Rewritten Bible at Qumran," 131–48; Brooke, "Scripture and Scriptural Tradition in Transmission," 1–17.

Judaean Desert series. It is interesting to note, however, that several fragmentary manuscripts of Leviticus have come to light and been published in various places, even since the appearance of the collection *Leviticus at Qumran*, which was intended to be comprehensive.[17] All the resources that have been used to assemble the data are cited in Chapter II.

The second stage of the research requires the identification of all the major explicit and implicit uses of Leviticus in the scrolls found in the caves at and near Qumran. The process of identification reflects two approaches. On the one hand, I have relied on handlists produced largely without the aid of computer technology. Chief among those has been the index of scriptural passages compiled by Johann Maier.[18] Such handlists can be problematic because the use of concordances can encourage scholars to make identifications of scriptural usage where none was originally intended or where an ancient author has unconsciously used scriptural idiom. Maier's list was produced with sensitivity to such problems and so is a trustworthy guide to what actually may have been the case. On the other hand, I have used electronically generated resources such as the lists in Armin Lange and Matthias Weigold's helpful volume, together with the files from Accordance Bible software.[19]

Accordance Bible software has also enabled me to generate my own searches for allusions to Leviticus. The principal method I used to search for references consisted of entering two or three words, commonly in Hebrew in their root form, in the search bar. Such searches were intended to discover verbal overlaps between Leviticus and some of the scrolls from the Qumran Caves. In addition, I searched for a distinctive theme word, such as "Covenant" or "Sabbath," using either Hebrew or English search terms. Such searches were intended to help in the identification of the use of similar phrases and ideas in Leviticus and some of the scrolls from the Qumran Caves. Overall, from all such searches I was able to compile lists of likely sources in Leviticus that might have been used in certain instances. I sorted through the lists to determine which passages of Leviticus were most likely to lie behind the newly formulated passages in the selected texts from the Qumran Caves.

I have cited throughout the dissertation many parallels between Leviticus and the scrolls and developed my own system for helping readers see the passages from Leviticus that have influenced the Scrolls found in

17. Kugler and Baek, *Leviticus at Qumran*.

18. Maier, *Die Qumran-Essener*, 3:161–82.

19. Lange and Weigold, *Biblical Quotations and Allusions in Second Temple Jewish Literature*, 81–88; *Accordance Bible Software: Version 12.0.6*.

the Qumran Caves. In these parallel examples, the English of **explicit quotations** are in bold type; explicit quotations are those which are marked in the text itself with a phrase such as "it is written" (e.g., the use of Lev 14:8 in MMT B 64b–67a). The English of implicit uses of Leviticus are categorized in three ways. First, **<u>verbal overlaps</u>** of two words or more are indicated in bold type with underlining (e.g., the use of Lev 26:25 in Jub. 1:10). This kind of overlap uses the same words and commonly those words have the same grammatical form as found in a known text of Leviticus. Second, *<u>similar use of phrasing and ideas</u>* are in italic type and underlined (e.g., as in the use of Lev 20:24 in 11QT[a] 51:16). In these examples some words of Leviticus are used, but they feature in rewritten or rephrased statements that share ideas with identifiable passages of Leviticus. Third, *compatible ideas* are in italic type without underlining (e.g., the use of Lev 19:24–25 in MMT B 62b–63).[20] These expressions do not share the same precise details but use similar words which are compatible with particular themes in Leviticus. The important aspect of these three types of implicit use of Leviticus is that, although there are echoes of or allusions to the base text, it is reworked in various ways some of which represent specific topics and others of which influence the structure of the passage in which implicit use occurs.

The third stage in the process of investigation has been the analysis of the uses of Leviticus in several compositions. In each composition it has been necessary to construct a set of categories for handling the uses of Leviticus. Sometimes those categories have focused on how Leviticus influences the overall structure and line of argument of the composition; sometimes those categories have been concerned rather with precise usages in well-defined passages of the text. The outcomes of the analysis are presented in each chapter as the influence of Leviticus on the ideology of the various compositions is described. I have extensively reviewed scholarly work that substantially assesses and analyzes certain key themes selective to the text as literature. My purpose has not been to show intertextuality or to study sociolinguistics. Rather, my focus is the close reading of selected biblical texts that are related to texts found in the Qumran Caves explicitly or implicitly in order to investigate the use of the structure, content, or ideology of Leviticus in some compositions. This thorough reading discloses why certain parts of Leviticus were used and others were not.

20. Sometimes two or more types of implicit use of Leviticus can occur in one and the same passage.

OVERVIEW OF THE VOLUME AND ITS ARGUMENT

This volume is constructed in six chapters. Chapter II describes and reviews twenty-five manuscripts of Leviticus from the Second Temple period as found among the Qumran Scrolls and elsewhere to determine whether the manuscripts display any features that would indicate how they were used. This chapter will help readers see the richness of the uses of Leviticus in the scrolls.

Chapters III and IV include and consider pre-sectarian materials, Jubilees, and the Temple Scroll. Those compositions are reviewed and discussed in relation to how Leviticus controls their structures and provides key ideological markers in their contents such as concerns over priestly issues, the covenant, and the Sabbath.

Chapters V and VI are discussions of two key sectarian texts, the Damascus Document, and MMT. Although there are some distinctive features of the use of Leviticus in the Damascus Document and MMT, both compositions develop and enhance several of the key uses of Leviticus in Jubilees and the Temple Scroll. In particular, it is very intriguing to notice how the Sabbath, warning, judgement, and covenant, all referred to in Lev 26, are reflected in these two sectarian texts. It is equally interesting to see how the so-called Holiness Code (Lev 16–27) plays a significant role in providing the ideology of the compositions, even though, of course, the Holiness Code was not known as such to the ancient authors and editors of the Damascus Document and MMT.[21] Leviticus is a foundational source for these compositions.

The final chapter treats briefly other compositions that contain Leviticus texts. These compositions offer more evidence, which is nevertheless fragmentary; some of these compositions were composed early in the life of the sect and others were composed later. The purpose of this chapter is to provide further comprehensive coverage of the influence of Leviticus in the Qumran literary corpus.

Throughout the volume my endeavour is to offer explanations that show how Leviticus influences the structure, content, and ideology of the various key compositions among the scrolls. My research has shown that Leviticus was very predominant and significant in the late Second Temple period. Therefore, the purpose of this volume is to show how closely Leviticus influenced the composition of texts in both the Qumran and pre-Qumranic communities or the wider movements of which they were a

21. I have included Lev 16 in my argument since this chapter deals closely with several sections found in the scrolls.

part. This supports my overall argument that Leviticus was a fundamental contributor to the creation of priestly sectarian ideology in the late Second Temple period, not least for those who had to some extent withdrawn from the Temple.

II

The Manuscripts of the Book of Leviticus

PRELIMINARY DISCUSSION

In this chapter, I will briefly describe twenty-five manuscripts:[1] the twenty-two manuscripts of Leviticus from the Qumran Caves,[2] two from Masada,[3] and one from En-Gedi.[4] There are further manuscript fragments containing small parts of Leviticus;[5] they are all described by Eibert

1. Some further fragments of Leviticus have recently been identified from Cave 11 by Émile Puech. Some of them seem to belong to 11Q1 and 11Q2. Puech has also suggested that some fragments in cryptic A script might also be a copy of Leviticus. In addition, he suggests that a papyrus fragment could be yet another copy of Leviticus (oral communication with Brooke, May, 2017).

2. The twenty-two scrolls from Qumran are: 1QpalaeoLev–Num^{a}, 2QpalaeoLev, 2QNum^{d}?, 4QExod–Lev^{f}, 4QLev–Num^{a}, 4QLev^{b}, 4QLev^{c}, 4QLev^{d}, 4QLev^{e}, 4QLev^{g}, 4QLXXLev^{a}, 4QpapLXXLev^{b}, 4QtgLev, 4QRPc. 4QRP^{d}, 4QRP^{e}, 4Qpap cryptA Lev^{h}?, 4Qpap cryptA Text Quoting Leviticus A, 4Qpap cryptA Text Quoting Leviticus B, 6QpalaeoLev, 11QpalaeoLev^{a}, 11QLev^{b}. For the principal publication of each of those scrolls, see the relevant sections in this chapter. For a preliminary list of the biblical passages in these scrolls, see Ulrich, "An Index of the Passages in the Biblical Manuscripts from the Judean Desert (Genesis–Kings)," 113–29.

3. For MasLev^{a} and MasLev^{b}, see Talmon, *Masada VI*, 36–50.

4. Segal et al., "An Early Leviticus Scroll from En-Gedi," esp. 3.

5. The details of the publication of the three major sets of fragments are as follows. 1)

Tigchelaar as unprovenanced and so will not be discussed in this chapter.[6] As Tigchelaar has stated: "the better part of wisdom is to set all those fragments apart to avoid contamination of our scholarly data."[7] The main purpose of this chapter is to review those manuscripts which most probably contained all or significant parts of the book of Leviticus as found among the Qumran Scrolls and elsewhere, for which the provenance is certain or very likely, to see whether or not the manuscripts display any features that might indicate how they were used. Many of the observations in this chapter are highly dependent on the descriptive work of others, but few scholars have commented on how the Leviticus manuscripts might have been used in the late Second Temple period.

My distinctive contribution is to comment on the functions of the manuscripts of Leviticus by focusing on their key features, including their contents, physical characteristics, scribal features, and textual affiliation. I am not providing a new edition of any manuscript in this chapter but rather trying to understand how the manuscripts of Leviticus might have functioned.

In addition, the Leviticus scrolls are both richly preserved and seem to have been widely used in the communities associated with the site of Qumran and the wider movement.[8] Leviticus was influential in many different Second Temple communities: it is written in three languages (Hebrew, Aramaic, and Greek) and the Hebrew manuscripts are in two scripts (palaeo and square). Leviticus is considered a significant book "not only [for its] view of cultural history, but also for the history of the biblical text and canon."[9] Unlike other books in the Torah, Leviticus does not show large-

---

ArugLev: Eshel et al., "Fragments of a Leviticus Scroll (ArugLev) Found in the Judean Desert in 2004." 2) MS 4611: Elgvin, "MS 4611. Mur/ḤevLev (Lev 26. 3–9, 33–37)." 3) NCF. SCR. 004742: Kutz et al., "Leviticus 23:24–28 (Inv. NCF. SCR. 004742)."

6. Tigchelaar, "A Provisonal List of Unprovenanced, Twenty-First Century, Dead Sea Scrolls-like Fragments." A similar list has been compiled by Arstein Justnes who lists the following Leviticus fragments on his website, "A List of 76 Unprovenanced, Post-2002 Dead Sea Scrolls-like Fragments": 1) Lev 1:2–5 (Lev 1:2–5 Bar Kochba); 2) Lev 10:4–7 (APU 2, DSS F.152 [Lev1]); 3) Lev 20:24, 18:28–30 (Dearing Fragment, DSS F.162 [Lev2]); 4) Lev 23:4 (?) (MOTB.SCR. 000122, DSS F.193 [Lev5]); 5) Lev 23:24–28 (MOTB.SCR.004742, DSS F.203 [Lev6]); 6) Lev 23:38–39 (ArugLev frg.a); 7) Lev 23:40–44; 24:16–19 (ArugLev frg. b-c). There is a strong possibility that some of these fragments might be forgeries, but the matter is under ongoing discussion: see Justnes, "The Lying Pen of Scribes: Manuscript Forgeries and Counterfeiting Scripture in the Twenty-First Century" https://lyingpen.com/2016/08/11/a-list-of-70-unprovenanced-post-2002-dead-sea-scrolls-like-fragments/.

7. Tigchelaar, "A Provisonal List," 178.

8. Kugler, "Rethinking the Notion of 'Scripture' in the Dead Sea Scrolls," esp. 348.

9. Fabry, "The Reception of the Book of Leviticus in Qumran," esp. 75–76.

scale editing; rather it presents a "general uniform state" by the late second century BCE and there appears to be only one edition in circulation.[10] The Leviticus scrolls are extant in various sizes,[11] from pocket-size to extra large, which is a strong indication that Leviticus might have been read in various settings.[12]

This chapter will lay the foundation for this work by comprehensively analysing the main features of all the Leviticus scrolls that have been published from the Qumran Caves and other sites. While it is not possible to draw firm conclusions now, the different sizes of scrolls suggest varied intended uses. We can categorize the Scrolls from the Qumran Caves into three groups based on size: small, medium, and large/deluxe. I am relying on the analytical descriptions of the manuscripts by Emanuel Tov and Armin Lange as a guideline to determine how to categorize each scroll.[13]

The scrolls that can be considered small have between five and thirteen lines of writing and their height is similarly small. The medium-sized scrolls in general have fourteen to eighteen lines. The large scrolls (deluxe editions) are characterized by significant top and bottom margins of around three centimeters and some of these scrolls have more than twenty-five lines in each column.[14]

Based on these data, we can postulate some uses for each category of size. The small scrolls seem likely to have been used in private settings where portability would be valued. Medium-sized scrolls could have been used in educational settings, possibly for the training of scribes. In this context, a small scroll would not be desirable, since readability would be important. However, considerations of cost may have kept the overall size somewhat compact. Finally, some large or deluxe scrolls may have been used for liturgical purposes. The fact that the large size seems to have been used mostly for authoritative biblical texts, with only some exceptions, supports this conclusion.[15] In this context, an overly large manuscript may have reflected the high esteem the contents of the scroll received from the community.

10. Metso, "The Character of Leviticus Tradition at Qumran."

11. The size of the scroll often depends upon the dimensions of the sheet and contents. See Tov, *Textual Criticism of the Hebrew Bible*, 110.

12. The earliest scroll is 4QExod–Lev[f] (4Q17) and has been dated palaeographically to 250 BCE. Fragments of Leviticus Scroll (ArugLev) have been dated to 75–100 CE, which indicates that Leviticus was in use for a long period.

13. Tov, *Scribal Practices*, 144; Tov, *Textual Criticism of the Hebrew Bible*, 111; Lange, *Handbuch*, 66–67.

14. Tov, "The Scribes of the Texts Found in the Judean Desert," 131–52; Tov, *Scribal Practices*, 144; Tov, *Textual Criticism of the Hebrew Bible*, 111. E.g., 1Q3 with 44 lines.

15. See Tov, *Textual Criticism of the Hebrew Bible*, 111. Lange, *Handbuch*, 66–67.

Further, considerations of cost would not have weighed as heavily upon the construction of the scroll, allowing for resources to be spent on luxuries such as large borders.

In the following discussion, I will utilise these categories in order to speculate about the nature of each of the Leviticus scrolls found in and near Qumran. This lays the foundation for considering the influence of Leviticus in the late Second Temple period. I argue that it was a diverse and popular book based on a single stable edition but containing some variant readings reflecting the range of text types present at the time.[16]

THE MANUSCRIPTS OF LEVITICUS

1Q3 (1QpalaeoLev–Num[a])

Contents

In 1955, Dominique Barthélemy published in DJD I a group of fragments that he labelled "1Q3: Lévitique et autres fragments en écriture 'Phénicienne'" and tentatively identified them as three or four separate manuscripts by grouping the fragments as follows: 1–15, 16–21, 22–23, and 24.[17] Mark McLean distinguishes three different manuscripts: 1Qpalaeo-Lev[a]: fragments 1–8, 10–15; 1Qpalaeo Lev[b]: fragments 22–23; 1Qpalaeo Lev–Num[a] fragments 16–21.[18] Eugene Ulrich suggests 1Q3 represents just two manuscripts: 1QpalaeoLev–Num[a] and 1QpalaeoLev[b].[19] Whichever scholar is followed, the number of Leviticus manuscripts from the Qumran Caves would increase yet further. This discussion only considers that the principal fragments all seem to belong together.

According to DJD I, fifteen fragments have been assigned to 1QpalaeoLev–Num[a], and this manuscript contains certain parts of Leviticus (Lev 11; 19–21; 23) and Numbers (Num 1:48–50; 36:7–8?). All the significant identifications of scriptural passages are indicated in the following table:

16. Lange and Tov, eds., *The Hebrew Bible*, 93–95.
17. Barthélemy and Milik, *DJD* I, 51–54 and plates VIII–IX.
18. McLean, "The Use and Development of Paleo-Hebrew," 41–42.
19. Ulrich, "1QpaleoLev–Num[a]"; Lange, *Handbuch*, 67.

Frg.	Passage	Frg.	Passage	Frg.	Passage
1	Lev 11:10–11	8	Num 1:48–50	22	Lev 27:30–31(?)
2	Lev 19:30–34	9	Num 36:7–8 (?)	23	Partial word
3 et 4	Lev 20:20–24	10–15	Partial words	24	Partial word
5 et 6	Lev 21:24–22:6	16	Num 1		
7	Lev 23:4–8	17–21	Partial words		

Since all the fragments of 1Q3 are written in Palaeo-Hebrew script, it is a challenge to date them since the style of Palaeo-Hebrew persisted for several generations. Richard Hanson suggests a date of 125–75 BCE.[20] 1Q3 frgs. 1–15 have been assigned to a single scroll of Leviticus and Numbers, though we cannot be sure that the manuscript contained both books. Currently, according to most scholars, frgs. 1–15 belong to one manuscript and frgs. 22–23 belong to another, but this conclusion is not clear.[21] The surviving portion of Leviticus texts in 1Q3 is heavily concentrated on cultic practices.

Physical Characteristics

According to the images of plates VIII and IX in DJD 1[22] and the Leon Levy digital library,[23] many of the fragments assigned to 1Q3 seem to be a well-prepared skin, though some of the fragments have a shady and dark colour. Fragments 22–23 have a clean and smooth surface and a soft reverse side, and frg. 24 is not preserved well. The fragments are inscribed on skin ranging in color from light to dark brown, and some are almost black, with defective orthography.[24]

20. Hanson, "Paleo-Hebrew Scripts in the Hasmonean Age," esp. 44.

21. Ulrich, "1QpaleoLev–Num[a]," 341–47; McLean, "The Use and Development of Palaeo-Hebrew," 42, 60.

22. Barthélemy and Milik, *DJD* I, 51–54, plates VIII–IX.

23. "Explore the Archive," Leon Levy Digital Library, http://www.deadseascrolls.org.il/explore-the-archive/manuscript/1Q3-1. B-278286. PAM M40.550.

24. Kugler and Baek, *Leviticus at Qumran*, 1.

Scribal Features

Many of the fragments were prepared with a clear horizontal line (a little over 0.5 cm, carefully ruled and very even) and the average vertical width of the columns is tall and thin. The columns average around 44 lines, roughly 45 cm,[25] and the average length of the lines is around 12 cm. For Tov, the principal fragments assigned to 1Q3 can probably be classified as deluxe.

Textual Affiliation

The contents of the fragments of 1Q3 could be classified as proto-Masoretic (or proto-Rabbinic).[26] However, Peter Flint considered the textual form of the fragments to be close in some respects to MT and in some respects to the P; it is possible to list the material as mixed.[27] Though not speaking about 1Q3 specifically, it is worth noting that according to Tov, Palaeo-Hebrew script may have been used by the Sadducees, but 1Q3 indicates that the use of Palaeo-Hebrew was probably not exclusively Sadducean.[28]

Conclusion

Even with the fragmentary nature of 1Q3 in mind, we can note that at least some of the fragments suggest the survival of at least one scroll of an extra large size and the surviving texts in 1Q3 are heavily concentrated on cultic practices. Thus, it is my preliminary analysis that the fragments of 1Q3 were likely crafted for authoritative cultic purposes or public use.

2Q5 (2QpalaeoLev)

Contents

One fragment has been assigned to 2QpalaeoLev and contains just one middle section of Leviticus (11:22–29; matters of purity). The suggested date for this fragment written in Palaeo-Hebrew script is first century BCE.[29]

25. Tov, *Scribal Practices*, 144; Tov, *Textual Criticism of the Hebrew Bible*, 111; Lange, *Handbuch*, 66–67; Barthélemy and Milik, *DJD* I, 51.

26. Tov, "The Biblical Texts from the Judean Desert," esp. 151.

27. Milgrom, *Leviticus 1–16*, 2; Flint, "The Book of Leviticus in the Dead Sea Scroll," esp. 324; Ulrich, "1QpaleoLev–Num[a]."

28. Tov, "Biblical Texts," 151.

29. Metso, "Evidence from the Qumran Scrolls for the Scribal Transmission of

Physical Characteristics

2QpalaeoLev is in fairly good condition and its skin is of average thickness and dark brown in colour.[30] The surface seems even, and the letters on the skin are very clear but line traces are not completely clean. The scribe did not use a sharp pen to write this manuscript, thus the letters are quite thick.

Scribal Features

Like other Palaeo-Hebrew manuscripts from the Qumran Caves, this text shares the characteristics of the Qumran scribal practice. The word-dividers in 2QpalaeoLev are shaped like small oblique strokes, which may be compared with vertical line dividers in many early lapidary texts; "the scribe of 2QpaleoLev placed the dots serving as word-dividers and short oblique lines guiding the drawing of horizontal lines at the end of the lines."[31]

The space between lines is 7–8 mm and is relatively even, indicating that the scribe was careful when writing. This fragment is at the left end of a sheet, and the marginal space of the left side is roughly 1.5 cm.[32] It appears from this fragment that the scribe did not use the highest quality of material; however, 2QpalaeoLev still demonstrates a fairly good standard of writing even though not much evidence survives.

Textual Affiliation

The orthography is apparently fuller than what one expects in MT, but the evidence is not enough to determine the affiliation of the fragment.[33]

Leviticus," esp. 78.

30. Baillet and Milik, DJD III, 56–57. Planche XII; "Explore the Archive," Leon Levy Digital Library, B-284858. Plate 742.

31. Tov, *Scribal Practices*, 121–24. As in texts written in the square script, most Palaeo-Hebrew texts use spacing in the middle of the line for the indication of closed sections (see 1QpalaeoLev, 4QpalaeoGen-Exod[l], 4QpalaeoExod[m], 4QpalaeoDeut[r] for clear evidence). On the other hand, the well-preserved 11QpaleoLev[a] does not use this device. More explanation will be provided in the 11QpalaeoLeva section since this scroll is considered to be an independent text. Tov suggests that the writing in two different scripts likely represents different scribal schools.

32. Many manuscripts have spaces at a distance of 0.5–1.0 cm from the edge of the sheet; however, 2QpalaeoLev (1.5 cm) has appeared at a considerable distance from the edge of the sheet. See Tov, *Scribal Practices*, 57.

33. Kugler and Baek, *Leviticus at Qumran*, 2.

Conclusion

While the scribe seems to have been somewhat careful at times in the writing of this manuscript, the hand is not nearly as clear as other Palaeo-Hebrew texts.[34] Further, the small amount of evidence does not allow us to draw firm conclusions about how the manuscript might have been used.

2Q9 (2QNum^{d}?)

Contents

Two fragments have been assigned to 2Q9 (Num 18:8–9? or Lev 23:1–3?). They are not well preserved and are very fragmentary. The few partial words preserved on this small fragment are not enough to identify the contents of the scroll. However, Baillet suggests that this may be a fragment of Numbers and others have reiterated his conclusion but he also allows the possibility that the manuscript contains the text of Lev 23:1–3.[35]

Physical Characteristics

The skin of these fragments is of medium thickness and their colour is very dark.[36] The margins of the interline are 6.5 mm, the right margin is at least 1.1 cm, and the column width is about 8 cm.[37] This manuscript is smaller[38] than the medium- or large-sized manuscripts, but very little text survives.

Scribal Features

Because this is such a small fragment, it is not easy to identify scribal features though the handwriting seems very careful and well-written.

34. Palaeo-Hebrew in manuscripts that contain Exodus appears to be used very carefully and with consistent workmanship, while Palaeo-Hebrew in Leviticus manuscripts reflects inconsistent workmanship. See Mathews, "The Paleo-Hebrew Leviticus Scroll from Qumran."

35. Baillet and Milik, *DJDJ* III, 59.

36. Baillet and Milik, *DJDJ* III, 59–60. Planche XII; "Explore the Archive," Leon Levy Digital Library, B-371431. Plate 742.

37. Baillet and Milik, *DJDJ* III, 59.

38. Tov suggests that 7–13 lines (6.2–8.2 cm) could be considered as a small size writing block. See Tov, "The Dimensions of the Qumran Scrolls," esp. 78–79.

Textual Affiliation

This manuscript was written in Hebrew, but it is not easy to tell its textual affiliation because there is very limited material.

Conclusion

Since this fragments only have a limited amount of text, it is difficult to speculate about the intended purpose of the manuscript but I include it here simply because it might possibly contain traces of Lev 23:1–3.

4Q17 (4QExod–Lev^f)

Contents

4QExod–Lev^f is one of the earliest manuscripts found in the caves at Qumran. This manuscript dates to the mid-third century (250) BCE.[39] Seven fragments have been assigned to 4QExod–Lev^f. These fragments contain the end of Exodus, the beginning of Lev 1, and possibly Lev 2. Fragments 3–4 contain a section of Lev 1 (1:13–15; 1:17) and frg. 4 contains Lev 2:1. The contents of 4Q17 are as follows:

Col.	Frg.	Passage	Col.	Frg.	Passage	Col.	Frg.	Passage
I	1i	Exod 38:18–22	II	1ii	Exod 39:20–24	III	3	Lev 1:13–15
						III	4	Lev 1:17–2:1
I	2i	Exod 39:3–19	II	2ii	Exod 40:8–26			

4QExod–Lev^f seems to contain Exodus and Leviticus in continuity but the joint between the two books has not been well preserved. It is common for Leviticus and Numbers to be on a single manuscript, but the scroll Exodus–Leviticus possibly included the Tetrateuch or possibly the whole

39. Along with 4QSam^b the manuscript of 4QExod–Lev^f is the earliest manuscript and letter-forms are broad and squat. See Cross, "4QExod–Lev^f," 133–44. Plate XXII; Metso, "Evidence," esp. 78; Ulrich, "The Evolutionary Growth of the Pentateuch in the Second Temple Period."

Torah.[40] The contents of 4QExod–Lev^{f} show clear evidence of the two books being written in order.[41]

Physical Characteristics

The surface is very dark and brown. The letters are very precise and sharply written.[42] The column width of frg. 2 is 12.75 cm, and the marginal rulings between columns are 2.0 cm. Column II (frgs.1ii and 2ii) can be calculated at roughly 60 lines of script of which only 31 lines are extant (including frgs. 1 and 2).[43] Based upon the data above, 4Q17 can be categorized as very large.

Scribal Features

The manuscript of 4QExod–Lev^{f} is one of the earliest manuscripts in the caves of Qumran and the script is not the formal script characteristic of the third century. It belongs to a less formal script tradition, which could be called "protocursive." The letter forms are broad and square.[44] The orthography is generally more *plene* than the MT, like other Leviticus manuscripts that often reflect the spelling of the Samaritan tradition.[45] Cross summarises by saying that 4Q17 is a "Proto-Samaritan" text with a tendency toward expansion.[46]

40. 4QExod–Lev^{f} is considered to be a very large-sized scroll that contains two or more books since a large number of lines often implies that the scroll was long. It is likely that several scrolls found at Qumran contained more than one book of the Torah and possibly all of the Torah in which case they would have measured 25–30 metres. See Tov, *Scribal Practices*, 71; Lange, "The Dead Sea Scrolls and the Date of the Final Stage of the Pentateuch," 289–304, esp. 291–92.

41. Callaway, *The Dead Sea Scrolls for a New Millennium*, 77.

42. Cross, "4QExod–Lev^{f}," 133. Plate XXII; "Explore the Archive," B-513029. Plate 1002, Frg. 2.

43. Cross, "4QExod–Lev^{f,}" 134.

44. Cross, "4QExod–Lev^{f}," 134.

45. Kugler and Baek, *Leviticus at Qumran*, 2.

46. Cross, "4QExod–Lev^{f}," 136; Tov, *Scribal Practices*, 217–18. Based upon Cross and Tov, 4QExod–Lev^{f} is an early direct, or better collateral, witness to the textual family, which has been called proto-Samaritan, and which I prefer to label "Palestinian." In the development during the Persian period of the final forms of certain letters in the square script there was a transition period during which certain scribes or scribal centres used the newly developed final forms, while others did not yet do so, or used them inconsistently. Thus, an early text like 4QExod–Lev^{f} (middle of third century BCE) did not use final forms.

Textual Affiliation

4QExod–Lev[f] preserves Exod 39:3–24 immediately before chapter 40, in agreement with the order of Mosoretic Text (MT) and some with Pentateuch (P) traditions, but contrary to the Septuagint, which places Exod 39:3–24 before 36:10–32.[47] Further, the early manuscript's textual character in many places stands against the readings of the Masoretic Text. 4QExod–Lev[f] appears to be an early, direct witness to the textual family, which has been called Proto-Samaritan and which has been suggested to be "Palestinian."[48]

Conclusion

4Q17 (4QExod–Lev[f]) is an extra large size; it probably was not used by an individual, but rather for cultic or public purposes. Also, the likelihood of this scroll containing multiple books, even the entire Torah or Tetrateuch, suggests public rather than private use.

4Q23 (4QLev–Num[a])

Contents

There are seventy-four fragments assigned to 4QLev–Num[a], twenty-six of which contain the latter sections of Leviticus. 4QLev–Num[a] contains some middle and end sections of Leviticus; this scroll contains both Numbers and Leviticus, but the joint between the two books has not been preserved.[49]

47. Cross, "4QExod–Lev[f]," 136.

48. Cross, "4QExod–Lev[f]," 136.

49. Ulrich, "4QLev–Num[a]," 153–76, esp. 153; Tov, *Dimensions of the Qumran Scrolls*, 71.

Frg.	Leviticus	Frg.	Leviticus	Frg.	Leviticus
1	13:32–33	7	15:19–24	21ii, 22–23	27:5–13
2	14:22–31	8–14i	16:15–29	24–26	27:14–22
3	14:31–34	14ii, 15	18:16–21		
4	14:40–50	16–19	19:3–8		
5	14:51–54	20	24:11–12		
6	15:10–11	21i	26:26–33		

Physical Characteristics

Many fragments are dark and some are in poor condition. The leather appears to have been light golden-brown and moderately thick.[50] The appearance of this scroll is relatively poor, which is likely due to deterioration.

Scribal Features

The manuscript is carefully and clearly inscribed in an early Hasmonaean formal script (150–100 BCE)[51] and is easy to read. 4QLev–Num[a] is large and the columns are wide. The number of letter spaces per line is normally 65–75 letter spaces but reaches 70–80 letter spaces in the column in frgs. 32ii, 34i–43. The vertical distance between the lines of the script ranges between 0.6 and 0.9 cm, and the reconstruction of columns suggests that the number of lines per column was 43 lines; thus the height of the inscribed column can be estimated at 35–37 cm.[52] 4QLev–Num[a] is very close to this standard format.

50. Ulrich, "4QLev–Num[a]," 154. Plates XXIII-XXX; "Explore the Archive," Leon Levy Digital Library, B371333. Plate 399.

51. Cross, "4QExod–Lev[f]," 133–44; Metso, "Evidence from the Qumran Scrolls," 67–79, esp. 78; Lange, *Handbuch*, 66–67.

52. Ulrich, "4QLev–Num[a]," 153; Lange, *Handbuch*, 68–69.

Textual Affiliation

The orthography of 4QLev–Num[a] shares some features with MT and some with P.[53] The text of this manuscript closely follows the MT with some notable exceptions[54]: Lev 14:24 and 45 are omitted, verse 43 is truncated, and verse 45 was added by a second hand.[55]

Conclusion

4QLev–Num[a] contains both Numbers and Leviticus on a large scroll without a joint between these texts. 4QLev–Num[a] is currently in poor condition but it was a well-written manuscript. Further, this manuscript is closely aligned with the MT. These characteristics suggest a liturgical purpose rather than a personal one.

4Q24 (4QLev[b])

Contents

There are thirty fragments surviving from 4QLev[b], which was written in a late Hasmonaean hand from approximately the mid-first century BCE.[56] This scroll contains the beginning as well as some of the final chapters of Leviticus. It might have contained the whole book of Leviticus, but we have no firm evidence for this conclusion.

Frg.	Leviticus	Frg.	Leviticus	Frg.	Leviticus
1–7	1:11–3:1	9ii, 11ii, 18–20i	23:2–25	27–28	25:45–49
8	3:8–14	21	23:40		25:51–52
9i, 10–17	21:17–20	20ii, 22–25	24:2–23		
	21:24–23:1	26	25:28–29		

Fragments 2–7 in which the right margin of the first column is partly preserved are darker than frg.1, probably due to deterioration. It is likely that a further two lines of writing were part of the bottom of the column to

53. Ulrich, "4QLev–Num[a]," 154.
54. Lange, *Handbuch*, 69.
55. Kugler and Baek, *Leviticus at Qumran*, 3.
56. Cross, "4QExod–Lev[f]," 133–44; Metso, "Evidence," esp. 78.

which frgs. 1–7 belong. Fragment 8—the top margin of col. II—is clearly preserved, but the text of 3:1–7 is not extant between the two columns. Ulrich suggests that 4QLev^{b} is missing a part of the text from Leviticus, probably most of Lev 3:1–7, which implies that either the *Vorlage* had an abbreviated text or that the scribe may have skipped some text since the wording of 3:1–4 and 3:6–11 is very similar.[57]

Physical Characteristics

The skin of this scroll seems to have been poorly prepared. The leather is moderately thin, possibly due to deterioration.[58] Many fragments are dark brown with greyish or dark grey tones.

Scribal Features

The manuscript is carefully and clearly inscribed in an early Hasmonaean formal script and lacks significant errors. The reconstruction of the columns from frgs. 9 i–17 have 41 lines, and the first column from frgs. 1–7 possibly had 41 lines also.[59] The height of these columns is 30.75 cm and the width is about 10 cm. The range of letters per line at the beginning of the manuscript is 60–65, later becoming 65–75. These characteristics place 4QLev^{b} in the category of large scrolls.

Textual Affiliation

The orthography shares some features with MT and some with P though there are minor variants[60], and there are no insertions and no signs of corrections by later hands.[61] 4QLev^{b} follows MT closely.

57. Ulrich, "4QLev^{b}," 177–87, esp. 177.

58. Ulrich, "4QLev^{b}," 177; "Explore the Archive," Leon Levy Digital Library, Plate 1077.

59. Ulrich, "4QLev^{b}," 177. Around twenty-eight texts preserve sections near the beginning of the book.

60. Lev 3:1–11 seems to have been shorter than MT, P and Lev 22:22 has a plus against MT, P and LXX. Kugler and Baek, *Leviticus*, 3.

61. Flint suggests that the text of 4QLev^{b} may be classified as *mixed*. See Flint, "Book of Leviticus," 326.

Conclusion

4QLev^{b} is a large scroll (41 lines) and contains the beginning and the final sections of Leviticus. It is a well-prepared scroll and deals with cultic practices from Leviticus in various places. Considering its size and contents, this scroll might have been utilised in a liturgical or public setting.

4Q25 (4QLev^{c})

Contents

4QLev^{c} is extant in six fragments, which include some verses from Lev 1–8. 4QLev^{c} is one of the scrolls among the Judean manuscripts that preserves a partial beginning of a text, similar to 4QLev^{b}. The beginning of a scroll is more likely to be damaged since it is often on the outside when the scroll is rolled up. Nonetheless, this scroll starts with the first verse of Leviticus.

Frg.	Leviticus	Frg.	Leviticus	Frg.	Leviticus
1	1:1–7	3	4:12–14	5	5:12
2	3:16–4:6	4	4:23–28	6	8:26–28

Scrolls that contain more than one biblical book have spaces between successive texts. However, 4QLev^{c} commences at the top of a column and 11QpalaeoLev^{a} ends in the middle of a column and is not followed by the book of Numbers. Thus, this scroll probably contained a single biblical book.[62]

Physical Characteristics

4QLev^{c} is made up of leather fragments and can be reconstructed as having a large writing block, similar to 4QLev^{b} (41 lines and 36.1–36.7cm).[63] It is possible that 4QLev^{c} is 36 lines long, if frg. 4 contains a top margin with Lev 4:23–28 (7 lines) and frg. 5 the bottom margin with Lev 5:12–13 (2 lines). If these two fragments are derived from the same column, it would have contained 36 lines (7+2+27 reconstructed).[64]

62. Milik, *The Books of Enoch*, 143.
63. Ulrich, "4QLev^{b}," 177.
64. Tov, "4QLev^{c}," 189–201, esp. 189.

Regarding the column size, frgs. 4 and 5 may serve as a point of departure. Since frg. 4 contains a top margin with Lev 4:23–28 (7 lines)[65] and frg. 5 the bottom margin with Lev 5:12–13 (2 lines), their relative position in the scroll can be calculated.[66]

Scribal Features

The six fragments of 4QLev[c] are dark brown. However, they were written carefully.[67] The material of 4QLev[c] is skin and its date has not been suggested by its editors. The top margins in frgs. 1 and 4 are 2.5–2.6 cm and the bottom margin of frg. 5 is 4 cm. The margin between the columns in frg. 1 is 2 cm. Also, in frg. 5 there are two stitches (with a piece of thread) repairing damage to the leather caused by frequent handling.

Textual Affiliation

While 4QLev[c] is very fragmentary, what is preserved is identical to MT and P orthographically (frgs. 1 and 2),[68] although there are minor orthographic variants in some. Flint suggests that this manuscript is mixed.[69]

Conclusion

4QLev[c], a large, high-quality scroll, might have been used in a regular setting of liturgical or public use. This eventually necessitated discontinuation of its use for cultic service, probably because of continuing damage during regular use.

4Q26 (4QLev[d])

Contents

4QLev[d] is extant in eleven fragments, with only the middle section of several chapters of Leviticus surviving.

65. Frag 4 (4:23–25) partially overlaps with 11QpalaeoLev[a], frg. A (Lev 4:24–26).

66. Tov, "4QLev[c]," 189.

67. Tov, "4QLev[c]," 189–192; "Explore the Archive," Leon Levy Digital Library, Plate 316.

68. Lange, *Handbuch*, 70.

69. Flint, "Book of Leviticus," 326.

Frg.	Leviticus	Frg.	Leviticus
1	14:27–29	4	17:2–11
2	14:33–36	5–11	unidentified
3	15:20–24		

Physical Characteristics

4QLev^{d} is in very poor condition and many parts of the fragments are deteriorated, probably due to poor preservation. These fragments are not easily readable since the ink has corroded and eaten through the skin, often creating the impression of a photographic negative.[70] The damage to the skin has continued, as can be seen in the photographs taken at different stages.[71]

Scribal Features

The spelling in the scroll is *plene* and 4QLev^{d} is written in an early Herodian script, dating between 30 BCE and 20 CE.[72] Due to the poor quality of the manuscript, the writing is not clear.[73] 4QLev^{d} frg. 4 is 5 cm wide and 11 cm high so this scroll can be considered small, but it could have been a large size if frgs.1–2 came from the same column. Tov suggests that frg. 4 probably included at least one additional line (0) before the preserved text, which would have contained the beginning of chapter 17, starting at the right margin of that line; therefore, it would be at least 18 lines. It averages 55 letters per line, while its average reconstructed width is 13.5 cm[74] and the distance between the lines is 0.7–1.0 cm on frg. 4.[75] Therefore, the reconstructed height of 4QLev^{d} could be 31 lines or more.

70. Tov's suggestion that different types of black ink were used to write is clear from the differing states of its preservation. In most cases, the ink has been preserved very well and 4QLev^{d} is one of those cases. See Tov, *Scribal Practices*, 50.

71. Tov, "4QLev^{d}," 193–98, esp. 193–95.

72. Flint, "Book of Leviticus," 326; Cross, "The Development of Jewish Scripts," 133–202, esp. 138. Cf. 4QNum^{b} was written 50–1 BCE.

73. Tov, "4QLev^{d}," 193–95, Plate XXXVI; "Explore the Archive," Leon Levy Digital Library, Plate 198.

74. 4QLev^{d} might not contain the whole book of Leviticus due to its size. See Lange, *Handbuch*, 71.

75. Tov, "4QLev^{d}," 193.

Textual Affiliation

4QLev[d] follows MT in frgs. 1 and 2, and in other fragments preserves variant readings suggesting a text that is mixed.[76]

Conclusion

The surviving fragments of this scroll contain only the middle section from Leviticus; nevertheless, its large size suggests that it might have been used in public.

4Q26a (4QLev[e])

Contents

4QLev[e] is extant in nine fragments, which contain some parts of Lev 3–22. 4QLev[e] might have contained the entire book, but this conclusion is not certain.

Frg	Leviticus	Frg	Leviticus
1	3:2–4	6	21:9–12
2	3:5–8	7	21:21–24
3	19:34–37	8	22:4–6
4	20:1–3	9	22:11–17
5	20:27–21:4		

Fragment 1 has a bottom margin of 2.3 cm; the fragment contains the beginning of Lev 3:2–4 and frg. 2 preserves Lev 3:5–8 without a top margin, but it seems to follow frg. 1 (3:2–4); therefore, there would have been a top margin just above what remains in frg. 2. Lev 1–2 are not preserved. In 2014, Tigchelaar offered corrections suggesting that frgs. 3, 4, and 8 are from a single column, with frg. 8 having been joined to the bottom of frg. 3; thus 4QLev[e] could have been a large scroll.[77]

76. Flint, "Book of Leviticus," 326–27; Kugler and Baek, *Leviticus at Qumran*, 11.
77. Tigchelaar, "A Partial Reedition of 4Q26a (4QLeviticus[e]," 234–39.

Physical Characteristics

The surface of the scroll is dark brown and it could be dated between 100–30 BCE.[78] This scrolls' frgs. 3, 5, and 8 show stitches;[79] it should be considered a large scroll that contained more than two-thirds of the book of Leviticus, possibly the entire book.

Scribal Features

4QLev[e] has a very low degree of scribal intervention showing no corrections or errors in any fragment, and the handwriting is very clear.[80] Further, it appears that the scribe used high-quality ink and pen for this writing. According to a reconstruction based on the MT between frg. 3 to the first word of frg. 5, there are about 44 lines.[81] There may be more lines in frg. 5 if the first word is not at the beginning, making 4QLev[e] a very large scroll.[82]

Textual Affiliation

Orthographically, 4QLev[e] agrees sometimes with MT and sometimes with P.[83] It was written in a Herodian hand and the preserved readings do not show any difference from the MT.

Conclusion

4QLev[e] is a very large scroll. The scribe's careful writing with a very low degree of scribal intervention indicates a high respect for the text. 4QLev[e] was almost certainly used for cultic purposes in public.

78. Metso, "Evidence," 67–79, esp. 78–79.

79. Tov, "4QLev[e]," 197–201, esp. 197; Tigchelaar, "A Partial Reedition of 4Q26a (4QLeviticus[e])," 234–39; Lange, *Handbuch*, 72 (30–1 BCE).

80. Tov, "4QLev[e]," 197–201, Plate XXXVII; "Explore the Archive," Leon Levy Digital Library, Plate 197.

81. Tov, *Scribal Practices*, 239–40.

82. Tov suggests that the large format was used mainly or only for authoritative texts, since this distinctive format gave the scroll prestige, as in the case of the luxury scrolls. These deluxe scrolls are recognized especially by their large top and bottom margins, but the size of the writing block is also of importance. These scrolls are characterized by their low level of scribal intervention, as may be expected among predominantly carefully written manuscripts, since the fewer mistakes that are made, the fewer the corrections needed. See Tov, *Scribal Practices*, 85, 119–21.

83. Flint, "Book of Leviticus," 327; Lange, *Handbuch*, 72.

4Q26b (4QLev^{g})

Contents

4QLev^{g} contains Lev 7:19–26; it is very hard to decipher the letters in this fragment. The poor quality of this manuscript provides few clues about its date and contents.

Physical Characteristics

One fragment has been assigned to 4QLev^{g}, which has a medium thickness and smooth surface. The leather was broken in many areas, the surface is very dark, and the material is of poor quality. The date of composition has not been suggested, but it could have been written very early because of its distinctive use of the Tetragrammaton.[84]

Scribal Features

This fragment differs from other manuscripts of Leviticus in its distinctive use of the Tetragrammaton in the Palaeo-Hebrew script.[85] Eugene Ulrich comments:

> The use of the Palaeo-Hebrew script for the Tetragrammaton in a text principally written in the Jewish (square) script had, in the early years, been considered an indication that the text was not biblical, because at that time the few published manuscripts displaying the phenomenon happened to be nonbiblical. However . . . it should be laid to rest now that a number of biblical scrolls in the Jewish script have surfaced that present the Tetragrammaton in the Palaeo-Hebrew script.[86]

84. The representation of the divine name (mainly the Tetragrammaton) in Palaeo-Hebrew characters in several Qumran manuscripts has been noticed from the earliest days of the Qumran discoveries, since it is found in several texts from Cave 1. See Tov, *Scribal Practices*, 225.

85. Tov, "4QLev^{g}," 203–4, esp. 203.

86. Ulrich, *Dead Sea Scrolls and the Developmental Composition of the Bible*, 197. The majority of the texts using the Palaeo-Hebrew characters for the Tetragrammaton are of a sectarian, nonbiblical nature. At the same time, the negative evidence must also be taken into consideration. No Hebrew texts of a non-sectarian nature or those clearly not written in the Qumran scribal practice, containing any of the aforementioned scribal systems for the writing of divine names, have been preserved. It is unclear why certain scribes used Palaeo-Hebrew characters for the Tetragrammaton, while others wrote the Tetragrammaton in square characters. This question is particularly relevant

In this text, as well as in others, the use of Palaeo-Hebrew script is extended to the preposition *lamed*.[87] The Tetragrammaton was always written in Palaeo-Hebrew characters and it is likely that this indicates that the manuscript has been read aloud since the use of Palaeo-Hebrew would warn the reader of the presence of the divine name.[88]

Textual Affiliation and Conclusion

Basically 4QLev[g] follows the system of MT. This scroll has only one fragment and it is preserved very poorly; therefore, it is hard to determine its size or purpose, but the use of the Tetragrammaton in Palaeo-Hebrew suggests that it was read in public.

4Q119 (4QLXXLev[a])

Contents

4QLXXLev[a] is extant in two fragments, which is the Septuagint text of Lev 26:2–16. 4QLXXLev[a], with 4QpapLXXLev[b], antedates other Greek witnesses to Leviticus by approximately four centuries.[89] The scribe used the customary *scriptio continua* but with occasional spaces for word divisions.[90]

Physical Characteristics

The leather appears to be of medium thickness and the surface is coarse on both sides. It is not easy to determine the original colour but it could range from dark brown to dark reddish.[91] The date of 4QLXXLev[a] is from the late

with regard to the texts written according to the Qumran scribal practices, since most texts using the Palaeo-Hebrew Tetragrammaton are written in this style. Tov, *Scribal Practices*, 208 and 225.

87. Tov, "4QLev[g]," 203. This manuscript uses Palaeo-Hebrew script for the divine name in line 8 (Lev 7:25), but not on other occasions that it appears in the fragment (line 2, Lev 7:21). See Kugler and Baek, *Leviticus at Qumran*, 5.

88. The Qumran texts differ internally with regard to the details of the use of Palaeo-Hebrew characters. Some scribes also wrote the prefixes and suffixes of the divine names in Palaeo-Hebrew characters (4QLev[g] 8 Lev 7:19): prefix. See Tov, *Scribal Practices*, 227. The idea that this text was probably read aloud was suggested in a private conversation with George Brooke.

89. Skehan et al., *DJD* IX, 163.

90. Skehan et al., *DJD* IX, 162.

91. Skehan et al., *DJD* IX, Plate XXXVIII, 162; "Explore the Archive," Leon Levy

second or early first century BCE,[92] and it has preserved the full height of one column, with top, left, and bottom margins partially preserved.

Scribal Features

Fragment 1 contains the full height, which is 28 lines. The lines are not straight in that the letters are suspended from the line.[93] The widths of the lines are approximately 10 cm and the left margin measures 0.8 cm. This scroll shows the scribe's regular writing style, especially at the top of the lines rather than the bottom. The distance between the tops of the lines varies from 0.55 to 0.7 cm.[94] 4QLXXLev^a of Lev 26 has a closed section together with a paragraph sign in frg. 1 21 (after Lev 26:13).[95] We can conclude that the scribe wrote this manuscript with care because we see no major corrections or errors. However, there are minor changes in lines 5, 10, 19, and 22.

Textual Affiliation

There are eight Septuagint or Septuagint-related manuscripts found at Qumran and two of them contain Leviticus.[96] The survey of Leviticus manuscripts among the Dead Sea Scrolls shows that there was a significant amount of text types available at the time of the translation of the book of Leviticus into Greek.[97] These Septuagint texts show textual variants. Ulrich states: "They contain many original readings, a certain number of unique errors, a certain number of errors inherited from parent texts, usually some intentional expansions or clarifications, and often some revisions (whether fresh or inherited) for a variety of purposes."[98]

Digital Library, B-497902, Plate 1004/1.

92. Skehan et al., *DJD* IX, 162; Metso, "Evidence," 78–79; Faulkenberry Miller, "4QLXXLev^a," 1–28, esp. 1.

93. Skehan et al., *DJD* IX, 162. Plate XXXVIII.

94. Skehan et al., *DJD* IX, 161.

95. *Paragraphos* is a horizontal or slightly curved line. Sometimes this *paragraphos* is formed as a straight line, but it often has a slightly curved downstroke to the left or right, and therefore is shaped like a fish hook, or a more developed downstroke in a 45-degree angle. Tov, *Scribal Practices*, 170.

96. 4QLXXLev^a and 4QpapLXXLev^b. See Himbaza, "Textual Witnesses and Sacrifical Terminology in Leviticus 1–7."

97. Peters, ed,. *XIV Congress*, 28.

98. Ulrich, *Dead Sea Scrolls*, 167.

The text of 4QLXXLev[a] is a representative within the MS tradition of the Old Greek (OG) of Leviticus, and thus Ulrich suggests that the text 4QLXXLev[a] penetrates further behind the other witnesses to provide a more authentic witness to the OG translation.[99] Wevers at first did not consider the Qumran evidence but later agreed with Ulrich's verdict and admitted that the Qumran Greek evidence is closer to the OG at times. Compared to Genesis and Exodus, it reflects more of the Hebrew tradition than of the Greek.[100] Tov notes, "these revisions reflected the need to use a Jewish-Greek text based on the content of the Hebrew Bible."[101]

Conclusion

This scroll is a large scroll and it contains part of Lev 26 in Greek. Based upon Greek language, size, and material, it could have been used for teaching purposes or during public assemblies.

4Q120 (4QpapLXXLev[b])

Contents

4QpapLXXLev[b] is extant in ninety-seven fragments, thirty-one of which contain parts of the first six chapters of Leviticus. In this chart, I have included only those fragments that contain a reference to Leviticus. Many of these fragments only contain one or two verses of Leviticus.

99. Skehan et al., *DJD* IX, 163; Aitken, ed., *The T. & T. Clark Companion to the Septuagint*, 51–52; Tov, *Hebrew Bible*, 186; Miller, "4QLXXLev[a]," 1–28, esp. 6–7.

100. Wevers, *Notes on the Greek Text of Leviticus*, xxvii. See also Metso and Ulrich, "The Old Greek Translation of Leviticus," 381–402.

101. Tov, *Textual Criticism of the Hebrew Bible*, 187; Metso and Ulrich, "Old Greek Translation of Leviticus," 266–67.

Frg.	Leviticus	Frg.	Leviticus	Frg.	Leviticus
1	1:1	9	4:3–4	22	4:30
2	2:3–5	10–11	4:4	23	5:6
3	2:7–8?	12–15	4:6–8	24–25	5:8–10
4	3:4	16	4:10–11	26	5:16–17
5	3:7	17–18	4:18–19	27–31	5:18–6:5
6–7	3:9–13	19	4:26		
8	3:13–14	20–21	4:26–28		

Physical Characteristics

The date of this scroll, written on thin papyrus, is likely around the first century BCE.[102] However, the quality of the material seems to be good.[103] The estimated number of letters per line in col. V (frgs. 4–7) is twenty-three to twenty-nine and one can estimate roughly thirty-eight lines for that column.[104] The height of this scroll would have been at least 31 cm high. Thus, this is very large scroll.[105]

Scribal Features

The quality of 4QpapLXXLev^b appears to have been moderately good, for the writing on frgs. 24–31 is still smooth and regular. The writing on frgs. 24 and 30 is clearer and originally most likely would have been in good condition. The orthography is similar to that of Septuagint codices, with customary *iota* adscript.[106] There is no evidence of corrections or supralinear insertions by the original scribe.

102. Skehan et al., *DJD* IX, 167; Metso, "Evidence," esp. 78–79.

103. Skehan et al., *DJD* IX, Plates XXXIX–XLI, 167; Tov, "Explore the Archive," Leon Levy Digital Library, Plate 376 and 378. Based upon these data, 4QpapLXXLev^b was written on well prepared materials.

104. Skehan et al., *DJD* IX, 167.

105. The relatively small number of papyrus fragments of biblical texts (four to six copies out of a total of two hundred biblical manuscripts) possibly served as personal copies. On the other hand, papyrus was used for almost all document texts from the Judean Desert and several literary works from Qumran. See Tov, *Scribal Practices*, 238.

106. Skehan et al., *DJD* IX, 168.

Textual Affiliation

The manuscript's textual character is, like 4QLXXLev[a], consistent with the LXX tradition.

Conclusion

Since these two scrolls, 4QLXXLev[a] and 4QpapLXXLev[b], contain the beginning of Leviticus (first six chapters) and Lev 26:2–16, it may be possible to assume that these scrolls each contained the whole book of Leviticus. 4QpapLXXLev[b] is a large scroll with very good skin quality. It might have been used for a public purpose such as cultic usage.

4Q156 (4QtgLev)

4QtgLev is extant in two fragments that contain a handful of verses from Lev 16:12–15 related to the ritual for the Day of Atonement.[107] The writing is from the second century BCE and Milik has noted the distinctiveness of this Aramaic version of Leviticus among the finds from the Qumran Caves.[108] The small amount of evidence does not permit us to conclude that the manuscript contained the whole of Leviticus in Aramaic. It is possible that just a part of Leviticus, notably the Day of Atonement chapter, was translated for some purpose, either ritual or didactic.[109]

4Q249j (4Qpap cryptA Leviticus[h]?)

"Leviticus is the only book of the Hebrew Bible which is represented by extensive quotes in the Cryptic A script."[110] Pfann has assigned two small fragments, each with a few extant letters, to this manuscript which he has combined to form part of Lev 26:14–16. He dates the fragments to the first half of the second century BCE, which would suggest that Leviticus played a significant role during the early years of the sectarian movement. Little else can be said about the character and value of this manuscript because what remains is so slight.

107. McNamara, *Targum and Testament*, 96.

108. Milik and de Vaux, *DJD* VI, 47.

109. Milik, *DJD* VI, 47; Stuckenbruck and Freedman, "The Fragments of a Targum to Leviticus," 79–95; Kugler and Baek, *Leviticus at Qumran*, 8.

110. Pfann, "Cryptic Texts," 575. The full edition of 4Q249j is found on 575–77.

4Q249k (4Qpap cryptA Text Quoting Leviticus A)

A single fragment has been assigned to this manuscript with a few letters extant in five lines. Pfann has proposed that the letters in lines 1–3 belong to Lev 26:16–17 in an adjusted form and so he concludes that the fragment as a whole contains a quotation or represents Leviticus in a previously unknown form.[111] The possible similarities with the way Leviticus is represented in the Reworked Pentateuch manuscripts means that I include this manuscript in the lists of possible copies of Leviticus for the sake of completeness, even though several questions remain about the status and content of the fragment.

4Q249l (4Qpap cryptA Text Quoting Leviticus B)

A single fragment has been assigned to this manuscript with a few letters extant in seven lines. Pfann has proposed that the letters in lines 1–3 belong to Lev 26:33–34 in a slightly adjusted form.[112] The words in lines 6 and 7 cannot be identified with the immediate context of Lev 26 so the fragment either contains a quotation alongside other text or a rewritten version of Leviticus. Once again, because of the possible similarities with the Reworked Pentateuch manuscripts, I include this manuscript in the lists of possible copies of Leviticus for the sake of completeness even though several questions remain about the status and content of the fragment.

4Q365 (4QReworked Pentateuch[c])

Contents

The surviving fragments of 4Q365 contain passages from Gen 21:9–10 to Deut 20:1, which suggests that the manuscript contained a version of the whole Torah. The principal edition of 4Q365 and the other Reworked Pentateuch manuscripts present the work as primarily exegetical. Subsequently, Tov has concluded that "4QRP constitutes a group of Scriptural manuscripts that had the same level of authority as the Hebrew texts underlying the LXX."[113] For this reason, I include 4Q365–367 in the list of copies of Leviticus in this chapter.[114] Fragments 14–26 contain parts of Leviticus 11–27.

111. Pfann, "Cryptic Texts," 578–80.

112. Pfann, "Cryptic Texts," 581–82.

113. Tov, *Collected Essays*, 3:59.

114. It is likely that the five fragments assigned to 4Q365a actually belong with

The Contents of Leviticus in 4Q365

Frg.	Leviticus	Frg.	Leviticus	Frg.	Leviticus
14	11:1–[3]	19	13:15–[19]	23	23:42–24:2+
15a-b	11:17–[25]	20	13:51–52	24	25:7–9
16	11:32–[33]	21	16:6–7 or 11–12 or 17–18	25a–c	26:17–32
17a–c	11:[39]–[46]	22a–b	18:[25]–[29]	26a–b	27:34 (?)
18	13:6–8				

Physical Characteristics

4Q365 is dated between the late Hasmonaean and early Herodian periods[115] and the text was written on well-prepared leather that survives in different shades caused by exposure or decay.[116] The reconstructed manuscript of 4Q365 contains 43 lines in narrow columns.[117] 4Q365 is a large scroll, possibly up to 25 metres long. Many of the fragments of 4Q365 have been damaged; many of them are small fragments that preserve just a few lines of text.[118]

Scribal Features and Possible Function

Tov and Sidnie White state that 4Q365 contains many corrections,[119] which seems to indicate that 4Q365 might have been edited to include variant textual information. The well-prepared leather might indicate that the scroll was produced for cultic purposes, but the corrections and changes could indicate that the manuscript was the basis of discussion and debate, which might more appropriately reflect an educational setting. The textual character of 4Q365, following a middle course between MT and P and its tendency

4Q365 as John Strugnell originally proposed. Those fragments do not contain any explicit section of Leviticus so for the purposes of this chapter it is not necessary to come to a firm conclusion about their status.

115. Tov and White, "Reworked Pentateuch," esp. 260, 336, 346.

116. Tov and White, "Reworked Pentateuch," 255.

117. Tov and White, "Reworked Pentateuch," 256; Tov, "Dimensions of the Qumran Scrolls," 69–91, esp. 83.

118. Tov and White, "Reworked Pentateuch," 255.

119. Tov and White, "Reworked Pentateuch," 258.

to use the so-called "Qumran practise" of orthography,[120] do not provide criteria that enable us to decide between cultic and educational use.

4Q366 (4QReworked Pentateuch[d])

4Q366 frg. 2 probably contains passages from Lev 24:20–22 (?) and Lev 25:39–43. It is similar to 4Q365 because it also has surviving passages from Exodus, Numbers, and Deuteronomy. This manuscript is very fragmentary and no firm conclusions can be reached about its original size and function, though as with 4Q365 it is likely that it should be considered as a scriptural manuscript.

4Q367 (4QReworked Pentateuch[e])

4Q367 has been classified as another example of Reworked Pentateuch. The three fragments assigned to this manuscript contain only some parts of Leviticus and so 4Q367 might simply be another copy of Leviticus itself. However, the contents of frg. 2 show that Lev 15 and 19 have been considerably adjusted in ways consistent with the character of the Reworked Pentateuch manuscripts.

The Contents of Leviticus in 4Q367

Frg.	Leviticus	Frg.	Leviticus
1a–b	11:47–13:1	3	Add.? + Lev 20:13; 27:30–34
2a–b	15:14–15		
	19:1–4, 9–15.		

4Q367 is a mid- or late-Hasmonaean formal hand[121] and the leather is medium thick.[122] Like 4Q365, 4Q367 contains text which is occasionally similar to P. Based upon the material of these fragments, it appears the manuscript was not prepared well with high quality material. As with 4Q366, not enough survives for scholars to determine the likely function of the manuscript.

120. Tov and White, "Reworked Pentateuch," 188.

121. Tov and White, "Reworked Pentateuch," 260, 336, 346.

122. Tov and White, "Reworked Pentateuch," 345.

6Q2 (6QpalaeoLev)

Contents

6QpalaeoLev (6Q2) contains Lev 8:12–13 and comes from the bottom of a column. The scroll was preserved very poorly, making it hard to be examined.

Physical Characteristics

One fragment has been assigned to 6Q2. The skin is of medium thickness and is not preserved well. This fragment has wormholes and is pocked. The surface is very rough and the skin is dark.[123] This fragment contains the end of the column, the lower margin is around 2.5 cm, and the space between lines seems to be 0.7–1.0 cm. The date is estimated to be between 250 and 150 BCE.[124] The space between words is quite broad, and it is medium to large size. The width is estimated to be around 10 cm.[125]

Scribal Features

6Q2 contains letters that were written carefully with a sharp instrument. The script is Palaeo-Hebrew, its orthography is full, and division dots were used to separate words.[126]

Textual Affiliation

6QpalaeoLev has a more *plene* orthographic character than the MT, but is textually similar to it.[127]

123. Baillet and Milik, *DJDJ* III, 106. Plate XX; "Explore the Archive," B-284843, Plate 894; B-298957, Plates 894, 893, 649.

124. Lange, *Handbuch*, 73; Metso, "Evidence," 67–79, esp. 78–79; de Troyer, "From Leviticus to Joshua," 29–78.

125. Baillet and Milik, *DJD* III, 106.

126. Baillet and Milik, *DJD* III, 106; Kugler and Baek, *Leviticus at Qumran*, 6.

127. Lange, *Handbuch*, 73.

Conclusion

The size of 6QpalaeoLev seems to be medium to large size, so it is not easy to speculate about its purpose. However, at the least this scroll shows that Leviticus was used in late second century BCE. If the contents of Cave 6 are the remains of a personal collection of manuscripts that would suggest that 6QpalaeoLev was a private copy.

11Q1(11QpalaeoLev[a])

Contents

11QpalaeoLev[a] contains partial elements of Leviticus, from chapters 4 to 27. This indicates that 11QpalaeoLev[a] likely contained the whole book of Leviticus.

Frg.	Leviticus	Frg.	Leviticus	Col.	Leviticus
A	4:24–26?	G (1–2), M	14:52—15:5/16:2–4	1	22:21–27
B	10:4–7	H (1and 2)	16:34—17:5	2	23:22–29
C	11:27–32	I (1and 2)	18:27—19:4	3	24:9–14
D	13:3–9	J (1and 2)	20:1–6	4	25:28–36
E	13:39–43	K, L 1	21:6–12	5	26:17–26
F (1and 2)	14:16–21	L 2	22:21–27	6	27:11–19

Physical Characteristics

The material of 11QpalaeoLev[a] was made out of the hides of either a young goat or a hairy sheep. Due to the pattern of the grain, a young goat is more likely. The skin is very thin, measuring 0.2–0.3 mm;[128] it was very well prepared and its remarkable clarity is a striking feature. Based on the letters and lines on the sheet, the scroll is 100.5 cm long, written very carefully with vertical and horizontal lines.[129] The column height of 25–26 cm contains about 42 lines of text; thus this scroll is considered large.

128. Freedman and Mathews, *The Paleo-Hebrew Leviticus Scroll*, 314. Plates 1–20; "Explore the Archive," B-497904, Plate 1039/1.

129. Freedman and Mathews, *Paleo-Hebrew Leviticus Scroll*, 4–5, 18. The regularity of the interlinear space assists the eye as it follows each line comfortably, and the clarity of outline leaves no question as to the carefulness of the scribal design—unlike the

Scribal Features

The scribe of 11QpalaeoLev[a] used dots that facilitated the observance of consistent word spacing.[130] A date around 100 BCE would seem to be appropriate for this Leviticus scroll because the shapes of the letters conform mostly to those appearing in the early Hasmonaean coinage. The scribe of 11QpalaeoLev[a] builds on the use of this preposition by using the *vav* method of demarcating larger units.[131] In 11QpalaeoLev[a], the *vav* occurs only in some open sections, possibly indicating a major sense division (J 1 [Lev 20:1]; II 2[Lev 23:23]; III 3, 8 [Lev 24:10,13]), while subdivisions lack this *vav* in the opening sections (I 7 [Lev 19:1]; II 6 [Lev 23:26]; K 6 [Lev 21:10].

The scribe copied this scroll very carefully so there are only minor corrections and textual notes. However, the writing is not consistent; therefore, more than one scribe may have written it.

Textual Affiliation

11QpalaeoLev[a] exhibits a paragraphing system that combines a peculiar feature with more common procedures among Qumran manuscripts, which might imply that it was an independent scroll[132] and that 11QpalaeoLev[a] is textually non-aligned.[133] The variants in the manuscripts, fairly considerable in number, are so insignificant vis-à-vis MT and P that the "manuscript is best thought of as falling into line with the single, relatively stable single literary tradition evinced by MT, P and LXX."[134]

---

writing itself, which is inconsistent. In contrast, the second largest exemplar penned in Palaeo-Hebrew script is 4QpalaeoExodm. This manuscript is restrained and formal in appearance, but the scribe of the Leviticus scroll endeavoured to put as much as he could on the scroll within the limits of neatness and ease of reading.

130. Dividing words by dots or strokes is an ancient practice well known from inscriptions of the third to first millennia BCE. See Freedman and Mathews, *Paleo-Hebrew Leviticus Scroll*, 8.

131. Freedman and Mathews, *Paleo-Hebrew Leviticus Scroll*, 11. In this scroll, *vav* and non-*vav* come into play (col. 2:3 and 2:6). The scribe in Column 3:3 at Lev 24:10 employed a *vav*-paragraph marker in accordance with this system.

132. Freedman and Mathews, *Paleo-Hebrew Leviticus Scroll*, 9.

133. Tov, *Collected Essays*, 3:310–11; Freedman, *Divine Commitment and Human Obligation*, 2:130, 161.

134. Kugler and Baek, *Leviticus at Qumran*, 7; Lange, *Handbuch*, 75; Kutz et al., "Leviticus 23:24–28," 110–24.

Conclusion

This scroll is easy to read; however, it has various writing styles. It might have been written by more than one scribe and at different times. Scribes divided the text into sections to help readers during the observances such as the Sabbath, first-month convocations (23:1–22), and the seventh-month convocation (23:23–44), and Lev 18 and 20 are presented in a harmonistic manner. Because this manuscript reflects the structure of Leviticus and was written in a very clear style, it seems plausible that it was for public use, probably for educational purposes.

11Q2 (11QLev^b)

Contents

11QLev^b is extant in nine fragments, seven of which contain various texts from the middle to the end of Leviticus. I have included only Leviticus fragments here. 11QLev^b is missing the beginning section and many fragments are dark and not clear. However, frg. 2 preserves Lev 9:23–10:2 very well. Fragment 2 shows careful writing and the space between letters and lines are regular. It was written elegantly with a pen that allowed both thick and very thin strokes.[135]

Frg.	Leviticus	Frg.	Leviticus	Frg.	Leviticus
1i	7:34–35	3	13:58–59	7	25:31–33
1ii	8:8 or 8:9	4	14:16–17		
2	9:23–10:2	5–6	15:18–19		

Although other fragments are not preserved well, the existing fragments contain Leviticus texts from various places, which make it possible to assume that this scroll might have preserved the complete book of Leviticus.

Physical Characteristics

The date of 11QLev^b is late Herodian (c. 50 CE). This manuscript also used the ancient Palaeo-Hebrew Tetragrammaton.[136]

135. García Martínez et al., *DJD* XXIII, 1–9.

136. Wilkinson, *Tetragrammaton*, 77–78; Siegel, "The Employment of Paleo-Hebrew Characters," 159–72.

Scribal Features

The skin is thicker than average, has a dull brown colour, and the horizontal and vertical ruling is very clear on most fragments. 11QLev[b] presents very careful writing with a high quality pen.[137] The average number of letter-spaces per line is around 40, the estimated width of the columns is calculated at 9–10 cm, the height of the inscribed section of the column would have measured 15–18 cm, and columns were likely around 20 lines.[138]

Textual Affiliation

The orthography is uniformly full, and the variants place the "textual character somewhere between MT and LXX" and thus 11QLev[b] is mixed.[139]

Conclusion

11QLev[b] contains only the middle section of Leviticus and part of chapter 25 with very careful writing. The manuscript is roughly medium-sized, but it is not easy to determine its usage due to the limited extant material.

Mas 1a (MasLev[a])

Contents

This scroll preserves the left half of 8 lines, containing Lev 4:3–9, and is identical to the MT, except at 4:8.[140]

Physical Characteristics

MasLev[a] consists of two pieces of very light brown, almost white, skin.[141] The restored text could have been 13.2 cm long. With an expected right-hand margin of some 1.2 cm, the width of the column comes to about 14.5 cm, which is wider than the average column of other manuscripts from Masada.

137. García Martínez et al., *DJD* XXIII, 1–9. Plate 1; "Explore the Archive," B-371386, Plate 566; Mathews, "The Leviticus Scroll," 171–207, esp. 172–73.

138. García Martínez et al., *DJD* XXIII, 1. See Lange, *Handbuch*, 76.

139. Kugler and Baek, *Leviticus at Qumran*, 8.

140. Ulrich, *Dead Sea Scrolls*, 254.

141. Talmon, *Masada VI*, 38. Illustration 3.

The average amount of letters and inter-word spaces is 70, which implies that the lines of this manuscript were longer and the columns accordingly wider than in other biblical fragments from Masada.[142] The comparatively large width suggests that the scroll was very long.

Scribal Features

The scroll from which this fragment stems was penned in an early Herodian formal script and can be dated to the last quarter of the first century BCE. The letters are well written, but at the end of the bottom line the letters are appreciably smaller and somewhat crowded, for no apparent reason.[143]

Textual Affiliation

The preserved MasLev[a] is identical to MT, except for the *plene* spelling of ישפוך (1.6).[144] The Masada corpus contains biblical texts that are all closely related to the MT, while the Qumran biblical texts present a wide textual variety.[145] Ulrich suggests that all the orthographic differences and variants are quite minor and routine, involving no change in meaning and exhibiting erratically changing patterns of affiliation.[146] Talmon suggests that the persuasive identity of MasLev[a] and MT becomes fully apparent in four instances of variants and pluses exhibited in an ancient version or versions.[147]

Conclusion

The text of MasLev[a] shows the stability of one form of Leviticus in antiquity.[148] This form seems to have been a fixed and stable text, which could have influenced other texts from various places. It is difficult to decide how the manuscript might have been used.

142. Talmon, *Masada VI*, 37–39.

143. Talmon, *Masada VI*, 37.

144. Ulrich, *Dead Sea Scrolls*, 255; Talmon, *Masada VI*, 38.

145. Young, "The Stabilization of the Biblical Text," 364–90, esp. 370.

146. Ulrich, *Dead Sea Scrolls*, 255.

147. Talmon, *Masada VI*, 38. Compare Lev 4:4 and MasLev[a] 1.3, Lev 4:5 and MasLev[a] 1.3, Lev 4:6 and MasLev[a] 1.5, Lev 4:8 and MasLev[a] 1.7. Lange, *Handbuch*, 77–78.

148. Kugler and Baek, *Leviticus at Qumran*, 9.

Mas 1b (MasLev^{b})

Contents

MasLev^{b} contains a large part of Leviticus chapters 8:31—11:40 and is identical with the MT, with spaces between the chapters.[149]

Leviticus	Leviticus	Leviticus
8:31	9:12–13	10:9–20
8:33–34	9:22–24	11:11–13
9:1–10	10:1	11:15–21, 23–40

Physical Characteristics

MasLev^{b} consists of over forty fragments that are not preserved well. Some fragments are just small pieces and others are the size of the palm of a hand; all are very dark brown.[150] The size of MasLev^{b} could have been 18 cm high (25 lines or col. II has possibly 26 lines) and col. V can be estimated at 9–10 cm. Thus, the five columns together covered 54 cm.[151] Also, some contain only a few words and some have complete lines by joining other sheets.

Scribal Features

The scribe wrote this fragment with straight lines and each line is parallel. The letters are very clear and thus it was most likely written by an expert scribe in a Herodian book hand. The text may be dated to the late first century BCE or the early first century CE.[152] There are no variants against the Qumran manuscripts and only a few variants against P.[153]

149. Talmon, *Masada VI*, does not assign numbers to each of the fragments but simply places them in the order of Leviticus.

150. Talmon, *Masada VI*, 40.

151. Talmon, *Masada VI*, 49.

152. Talmon, *Masada VI*, 40–41. Illustrations 4; “Explore the Archive,” Leon Levy Digital Library, Plate 198.

153. Ulrich, *Dead Sea Scrolls*, 257; Lange, *Handbuch*, 77–78.

Textual Affiliation

MasLev[b] and MT are very similar, whereas the P, which adds more material, is quite different from these two text types. Despite the similarity of MasLev[b] and MT, there are still different spellings, suggesting that MasLev[b] may have been copied at a time in the transmission history of the biblical text when it was not yet orthographically stabilized.

Manuscript finds from Masada and Qumran suggest that five was the standard number of columns on a sheet of skin.[154] This observation of MasLev[b], that it is identical with MT, supports the view that MasLev[b] could have contained the book of Leviticus or possibly the entire Pentateuch.

Conclusion

MasLev[b] seems to have been a medium-sized scroll. It is not easy to determine what the purpose of this scroll might have been, but it could possibly have been produced for public usage in a cultic or educational setting since it was penned in a very careful and clear expert handwriting.

En-Gedi

Discovery and Date

An early Leviticus scroll from the debris of the ark of the synagogue at En-Gedi contains text from the first two chapters of Leviticus. The location of the discovery is significant for my analysis as it strongly suggests a cultic context for the use of the scroll. The scroll could have been copied between the third and fourth centuries CE, or in the second century CE.[155] The two columns have been preserved on one sheet of a leather scroll, with no stitches between one sheet and the next. This manuscript from En-Gedi was not a complete Torah scroll, but rather contained only one, two, or three books.[156]

154. Talmon, *Masada VI*, 42.

155. Segal et al., "An Early Leviticus Scroll," esp. 3. The two outer segments contain the text of Lev 1 and 2, with Lev 1 wrapped inside Lev 2, while the innermost segment that has been analysed has a large black area. We can therefore conclude that the scroll was rolled from its beginning, and the outer layers contained subsequent passages. This scroll was burned so it is not easy to determine the original length of the scroll.

156. Segal et al., "An Early Leviticus Scroll," esp. 6.

Physical Characteristics

According to the calculations of Segal et al., the two columns originally contained 35 lines each, of which 18 lines have been preserved and another 17 need to be reconstructed at the bottom of the columns. The published segment is 16.8 cm long and 7.8 cm high. Based on these measurements, the reconstructed height of the columns would be 18–19 cm, making this a medium-sized scroll.[157]

Scribal Features

The script of this Leviticus scroll from En-Gedi has many affinities with the fragments from the Judean Desert. It definitely belongs to the style of the "Jewish" book-hand attested in the scrolls of the Judean Desert.[158]

Textual Affiliation

The preserved text of Lev 1–2 matches the consonantal text of the medieval MT of Leviticus. There is not a single variant vis-à-vis MT and En-Gedi. This scroll can be characterized as strictly proto-Masoretic.[159]

Conclusion

The En-Gedi Leviticus scroll can be characterized as proto-MT, which supports the model(s) of textual development that had already been developed by scholars before its discovery. The text does not contribute to any new reading but its significance lies in its confirmation of textual history and in the location of its discovery in the synagogue. This scroll could have been used for cultic purposes.

CONCLUSION

The twenty-five Leviticus manuscripts analysed above are not all the same size and the same language, which implies that the book of Leviticus had a broad influence and various uses during the Second Temple period.

157. Segal et al., "An Early Leviticus Scroll," esp. 7–8.
158. Segal et al., "An Early Leviticus Scroll," esp. 20.
159. Segal et al., "An Early Leviticus Scroll," esp. 11.

Thirteen Leviticus manuscripts can be classified as large or very large scrolls: 1Q3 (1QpalaeoLev–Num[a]), 4Q17 (4QExod–Lev[f]), 4Q23 (4QLev–Num[a]), 4Q24 (4QLev[b]), 4Q25 (4QLev[c]), 4Q26 (4QLev[d]), 4Q26a (4QLev[e]), 4Q26b (4QLev[g]), 4Q119 (4QLXXLev[a]), 4Q120 (4QpapLXXLev[b]), 4Q365 (4QRP[c]), 6Q2 (6QpalaeoLev-medium or large), and 11Q1 (11QpalaeoLev[a]).

Due to deterioration and the fragmentary nature of many manuscripts, it is hard to determine the contents and size of each scroll. Nevertheless, enough information survives for us to conclude that the book of Leviticus was definitely treated as important, because many of these manuscripts were well prepared with few major corrections or scribal interventions. As an example, 11QpalaeoLev[a] was written on well-prepared skin with very careful handwriting. It is likely that at least some of these large scrolls were written for public use or for cultic purposes in the late Second Temple period.

These twenty-five Leviticus manuscripts are probably not all that survived from antiquity. Other small fragments are in the process of being identified and might enlarge the extant corpus. The survey in this chapter has shown that Leviticus was copied from 250 BCE (4QExod–Lev[f]) to the early first century CE (MasLev[b]), in various shapes and sizes, which probably indicates its significance in several different settings.

The book of Leviticus was sometimes copied with other texts, such as Numbers or Exodus, on a single manuscript. Leviticus seems to maintain textual stability since the majority of Leviticus scrolls do not show major textual variants. The text of MasLev[a] shows the particular stability of the form of Leviticus that preceded the later authoritative rabbinic text.

By closely observing Leviticus scrolls from Qumran, Masada, and elsewhere, several distinctive features can be highlighted. Leviticus survives in three languages: Hebrew (attested in square Hebrew, Palaeo-Hebrew, square Hebrew with Palaeo-Hebrew words, especially the Tetragrammaton), Aramaic, and Greek. Leviticus seems to have been popular, not only for the sectarians who lived at Qumran; even at Masada two of the seven surviving scriptural manuscripts are copies of Leviticus, indicating that it was amongst the more popular books there.

As this survey has shown above, all of these Leviticus scrolls reveal that there was probably a single edition of Leviticus in circulation. There are minor variant readings and manuscripts in different sizes and formats. As Ulrich states, "large parts of the book [Leviticus] appear as though they may simply have constituted the manual or instructions and regulations for the priest and the ritual and worship life of Israel prior to incorporation into the Pentateuchal narrative."[160] The significant conclusion is that Leviticus clearly influenced various communities in cultic, school, and private life.

160. Ulrich, "1QpaleoLev–Num^{a}," 341–47, esp. 346.

III

Jubilees and Leviticus

INTRODUCTION

In this chapter, I will focus on the influence of Leviticus on the structure and content of Jubilees. Though the Torah as a whole played a major role in the construction of Jubilees, Levitical themes stand out as central to this book. This has not gone unnoticed by scholars. For example, James Kugel argues that Leviticus closely influences and controls the structure of the beginning of Jubilees. He also argues that the purpose of Jubilees is to reveal the sins of Israel and to disclose God's covenant with them (Jub. 1:16),[1] a central theme of Leviticus (Lev 25–26). Jubilees opens with the concept that the people will return to God from their disobedience and keep the commandments (Jub. 1:15, 23), a theme with various allusions to Lev 25 and 26, as can be seen in this passage:

> But if they confess their iniquity and the iniquity of their ancestors, in that they committed treachery against me and, moreover, that they continued hostile to me—41 so that I, in turn, continued hostile to them and brought them into the land of their enemies; if then their uncircumcised heart is humbled and they make amends for their iniquity—42 then will I remember my covenant with Jacob; I will remember also my covenant with

1. Kugel, *A Walk through Jubilees*, 6.

> Isaac and also my covenant with Abraham, and I will remember the land. (Lev 26:40–42)

Another scholar who explores the relationship between Jubilees and the Torah is Michael Segal. He argues that the central themes of Jubilees[2] are based on Lev 25 and that Jubilees thus transformed the biblical law.[3] Kugel and Segal are not alone in their view of Jubilees, since most scholars conclude that the various themes of Jubilees are based on the Torah. However, the significance of Leviticus for the formation of Jubilees has not been fully developed by many scholars.

Thus, this chapter shows how the book of Leviticus, especially chapters 16–27, heavily influenced the formation of Jubilees. There are multiple implicit use of Leviticus including some verbal overlaps but several similarities in phrasing and ideas.

Background to the Book of Jubilees

Scholars commonly agree that Jubilees was written in Hebrew, but until the Dead Sea Scrolls were discovered, there was no textual evidence to support this conclusion.[4] The Hebrew version of Jubilees was likely translated into Greek and Syriac, and then from Greek into Latin and Ethiopic.[5] Yet only one fragment of the Greek text survives. Other evidence for the Greek version of Jubilees is found in the form of quotations and summaries in Greek sources. In fact, only the Ethiopic version has survived in a virtually complete state.[6] The discovery of Qumran fragments provided direct evidence that Jubilees was likely composed in Hebrew. Wintermute states, "the manuscripts from Qumran are near enough to the date of the text's composition and close enough to its original social matrix to exclude the possibility that they were translations from another language."[7] Nevertheless, because the Ethiopic text is the only complete version, the various parallels between Jubilees and Leviticus discussed in this chapter are, for the most part, dependant on juxtaposing the English[8] translation of the Ethiopic

2. Segal, *The Book of Jubilees*, 5–9; Monger, "The Transmission of Jubilees," 153–71.

3. Segal, *The Book of Jubilees*, 7.

4. VanderKam, *Textual and Historical Studies*, 4–5; Wintermute, "Jubilees," 2:43.

5. Fourteen Hebrew MSS from Qumran, one partial Greek MS, and nearly thirty Ethiopic copies are preserved.

6. Wintermute, "Jubilees," 2:41–42.

7. Wintermute, "Jubilees," 2:43.

8. Wintermute, "Jubilees," 2:52–142.

text with the Hebrew of Leviticus.[9] This means that some of the parallels are less precise than might be desirable, and some are implicit rather than explicit. However, I believe there are enough examples to show that Leviticus influenced the formation of Jubilees.

Date and Authorship

Though scholars have debated the date of Jubilees' composition, most have located its date in the second century BCE.[10] VanderKam used palaeographic evidence of the Qumran copies of Jubilees to date the text within the second century BCE.[11] The earliest of the Qumran Hebrew MSS comes from approximately 125 BCE. There are also two texts from Qumran dated to the first or second centuries BCE that may have used Jubilees (CD 16:2–4 and 1QapGen). This evidence also supports a composition date prior to 100 BCE for Jubilees.[12]

Scholars disagree regarding who the author of Jubilees may have been. For example, Wacholder maintained that a member of the Qumran community wrote Jubilees,[13] but support for this position is tenuous. Simply put, because the manuscripts were found in the Qumran Caves does not necessarily suggest the author of Jubilees was a member of the community. It may be as reasonable to assume that Jubilees is a work composed in Palestine before the settlement at Qumran was established, copied, and preserved by the Jewish community living there.[14]

9. VanderKam states, "the Ethiopic text of the book is very reliable and accurate" since almost all textual variants between Ethiopic and Qumran Hebrew texts occur in extra-biblical texts. See VanderKam, *Textual and Historical Studies*, 106.

10. Segal, *The Book of Jubilees*, 35. Zeitlin sees the date of *Jubilees* as earlier than second century BCE because the authors opposed the laws and traditions of the Torah, a position that would have been unacceptable in the Hellenistic period. See Zeitlin, *The Book of Jubilees*, 8–16.

11. VanderKam, "The Manuscript Tradition of Jubilees," 3–21, esp. 4–6; VanderKam, *Book of Jubilees*, 17–21.

12. Wintermute, "Jubilees," 2:43.

13. Wacholder, *The Dawn of Qumran*, 96–98. If Jubilees is written in the second century BCE and Qumran was not occupied until about 75 BCE by sectarians at the earliest, then assigning authorship to a member of the Qumran community is obviously not possible.

14. Fitzmyer, *The Genesis Apocryphon*, 23.

THE INFLUENCE OF LEVITICUS 26 ON THE STRUCTURE OF JUBILEES

The author of Jubilees describes this book as divine revelation that everyone should listen to and keep.[15] Jubilees 1:1, "come up to me on the mountain, and I shall give you two stone tablets of the Law and the commandments, which I have written, so that you may teach them." Jubilees is presented as divine speech[16] that needs to be taught to the people of Israel; many of the legal and halakhic passages are similar to the contents of the Pentateuch. However, the theme and commandments found in Lev 26 extensively control the structure and ideology of Jubilees with its focus on Sabbaths, covenant, and warnings.[17] In the example below it is possible to see some verbal overlaps between Lev 26 and Jub. 1 as well as several similarities in phrasing and ideas. The use of Leviticus remains implicit but is sufficiently frequent to be recognized by readers ancient and modern as deliberate on the part of the author or editor of this section of Jubilees. The following examples are based on my use of electronic search instruments and offer new insights to the discussion of Leviticus in the book of Jubilees.

Lev 26:25

I will bring the sword against you, executing vengeance for the covenant; and if you withdraw within your cities, *I will send pestilence among you,* **and you shall be delivered into enemy hands**.

Lev 26:2

You shall keep **my sabbaths** and reverence **my sanctuary**: I am the Lord.

Jub. 1:10

And many will be destroyed and seized and **will fall into the hand of the enemy** because they have forsaken my ordinances and my commandments and the feasts of my covenant and **my Sabbaths** and my sacred place, which I sanctified for myself among them, and my tabernacle and **my sanctuary**, which I sanctified for myself in the midst of the land so that I might set my name upon it and might dwell (there).

15. Najman, "Interpretation as Primordial Writing," 379–410.

16. George Brooke suggests that for the author of Jubilees the angel of the presence is commanded to dictate everything to Moses, rather than to write it all by himself since the Ethiopic text at this point (Jub. 1:27) has the angel being commanded to do the writing. See Brooke, "Exegetical Strategies in Jubilees 1–2," 39–58; Najman, *Past Renewals*, 135–6; Dominik Markl, "Sinai," 23–43.

17. The plan in Jub. 1–2 should be brought to fulfillment. The author of Jubilees describes the covenant, Sabbaths, and other laws throughout the book, heavily influenced by Leviticus. See Gilders, "The Concept of Covenant in Jubilees," 179–92.

Lev 26:34	Jub. 50:2
Then the land shall enjoy[a] its sabbath years as long as it lies desolate, while you are in the land of your enemies; **then the land shall rest**, and **enjoy[b] its sabbath** years.	And I also related to you **the Sabbaths of the land** on Mount Sinai.
	Jub. 50:3
	And **the land will keep its Sabbaths** when they dwell upon it. And they will know the year of jubilee.

First, the parallel examples from Leviticus and Jubilees provide evidence that Jub. 1:10 echoes Lev 26:25, with its warning for the future. The beginning section of Jub. 1 is reminiscent of the judgement and promise of Lev 26. Then, Jub. 1:10 ("many will be destroyed and seized and will fall into the hand of the enemy") has a verbal overlap with Lev 26:25 ("and you shall be delivered into enemy hands" [cf. Psa. 31:8; Lam 2:7]). Both Jub. 1 and 50 echo Lev 26, issues which the author continues to highlight throughout the book.

Second, the Sabbath theme from Lev 26 heavily controls the structure and contents of both Jub. 1 and 50.[18] The Sabbath in Lev 26 deals not only with human beings but also with the land given to the Israelites. The command to provide Sabbath to the land in Lev 26:34 is also found in Jub. 50:2–3.[19] In fact, the theme of the Sabbath dominates Jubilees and is clearly dependent on Lev 26.

Third, the author of Jubilees echoes the covenant with Abraham in Jub. 1:7–8, 18, which reminds the reader of the covenant with Jacob, Isaac, and Abraham mentioned in Lev 26:42. Leviticus' statement of God's assurance (26:12) is repeated in Jub. 1:18.[20] In addition, Levi, who was a son of Jacob,[21] becomes a significant figure in Jubilees. Jacob, not Abraham, is mentioned first. This is also evident in Jacob's actions toward Levi: putting a garment of priesthood upon him, filling his hands (32:3), giving him tithes (32:2),

18. A detailed discussion in terms of the Sabbath theme from Leviticus in relation to the book of Jubilees will be provided in the Sabbath section below.

19. More discussion will be provided in Expansion of the Sabbath in this chapter.

20. More discussion will be provided below.

21. The author of Jubilees considers Jacob and Levi as significant individuals in relation to the covenant of God. Jacob is called God's first-born son (Jub. 2:19–21); however, that does not just mean "individual patriarch" here (Jub. 2:19; 21:24). See Shemesh, "4Q265 and the Authoritative Status of Jubilees at Qumran," 247–60; Najman, *Seconding Sinai*, 57–58, 122–23; Hanneken, *The Supervision of the Apocalypses*, 99; Livneh, "The Biblical Background," 123–35; van Ruiten, "Divine Sonship in the Book of Jubilees," 85–105, esp. 92–93.

and giving all his ancestors' books to him (45:16).[22] Thus, it seems that the author of Jubilees wants to demonstrate how God's covenant with Noah and Abraham has continued to the time of Moses.[23]

Finally, the warning with conditional clauses in Lev 26 has influenced the beginning of Jub. 1:10, where the reason is revealed why the Israelites were under God's judgement.

Lev 26:14	Jub. 1:10
But if you will not obey me, and do not observe all these commandments	. . . *because they have (forsaken) my ordinances and my commandments and the feasts of my covenant and my Sabbaths and my sacred place*

Jubilees points out Israel's broken relationship with the Lord, but the author redefines God's will for his faithfulness and covenant.[24] In Jub. 1:1–4a the author sets out his own method for establishing the scriptural basis of his material, which shares similar teachings to the Torah.[25] In subsequent paragraphs the scriptural basis becomes similar usages of phrasing and ideas. The warning of their fathers' iniquity in Lev 26:39 and 40 is repeated in Jub. 1:22. The expression "iniquity of their fathers" is also found in Neh 9:2 and Jer 11:10, but Jub. 1:22 is closer in emphasis to the Leviticus text in that Jub. 1 echoes "enemies' hands" found in Lev 26.

22. Jubilees considers Levi to be a significant figure; however, the book of Jubilees does not only mention certain people, it is a book for all Israelites (Jub. 30:21). See Endres, *Biblical Interpretation in the Book of Jubilees*, 243–44; Himmelfarb, *A Kingdom of Priests*, 57–59.

23. The laws of circumcision were also required to be kept throughout the generations, which became an eternal ordinance (15:23–24, 28). At the same time, however, God predicted that the sons of Israel would break these laws and not circumcise their children (15:33). See Najman, *Past Renewals*, 47–48.

24. Cf. Jub.1:6 // Lev 26:9, 42.

25. Davenport, *The Eschatology of the Book of Jubilees*, 11.

Lev 26:39	Jub. 1:22
And those of you who survive shall languish in the land of your enemies because of their iniquities; also they shall languish because of *the iniquities of their ancestors*.	And the LORD said to Moses, I know their contrariness and their thoughts and their stubbornness. And they will not obey until *they acknowledge their sin and the sins of their fathers*.
Lev 26:40	
But *if they confess their iniquity and the iniquity of their ancestors*, in that they committed treachery against me and, moreover, that they continued hostile to me.	

Jubilees 1:22 depends upon Lev 26 for its ideology that repentance for their sins and their forefathers' sins is required before they experience the Lord's purification (Jub. 1:23). Richard Bautch states, "Jubilees 1:22–25 encapsulates the people's disobedience and their return to the God who loves them as a father loves his son."[26] In Lev 26 both forefathers' iniquities and God's covenant with forefathers are reflected in Jub. 1 and 50.

LEVITICUS 16–27 AND FOUR THEMES IN JUBILEES

Introductory Comments

Although there are significant uses of cult and purity regulations in Lev 1–16 (sacrificial regulations 1–10, purifications 11–16), it is important to note that the dominant use of Leviticus in Jubilees covers Lev 16–27,[27] chapters which have, in modern scholarship, commonly been associated with the Holiness Code. Martha Himmelfarb argues, "Jubilees arrives at its understanding of the implications for the temple of the behaviour of lay people through its innovative reading of the Holiness Code (Leviticus 17–26)."[28]

26. Bautch, *Glory and Power*, 127.

27. I have included Lev 16 since Lev 16:31 includes the theme of Sabbath. See VanderKam, "Moses Trumping Moses," 25–44, esp. 20–30.

28. Based upon Himmelfarb and Doering, the author of Jubilees is concerned with holiness not only in the sanctuary but also throughout the land. Doering says, "under the influence of the Holiness Code (H), this holiness becomes a reflection of God's own holiness (Jub. 16:26; cf. Lev 19:2). He further focuses on the land defiled by sexual impurity (16:5; 33:10, 14)." The expansion of this holiness in the book of Jubilees appears to be dependent upon Leviticus, especially the Holiness Code. The author of Jubilees seems to combine temple ritual, calendrical system, and covenant into a single format, already present in the Torah. See Himmelfarb, *A Kingdom of Priests*, 61–63; Doering,

Thus, the contents and ideology of Lev 16–27 appear to have been a basic foundation for the composition of the themes of Jubilees. This concept is supported by John Endres: "the Chronicler, but also of priestly collections of Torah and narratives connected with them (especially on issues of priestly purity). These traditions encompass concerns of both Levitical and priestly groups, and they hint at this author's theological deconstructionism."[29]

The structure and contents of Jubilees clearly reveal its dependence on Leviticus, especially Lev 16–27. The following summary of the main themes of Lev 16–27 lays a foundation for more detailed discussion of Jubilees' reliance on Leviticus as the core of the ideology found both in Leviticus and Jubilees. I will support this position by following four lines of argument.

First, the term *Jubilees* comes from Leviticus, which also describes festivals in Lev 23, indicating that both chronological and calendric systems in Lev 23 influenced Jubilees. Though Exodus, Leviticus, and Numbers use the 364-day calendar to help the Israelites follow God's commands,[30] the appointed festival times in Lev 23 have a greater influence on Jubilees, since its author eschewed following the 364-day calendar (Jub 6:32–38).

Second, Leviticus' use of the possessive form of Sabbath and the expansion of a sabbatical year to the land as well as to the people strongly influenced Jubilees (Lev 25).[31]

Third, the theme of holiness in Leviticus markedly influences the composition of Jubilees in that the combinations of holiness/purity, and covenant/restoration are reflected therein.

Finally, various other priestly motifs in Leviticus influence Jubilees: obedience and blessing (26:3–13), future warning, cursing and blessing (26:14–39), and repentance and restoration (26:40–45).

Four Significant Themes

Chronological and Calendrical Systems of Jubilees

The author of Jubilees uses a chronological frame heavily dependent on Leviticus throughout the composition of these texts.[32] Jubilees claims that the

"Purity and Impurity in the Book of Jubilees," 261–75, esp. 270–71; Najman, *Seconding Sinai*, 45; Olyan, "Defects, Holiness, and Pollution," 1018–28.

29. Endres, *Biblical Interpretation*, 235.

30. See Himmelfarb, *A Kingdom of Priests*, 54.

31. Guillaume, *Land and Calendar*, 138.

32. The division of the times of the law, weeks, and jubilees (Jub. 1) occurs four times (vv. 4, 26, 29) and again in the last verse of the book (50:13). Segal, *The Book of Jubilees*, 83.

chronological system is derived from the heavenly tablets and that the presence of angels allowed Moses to understand it; however, the chronological system was already in place in Leviticus.[33]

In this section, three points will be discussed: The term *jubilee* and its connection with Leviticus, the understanding of main festivals and the use of the calendar in Jubilees, and the influence of the eschatological theme in Leviticus on Jubilees.

The Term *Jubilees*

The term *jubilees* appears eighteen times in Lev 25–27 and one time in Num 36:4.[34] Undoubtedly, "Lev 25:8–17 is the biblical origin for the concept of a jubilee"[35] and the Levitical understanding of the jubilees influences the book of Jubilees extensively. Matthias Henze says:

> Already Jubilees' prologue underscores the primary importance the author places on the exact calculation of the biblical events according to a sabbatical calendar. The essential measurements of time are "years," "weeks," and "jubilees." These are mentioned throughout the book and form a chronological grid that is underlying the whole of the composition.[36]

The term *jubilee* in Lev 25 and 27 is used in various ways: return (25:10–13; 27:24), holiness (25:12), and release (25:28, 30–33), all of which influence the composition of Jubilees.[37] This term, used mainly in Lev 25 and 27, as incorporated into the book of Jubilees invites an examination of the larger context of the jubilee concept.[38] The author of Jubilees has grasped the importance of the chronological system from Levitical texts, thereby

33. Charles, *The Book of Jubilees*, xvii; Segal, "The Composition of Jubilees," 22–35.

34. The implication of restoration in Jubilees was not fully realized by the partial return of the Judeans from exile in Babylon. The chronological value of the jubilee comes to the foreground, in part as an aid in deciding when the restoration would be perfectly realized. The key text in this respect is Dan 9, where the angel Gabriel is said to specify a period of 490 years until the eschaton arrives. See Bergsma, *The Jubilee from Leviticus to Qumran*, 4; Hanneken, *Supervision of the Apocalypses*, 57–58; Doering, "The Reception of the Book of Exodus in the Book of Jubilees," 485–510.

35. Davenport, *Eschatology of The Book of Jubilees*, 69; Wellhausen, *Prolegomena*, 118–19; Abegg, "The Calendar at Qumran," 145–72.

36. According to Matthias Henze, the foreshadowed freedom and restoration in Lev 25 influences the eschatology in Jubilees, which urged the author of Jubilees to emphasize the heptatic chronology. See Henze, "Daniel and *Jubilees*," 35–65, esp. 64–65.

37. Jub. 1:18, 22; 23:31; 30:8b; 50:5

38. VanderKam, *From Revelation to Canon*, 542.

exegetically incorporating Jubilees into it. It is the presence of the term *jubilees* in the book of Leviticus that seems to have prompted the author of Jubilees to compose Jubilees, its jubilee cycle, and its ideology.

Festivals

Several of the festivals in Lev 23 heavily influenced the book of Jubilees. Interestingly, Lev 23 commands the reader to observe the Sabbath of full rest in all dwelling places (Lev 23:3) prior to its description of some festivals. Karl Weyde says "the theme of Sabbath in Lev 23:3 is another indication that the Sabbath was juxtaposed with the other festivals in question."[39] The author of Jubilees emphasizes a chronological determination for all the significant events in Israel's observance of the Sabbath (Jub.1 and 50). Bergsma comments, "the Book of Jubilees is the premiere example of the historical-chronological use of the jubilee in Second Temple literature."[40] Leviticus with its emphasis on festivals, leftover meals, and the feast of booths, significantly influenced the composition of Jubilees.

The expression in Jub. 49:1, "in its time, on the fourteenth of the first month . . .," depends on Lev 23:5 and uses Lev 19:6 as a combined text. In the following examples I have considered serveral more verses, such as Lev 23:5; 19:6, 37 to support this assertion.

Lev 23:5

In the first month, **on the fourteenth** *day of the month, at twilight*, there shall be a passover-offering to the Lord.

Lev 19:6

It shall be eaten on the same day you offer it, or on the next day; and anything left over until the third day shall be consumed in fire.

Jub. 49:1

Remember the commandment which the Lord commanded you concerning Passover, that you observe it in its time, **on the fourteenth** *of the first month*, so that you might sacrifice it before it becomes evening and so that *you might eat it during the night on the evening of the fifteenth from the time of sunset*.

39. Weyde, *The Appointed Festivals of YHWH*, 15.

40. Bergsma, *Jubilee from Leviticus to Qumran*, 302.

Lev 19:23–25	Jub. 7:1–2
(23) When you come into the land and plant all kinds of trees for food, then you shall regard their fruit as forbidden;[a] **for three years** *it shall be forbidden to you; it must not be eaten*. (24) **In the fourth year** *all their fruit shall be set apart for rejoicing in the Lord.* (25) But in the fifth year you may eat of their fruit, that their yield may be increased for you: I am the Lord your God.	And *it produced fruit* **in the fourth year** . . . and he made wine from it, and he put it in a vessel, and he guarded until the fifth year.
	Jub. 7:36
	For three years *its fruit will not be gathered* from everything which may be eaten, but **in the fourth year** *its fruits will be gathered, and let one offer up the first fruits which are acceptable before the Lord Most High* . . .
Lev 19:37	Jub. 49:7
You shall keep [observe] all my statutes and all my ordinances, and observe them: I am the Lord.	And you, *remember this day all of the days of your life and observe it* from year to year all the days of your life.

In Leviticus, the appointed day, month, and year is significant to help the Israelites keep all the festivals on time, but Jubilees argues that the Israelites did not keep these rules since they did not understand the chronological system. This is made evident in Jub. 1:4: "and the Lord revealed to him both what (was) in the beginning and what will occur (in the future) the account of the division of all of the days of the Law and the testimony."

According to the author's understanding of festivals, God set the time for these events; therefore, the people should keep these festivals and Sabbaths at their appointed time.[41] This observance is only possible if the people use the ideal solar calendar, which has 364-days.[42] James Scott argues "the sins of Israel in the land will include, among other things, violations of the calendar: abandoning God's covenantal festivals, his Sabbaths, and the jubilees (1:10, 14)."[43] Most of these violations are mentioned in

41. Jubilees 6:11; 14:1, 10, 18; 15:1; 16:3; 22:14; 44:1–8.

42. Jubilees 2:9, "And the LORD set the sun as a great sign upon the earth for days, Sabbaths, months, feast (days), years, sabbaths of years, jubilees, and for all of the (appointed) times of the years." The calendar in Jubilees rejects any lunar calendar (Jub. 6:17–38). See VanderKam, "The Origins and Purposes of the Book of Jubilees," 3–24, esp. 4. Kugel suggests that the author of Jubilees inaugurated the celebration of this festival on its own initiative (Jub. 16:5–35) by which God told Moses to promulgate a law in the Torah (Lev 23:33–35), commanding Israelites to celebrate the festival that Abraham initiated. See Kugel, *A Walk through Jubilees,* 8; Baumgarten, *Studies in Qumran Law*, 113–14.

43. Scott, "The Chronologies of the Apocalypse of Weeks and the Book of Jubilees," 67–81, esp. 76; Grabbe, "Jubilees and the Samaritan Tradition," 145–59; Stackert, "How

Leviticus. Moshe Bernstein states, "all this is unsurprising considering the well-known stress which Jubilees places on issues of the 'true' calendar versus deviant ones."[44] Jubilees uses the ideal solar calendar to construct an elaborate chronological system based on the number seven, and the idea of the Jubilee period is based on Lev 25:8–12.[45] Leviticus 25 is composed of two sections: concerning the sabbatical year and jubilees (25:1–22) and the jubilee legislation (25:23–55). The most detailed scriptural account of the sabbatical and jubilee year is found in Lev 25. The use of the term *jubilee* for a forty-nine-year period gives evidence for the development of this concept from the biblical text. Leviticus 25:8–55 prescribes the laws for the jubilee, but in this pericope the word always refers to a single year—the fiftieth. While the author of Jubilees employs a biblical term, he assigns to it a different meaning: for the author it is not the fiftieth year but the preceding period that stretches between two jubilee years.

The Passover in Jub. 49:1 echoes the Passover in Lev 23:5.[46] All the appointed dates in Lev 23 are more detailed than in other books. As an example, both Lev 23 and Num 28 describe an appointed time of sacrifice, but the Leviticus passage provides more detailed information. Thus Leviticus 23:24 says, "Speak to the people of Israel, saying: In the seventh month, on the first day of the month, you shall observe a day of complete rest, a holy convocation commemorated with trumpet blasts." The Leviticus passage provides a very specific time frame that obviously influences Jubilees.

The author of Jubilees expands the purpose of the Passover in Jub. 49:1 by adding more emphasis on the Lord's commandment. Leviticus 19:6 says that the peace offering may not be eaten on the third day; Jubilees agrees with this passage when it states that the paschal lamb is to be consumed on the fifteenth day.[47] Thus, it appears that the laws from Lev 19 and 23 influence the Passover rule in Jub. 49. And later, Jubilees provides detailed information about planting a vine and picking its fruit in the fourth year in

---

the Priestly Sabbaths Work," 79–111, esp. 98–104.

44. Bernstein, *Reading and Re-Reading Scripture at Qumran*, 679.

45. Bergsma, *Jubilee from Leviticus to Qumran*, 250. See Jub. 6:32, where the Israelites only recognized a 364-day (solar) year, VanderKam, *From Revelation to Canon*, 524. Jubilees and the Temple Scroll operate with the same 364-day cultic calendar, never conflict with one another regarding festivals, and agree almost completely about sacrifice and procedures for their holidays. See VanderKam, "The Scroll and the Book of Jubilees," 231; Schiffman, "The Book of Jubilees and the Temple Scroll," 99–115; Ben-Dov, "Tradition and Innovation in the Calendar of Jubilees," 277–93.

46. Cf. Num 9:5, 28:6; Josh 5:10; 2 Chr 30:15, 35:1; Ezra 6:19; Ezek 45:21.

47. Baumgarten, *Studies in Qumran Law*, 126. Cf. CD 10:14–17. The Festival of Oaths in Jub. 6:17–18 echoes Lev 23:15–21 and Deut 16:9–11.

Jub. 7:1–2, which is clearly based on Lev 19:23–25.[48] Jubilees adapts the concept of producing first fruits in the fourth year from Lev 19:23–25, though putting the product in containers and keeping it until the fifth year echoes Lev 19:25.[49]

The regulations of the Feast of Booths in Jub. 16:28–31 echoes Lev 23:6, 34, 44. These texts describe both the Feast of Booths as taking seven days and also characterising it as requiring rejoicing before the Lord (Lev 23:40). The author of Jubilees respects the laws of Lev 25 and the chronological continuity at Sinai presented there.[50] This point is highlighted in the following verses:

Lev 23:6	Jub. 16:29
And on the fifteenth day of the same month is *the festival of unleavened bread to the Lord; for* **seven days** you shall eat unleavened bread.	. . . that they will be observers of **the Feast of Booths seven days** with joy in the seventh month which is acceptable before the Lord as an eternal law in their generations throughout all (time), year to year.
Lev 23:34	
Speak to the people of Israel, saying: On the fifteenth day of this seventh month, and *lasting* **seven days**, *there shall be* **the festival of booths** to the Lord.	
Lev 23:40	Jub. 16:30b–31
On the first day you shall take the fruit of majestic trees, branches of palm trees, boughs of leafy trees, and willows of the brook; and *you shall rejoice before the Lord your God for* seven days.	(30b) They should dwell in tents and that they should place crowns on their heads and so that they should take branches of leaves and willow from the stream . . . (31) *he (Abram) was praising and giving thanks to his God for all things.*

The author of Jubilees borrows the idea of the Feast of Unleavened Bread from Lev 23:6 and 34 without mentioning eight days.[51] Instead, the

48. In Israel, this would hardly occur near the first day of the first month. Noah's procedure, which does not serve as a precedent for an explicit law in Jubilees, simply indicates that what he did was in harmony with Lev 19:23–25. See VanderKam, "The Scroll and the Book of Jubilees," 228; Kugel, "Jubilees," 272–465.

49. Kugel, *A Walk through Jubilees*, 69. Cf. Jub. 7:35–36.

50. Segal, *The Book of Jubilees*, 84.

51. Cf. the mention of eight days in Lev 23:36–39 and Num 29:35. Kugel suggests that the author sought to attribute to Jacob the institution of an eighth day of celebration following those seven days, as stipulated in the Torah (Lev 23:34–36; Num 29:35).

author maintains the expression "seven days" in Jub. 16:18–29, 32:6, which automatically implies a basis for sacrifice on the eighth day.[52]

Jubilees provides further detailed information about the festival celebrations in 16:18–31, clearly based on Lev 23. Jubilees 16:18–31 omits the statement, "you shall rejoice before the Lord your God for seven days" (Lev 23:40), without providing a reason, but Jubilees, according to Kugel, instructs the people "to live in tents (booths), [and] the Israelites are to place wreaths on their heads . . . the only festival on which the Torah commands that people rejoice."[53] The calendric system of festivals in Leviticus is clearly a structure that also influences Jubilees.

Eschatology

The final theme connected to chronology is eschatology. As discussed above, the two chapters, Lev 25 and 26, focus on warning and punishment for the future, themes that influence eschatology in Jubilees.[54] Bergsma suggests that Lev 25 looks forward to the eschatological dwelling of Israel in her own land, and enacts measures to ensure that this ideal will be renewed and restored. According to the eschatological section of Jubilees (23:9–32),[55] much of the evil derives from various sexual sins and uncleanness that destroy the purity of the community. Yet this text also provides the hope of peace and happiness for the future,[56] concepts which often echo Lev 25–26.

See Kugel, *A Walk through Jubilees*, 157.

52. García Martínez, "The Heavenly Tablets in the Book of Jubilees," 243–61, esp. 254.

53. Kugel, *A Walk through Jubilees*, 105, 244. Cf. Deut 16:14. The memorial days from Lev 23:24 may have influenced Jub. 6:23–31 and 11QT 25:3 ("[the month, you shall observe a day of rest, a mem]orial proclaimed by trumpets, a [holy] con[vocation]" (Lev 23:24).

54. Daniel 9 associates the coming of a messiah with the inauguration of a jubilee for Jerusalem and its people. Daniel 9 seems to assume the same association of Jer 25:11, 29:10 with Lev 26:34–35, 43 as was seen in 2 Chr 36:20–21. Cf. Dan 12:1–3 and Jub. 23:30–31; both texts share an eschatological scene consisting of the resurrection and judgements that are closely intertwined, a significant theme of Lev 25–27. See Henze, "Daniel and *Jubilees*," 35–65, esp. 58; DiTommaso, "Penitential Prayer and Apocalyptic Eschatology," 115–33.

55. The angelic speaker of Jubilees goes on to tell of a time when the divine punishment will come to an end and mankind's missing year will be restored. See James L. Kugel, "The Jubilees Apocalypse," 322–37, esp. 333. Cf. Lev 26:14–26 and Jub. 23:12–13, which is based on Lev 26:14–26; Deut 28:20–22; and Ps 90:10.

56. Endres, "Revising The Rebekah of the Book of Jubilees," 765–82, esp. 773.

Leviticus 25–26 concerns future punishment and judgment. However, that is not the end. Davenport suggests that in Jub. 1:4b–26 the angelic discourse teaches that Torah must be obeyed, that the people's disobedience brought them hard times, yet the book proclaims God's faithfulness to Israel (Lev 26:42).[57]

The author of Jubilees brings the Pentateuchal call to confession to bear on his own generation because he knows that the scattering is described as a warning in Lev 26:14–45.[58] The eschatological view of judgement and God's restoration from Lev 25–26 compelled the author of Jubilees to show the Israelites the mistakes that they and their forefathers had made. Jubilees 1:22–23a depends upon Lev 26:40 by making clear that the Israelites' problem is their disobedience of the commands in the Torah. The next parallel is an example of how ideas compatible with Lev 26:40 are found in the book of Jubilees.

Lev 26:40	Jub. 1:22–23a
But *if they confess their iniquity and the iniquity of their ancestors, in that they committed treachery against me and, moreover, that they continued hostile to me*	. . . *and they will not obey until they acknowledge their sin and the sins of their fathers.* But after this they will return to me in all unrigheousness and with all their hearts and soul.
Lev 25:10	Jub. 23:26
And you shall hallow the fiftieth year and you shall proclaim liberty throughout the land to all its inhabitants. It shall be a jubilee for you: *you shall return, every one of you, to your property and every one of you to your family.*	And in those days, children will begin to search the law. And to search the commandments and *to return to the way of righteousness*
Lev 26:42	Jub. 23:31
Then *will I remember my covenant* with Jacob; *I will remember also my covenant* with Isaac and also *my covenan*t with Abraham, *and I will remember the land*	. . . and they know that the Lord is an executor of judgement: but *he will show mercy to hundreds and thousands, to all who love him.*

The ideology of Leviticus with its emphasis on disobedience, return, and God's faithfulness is reflected in Jubilees. Returning to God and receiving freedom are part of the Jubilee period. "Returning to the mother" bears conceptual analogy to the jubilee mandate to "return" (שוב) to the family

57. Davenport, *Eschatology*, 14; Bergsma, *Jubilee from Leviticus to Qumran*, 293; Livneh, "Love Your Fellow as Yourself," 173–99, esp. 187–89, 198–99.

58. Davenport, *Eschatology of the Book of Jubilees*, 27.

clan (משפחה) and familial inheritance in Lev 25:10.[59] Jubilees 23:11–31, often called "the Jubilees apocalypse,"[60] describes warning and judgement as the result of disobedience along with hope for restoration, which is directly and indirectly influenced by Lev 25 and 26.

Sabbath

The Sabbath laws are central to much of Leviticus.[61] Leviticus emphasizes the fact that the Sabbath belongs to God ("my Sabbath") and the Sabbath is meant for the land.[62] This section discusses these two aspects of the Sabbath as found in Leviticus and their influence on the book of Jubilees.

Possessive Form of the Sabbath

The possessive form of the term *Sabbath* in Leviticus heavily influences the book of Jubilees. The book of Leviticus uses the possessive form to refer to various things: my food offerings (16:17), my house (14:35), my tabernacle (15:31), my face, my rules, my statutes (17:10; 18:4), my Sabbaths,[63] and my sanctuary.[64]

The use of שבתתי forms for the Sabbaths and the first person possessive forms of sacred places are a distinctive feature of Leviticus,[65] which is also found in Jub. 1:10:

> And many will be destroyed and seized and will fall into the hand of the enemy because they have forsaken *my ordinances* and *my commandments* and *the feasts of my covenant* and *my Sabbaths* and *my sacred place*, which I sanctified for *myself* among them, and *my tabernacle* and *my sanctuary*, which I sanctified for *myself* in the midst of the land so that I might set my name upon it and might dwell (there).

59. Bergsma, *Jubilee from Leviticus to Qumran*, 22.

60. Collins, "The Genre of the Book of Jubilees," 737–55, esp. 753; Hanneken, *Supervision of the Apocalypses*, 173–74.

61. Leviticus 19:3, 30; 20:3; 21:23; 26:2, 43.

62. Leviticus 25:2, 4, 6; 26:34, 43.

63. Leviticus 19:3, 30; 26:2, 43.

64. Leviticus 19:30; 20:3, 23; 26:2.

65. The plural form and possessive form of Sabbaths are used in Isaiah (56:4) and Ezekiel (20:12, 13, 16, 21, 24; 22:26; 23:38; 44:24) and Leviticus and Ezekiel combine my sanctuary and my Sabbaths. However, Jubilees depends upon Leviticus since Jubilees echoes Levitical expressions, especially Jub. 1 and 50.

Jubilees 1:10 uses the possessive form extensively, many of these forms are found in Leviticus. Among the many of these possessive forms in Jub. 1:10, *my Sabbaths* is found one time in Exodus (31:13) and four times in Leviticus (19:3, 30; 26:2, 43).[66] Milgrom observes that "in these passages, [Sabbath] is always found with a suffix or as a construct. The first-person plural suffix always refers to God; one never finds the singular šabbattî."[67] The emphasis on ownership of Sabbaths in Leviticus seems to influence the author of Jubilees as seen in Jub. 1:10.

Expansion of the Sabbath

Jubilees depends upon the expansion of the Sabbath from Leviticus, where Sabbath law is not limited to human beings only, but is also expanded to materials and land (Lev 25:2, 4; 26:34), as seen in Jub. 50:2–3. The majority of the references to the Sabbath are in Jub. 1:10, 2:17–33 and 50:6–13.[68] The Jubilees calendar does not allow any of the festivals or beginnings of the months to occur on the Sabbath. The stringent observance of the Sabbath is a central concern to the author of Jubilees (Jub. 50:10–11). Jubilees adds other halakhic proscriptions like festivals, sacrifices, blood, priestly shares, criminal law, and forbidden sexual relations.[69]

The author of Jubilees expands the term *Sabbath* from human beings to material objects, including the sanctuary and land,[70] and increases the

66. Isaiah and Ezekiel use the possessive form of Sabbath, Ezekiel especially deals with my Sabbaths and sanctuary (Ezek 23:38). However, Ezekiel uses the past tense while Leviticus uses the future tense. And warning for the future in Lev 26 probably influences the book of Jub. 1:10 ("will fall into the hand of the enemy").

67. Milgrom, *Leviticus 17–22*, 1612.

68. See Baumgarten, *Studies in Qumran Law*, 105–14; Najman, "Interpretation as Primordial Writing," 379–410, esp. 396–97. Cf. CD 3:14–15; 6:18–19; 12:3–6.

69. They include God's own holiness (Jub. 16:26; cf. Lev 19:21) and the land that was defiled by sexual impurity (Jub. 21:21–22; 30:22; 33:19; cf. Lev 18:25, 28; 20:22). Within this framework, Jubilees applies H's provision for a priest's daughter engaging in "fornication" (Lev 21:9) to all Israelite women and girls (Jub. 20:4). The forbidden sexual behavior (Lev 18:29) is related to suffering for the whole people (Lev 18:28) and defiling the land (Lev 18:24–30). See Himmelfarb, *Kingdom of Priests*, 67; Doering, "The Concept of the Sabbath," 179–203, esp. 180; Doering, "Purity and Impurity in the Book of Jubilees," 261–75, esp. 272; Lambert, "Last Testament in the Book of Jubilees," 82–107; Segal, "Legal and Narrative Passage in Jubilees," 203–28; Frevel, "Separate Yourself from the Gentiles," 220–50; Livneh, "The Biblical Background of an Extra-Biblical Conflict Account," 123–35; Frisch, "The Body in Qumran Literature," 155–82.

70. The Sabbath is linked to Israel's dwelling in the land and is thus an unalterable constituent of its existence. See Doering, "The Concept of the Sabbath," 201; Guillamue, *Land and Calendar*, 102–3; VanderKam, "The End of the Matter?," 267–87, esp.

importance of the Sabbath in terms of the degree of holiness attributed to this day (Jub. 2:26, 30). The concept that the Sabbath is one of the most important times for Israel to be considered holy and most scrupulously observed indicates heavy reliance upon the Levitical theme of holiness.[71]

Leviticus applies Sabbath observance, not only to human beings, but also to the land (and objects), which belongs to the Lord. The land itself needs rest during the Jubilee, a concept closely related to the notion that rest purifies the land from defilement.[72] The following example contains similar use of phrasing and ideas and this example is based on my own use of electronic search facilities.

Lev 25:2 Speak to the people of Israel and say to them: When you enter the land that I am giving you, *the land shall observe a sabbath* for the Lord.	Jub. 50:2 And I also related to you *the Sabbaths of the land* on Mount Sinai.
Lev 25:4 But in the seventh year *there shall be a sabbath of complete rest for the land*, a sabbath for the Lord: you shall not sow your field or prune your vineyard.	Jub. 50:3 And *the land will keep its Sabbaths* when they dwell upon it. And they will know the year of jubilee.
Lev 26:34 Then *the land shall enjoy its sabbath years* as long as it lies desolate, while you are in the land of your enemies; then *the land shall rest*, and enjoy its sabbath years.	

Jubilees 50:2–3 thus echoes the concept of the land's Sabbaths (Lev 25:2–7) and the years of Jubilee (Lev 25:8–12). In the last chapter of Jubilees (Jub. 50), the author reemphasizes the significance of keeping the Sabbath in relation to land. Jubilees 50:1–3, depending upon the Sabbath of the land in Lev 25 and 26, uses the plural form of Sabbaths, the usual form in Leviticus. The command, "the land shall keep a Sabbath," is not found in other texts, only in Lev 25–26. The expansion of the Sabbath to include objects and

267–69.

71. Doering, "The Concept of the Sabbath," 194.

72. Bergsma suggests that the common lexemes and themes that tie Lev 27 to Lev 25, as well as the indications of the antiquity of Lev 27, indicate that both pieces of legislation originated from the same or similar legislator(s) in the same or similar historical-cultural location(s). Thus, Lev 27 pertains more to the "original" jubilee legislation. See Bergsma, *Jubilee from Leviticus to Qumran*, 113.

land, as well as human beings, is a Levitical ideology that heavily influences Jub. 50:2–3, and is a theme that occurs both at the beginning and end of the book of Jubilees.

Levitical Combinations

Holiness and Purity

One of the most significant characteristics of Jubilees is the addition of legal passages to the patriarchal narratives. Jubilees does not include collections of laws like Leviticus. However, Jubilees reflects on many of the laws from biblical texts, in particular the intentional separation of God's people from all the nations. Leviticus 15:31 declares, "Thus you shall keep the people of Israel separate from their uncleanness, so that they do not die in their uncleanness by defiling my tabernacle that is in their midst" and Lev 20:24–26 specifically describes the separation of God's people from other people.

Lev 20:24	Jub. 2:19
I am the Lord your God; *I have* separated *you from the peoples*.	Behold *I shall* separate *for myself a people from among all the nations.* And **I will sanctify** them for myself and I will bless them. Just as **I have sanctified** and **shall sanctify** the Sabbath day for myself (cf. Exod 31:13; Ezek 20:12) thus shall I bless them. And *they will be my people and I will be their God*
Lev 20:26	
And *I have separated you from the other peoples to be mine.*	
Lev 20:8; 21:8; 22:9, 16, 32	
Keep my statutes, and observe them; I am the Lord; **I sanctify** you.	

The ideology of separation of God's people from others appears primarily in Leviticus. The purpose of this separation is to maintain God's holiness. Though the idea of sanctifying Sabbaths is based upon Ezek 20:12, the separation of God's people from other people and the concept of sanctifying God's people are themes that echo Levitical texts. Jubilees 2:19 includes the separation of God's people, sanctifying them, and the Sabbaths, accompanied with a blessing. This verse uses themes from Leviticus, Exodus, and Ezekiel, but the main point of separating God's people to be holy is based on the theme of holiness in the Levitical texts.

Holiness in Leviticus is related to the land and its uncleanness, defilement, and Sabbaths. The ideology of Jub. 50:5, though not based upon Levitical texts, is very similar in terms of its treatment of previous sins (Lev

18:27a), the enemy's dwelling (Lev 26:42), and purifying the land (Lev 26:43). The following example contains compatible ideas in terms of land.

Lev 18:25	Jub. 50:5
Thus *the land became defiled*; and I punished it for its iniquity, and the land vomited out its inhabitants.	And jubilees will pass until Israel is purified from *all the sin of fornication, and defilement, and uncleanness, and sin and error*. And they will dwell in confidence in all the land. And then it will not have any Satan or any evil (one). And *the land will be purified from that time and forever*.
Lev 18:27	
(For the inhabitants of the land, who were before you, *committed all of these abominations, and the land became defiled*).	
Lev 26:32	
I will devastate the land, so that your enemies who come to settle in it shall be appalled at it.	
Lev 26:42–43	
(42) . . . and I will remember the land. (43) For *the land shall be deserted by them, and enjoy its sabbath years by lying desolate without them*, while they shall make amends for their iniquity, because they dared to spurn my ordinances, and they abhorred my statutes.	

Both sections of Lev 18 and 26 describe the purity of the land, evident in the book of Jubilees. The ideology of purification of the land depends on Leviticus since land is considered to be the people's inheritance from God (Lev 20:24). Leviticus uses the past tense to describe the situation of the land but also uses the future tense regarding God's promise to purify the land. Jubilees' dependence on this ideology is evident in the phrase "the land will be purified from that time and forever" (Jub. 50:5b).

The purity law from Lev 12:2–5 and the law of tithes from Lev 27:30 seem to influence Jub. 3:8–15; there are verbal overlaps and similar uses of phrasing and ideas. Jub. 13:25–26 exclusively in terms of the time required for purification:

Lev 12:2	Jub. 3:8
. . . If a woman conceives and bears a male child, *she shall be ceremonially unclean for* **seven days**; as at the time of her menstruation, she shall be unclean.	. . . **seven days** *for male*, but *for a female* **twice seven days** *in their impurity*
Lev 12:4	Jub. 3:10–11
Her time of blood purification shall be **thirty-three days; she shall not touch any holy thing**, *or come into the sanctuary, until the days of her purification are completed.*	. . . if she bears a male, she shall remain seven days in her impurity like the first seven days. And **thirty-three days** *she shall remain in the blood of her purity*. **She shall not touch anything holy**. *And she shall not enter the sanctuary until she has completed these days* . . .
Lev 12:5	Jub. 3:11
If she bears a female child, she shall be unclean **for two weeks**, *as in her menstruation; her time of blood purification shall be* **sixty-six days**	. . . and **sixty-six days** *she shall remain the blood of her purity*. And their total will be eighty days.
Lev 27:30	Jub. 13:25–26
All tithes from the land, whether the seed from the ground or the fruit from the tree, are the Lord's; they are holy to the Lord (Cf. Num. 18:21–24; Deut 14:22–23).	*. . . upon Abram and his seed a tenth of the first fruits to the Lord*. And the Lord ordained it (as) an ordinance forever that they should give it to the priest . . .

The purity law in Lev 12:2–5 clearly influences the author of Jubilees in 3:8–15. Based upon the description of Adam and Eve in Genesis, they were not born but created as mature adults by the hand of God, and the law in Leviticus says nothing about a child being impure, only the mother.[73] The author of Jubilees had Lev 12:2–5 in mind when he specified a further waiting period beyond the one and two weeks and several days to become pure.

Jubilees 34:12–13, 18 depends on Lev 16:29, 34; 23:27; 25:9, especially the themes of becoming clean before the Lord for their and their fathers' sins and the commands to offer atonement once a year.

73. See Kugel, *A Walk through Jubilees*, 231–32; VanderKam, "Exegesis of Pentateuchal Legislation," 177–200, esp. 188–90.

Lev 16:29 This shall be a statute to you for ever: *In the* **seventh month, on the tenth** *day of the month . . .*	Jub. 34:12–13 . . . **on the tenth of seventh month.** And he lamented all that night, because they had brought it to him in evening . . . and it happened as they were mourning and lamenting with him all that day . . .
Lev 23:27 Now, **the tenth day of this seventh month** is *the day of atonement*; it shall be a holy convocation for you: you shall deny yourselves and present the Lord's offering by fire.	Jub. 34:18 Therefore it is decreed for the children of Israel that they mourn **on the tenth (day) of the seventh month** . . . so that *they might atone for them(selves)* with a young kid **on the tenth (day) of seventh month**, *once a year, on account of their sins* because they caused the affliction of their father . . .
Lev 25:9 Then you shall have the trumpet sounded loud; **on the tenth day of the seventh month**—*on the day of atonement*—you shall have the trumpet sounded throughout all your land.	
Lev 16:34 This shall be an everlasting statute for you, to make atonement for the people of Israel *once in the year for all their sins*. And Moses did as the Lord had commanded him.	

Though Exod 30:10 also commands this atonement once a year, it is not related to their sins or their fathers' sins, as stated in Lev 16:29 and 34. Jubilees 34:18 exclusively uses Lev 16:19 and 16:34 for composing its texts to sanctify the entire people in Israel. The commandments in Lev 16 are not just directed to an individual's sins, but to the present and past sins of an entire group. This makes the issue much more complex: how to set sin aside, how to save guilty consciences, and how to deflect divine displeasure,[74] all of which are echoed in Jubilees.

Leviticus 16 provides the way the people become clean before the Lord by making atonement (Lev 16:30, 34), which is repeated in Jub. 5:17–18; 34:18. The author of Jubilees added the phrase in 5:17, "if they return to him

74. Carmichael, *Illuminating Leviticus*, 43; Debel, "Anchoring Revelations in the Authority of Sinai," 471–91.

in righteousness," while Lev 16:30 sounds as though the Day of Atonement were automatic.[75]

Covenant and Restoration

The author of Jubilees reflects the theme of the covenant in Jub. 1:17–18; 14:17–20; 15:4 and Jub. 50. John C. Endres argues:

> Israel's covenant theology has been mediated through priestly texts as well as those considered 'Levitical,' and it emphasizes actions and effect (blessings and curses) along with the holiness of persons, places and times. In Jubilees, however, the priestly concern with holiness achieved even greater prominence as the author masterfully blended it into his concept of a covenant community.[76]

The following examples illustrate this point:

Lev 26:44	Jub. 1:5
. . . *I will not spurn them, or abhor them* so as to destroy them utterly and break my covenant with them; for I am the Lord their God;	. . . *I have not abandoned them* on account of all of the evil which I am establishing between me and you today on Mount Sinai for their descendants.
Lev 26:12	Jub. 1:17
And I will walk among you, and *will be your God, and you shall be my people*.	*And I shall be their God and they will be my people* truly and rightly.
	Jub. 1:18
	And *I shall not forsake them, and I shall not be alienated from them because I am the Lord their God*
Lev 19:2	Jub. 30:8b
Speak to all the congregation of the people of Israel and say to them: *You shall be holy*, for I the Lord your God am holy.	. . . *for Israel is holy unto the Lord*, and every man who has defiled (it) shall surely die; they shall stone him with stones.

The influence of law and covenant in Lev 26[77] appears at the beginning of Jub. (1:5), and later in the chapter where Jub. 1:17–18 affirms the

75. Kugel, *A Walk through Jubilees*, 56.

76. Endres, *Biblical Interpretation in the Book of Jubilees*, 236.

77. Most importantly, Lev 26 manifests an interest in Abraham and the Abrahamic

re-established covenant from Lev 26:12. This is, in fact, one of the major themes in Jubilees.[78] Jubilees 1:17 depends upon Lev 26:12 with its command that the Israelites return to God in repentance so restoration will be given to them as God promised (cf. Jub. 1:15–18).

The idea of "return" is a significant motif in Lev 25 and 26. Leviticus 25:10 warns people to return to their property and their clan (משפחה) in order to obey his commands. Bergsma suggests that the idea of "returning to the mother" bears a conceptual analogy to the jubilee mandate to return to the family-clan and familial inheritance in Lev 25:10.[79]

The author of Jubilees predicts a restoration of the people,[80] a topic which dominates Lev 26. God's purification of his people is one of the major themes in Leviticus, a point which the book of Jubilees echoes by mentioning their sins and their fathers' sins from Lev 26:40. The texts in Leviticus, declaring the Lord's sanctification of his children, have been adapted in Jub. 1:23. The Levitical covenant and restoration provides the basic ideology for the composition of Jubilees.

Priestly Concerns: Levi (Genealogy), Priestly Books (Cultic Laws and Lore)

The final set of themes that I will discuss in this chapter is all related to the priesthood: Levi the person, and cultic images. The book of Jubilees focuses on Levi, who is the only one of Jacob's sons to inherit his father's and ancestors' books (Jub. 45:15); and Levi as a priest might have had the responsibility to renew them for his descendants. Levites later took priestly roles, and Jub 31:16 connects Levi to all other sons of Jacob and to the Lord.[81] Leviticus does not mention Levi; however, Lev 26:42 reflects on the reestablishment

covenant (26:9, 42), but that is not exclusive. See Bautch, *Glory and Power*, 54–56; Watts, "The Historical and Literary Contexts of the Sin and Guilt Offerings," 85–93; Rooke, "The Blasphemer," 153–69.

78. Kugel, *A Walk through Jubilees*, 21. The point of the book of Jubilees is that none of these judgements came because God abandoned Israel, but because of their own contrariness, which is the theme of Lev 26 as well.

79. Bergsma, *Jubilee from Leviticus to Qumran*, 22; Ruiten, "Divine Sonship in the Book of Jubilees," 85–105, esp. 86–87.

80. Jubilees 1:22–25 encapsulates the peoples' disobedience and their return to God who loves them as a father loves his son, a concept which Lev 26 strongly presents. See Bautch, *Glory and Power*, 127.

81. Ruiten, "Divine Sonship in the Book of Jubilees," 93–94; VanderKam, "Genesis 1 in Jubilees 2," 300–21; de Jonge and Tromp, "Jacob's Son Levi," 203–36.

of God's covenant with the patriarchs where Jacob is given priority, which appears to influence the author of Jubilees.

Lev 26:42	Jub. 2:20
Then *will I remember my covenant with Jacob; I will remember also my covenant with Isaac and also my covenant with Abraham*, and I will remember the land.	And *I have chosen the seed of Jacob from among all that I have seen*. And I have recorded him as my firstborn son, and have sanctified him for myself for ever and ever.
	Jub. 15:9
	And *I shall establish my covenant between me and you and your seed after you in their generations for an eternal ordinance* so that I might be God for you and your seed after you.

Jubilees names Jacob as God's firstborn in Jub. 2:20 and affirms the establishment of the covenant through Jacob and his descendants in Jub. 15:10. This theme is found clearly in Lev 26:42, where Jacob is listed before Isaac and Abraham. According to Jub. 30–32, the author affirms Levi as the seed of Jacob and raises him to the level of a priest who had received blessings and was elevated above his brothers. God's remembrance of his covenant with the patriarchs in Lev 26:42 is rewritten in Jubilees by extending the blessings to Jacob's descendants.[82] The patriarchs behaved like priests (Jub. 3:27; 4:25); other forefathers brought sacrifices (Adam, Noah, Abraham) but these concepts are not limited to Jubilees.[83] In Jubilees, the author seems to acknowledge the patriarchs' covenant, which is mentioned in Lev 26:42, and thereby Jacob's son Levi becomes a significant figure.

Jubilees connects the covenant with Abraham's faithfulness to God's commands.[84] The covenant with Abraham gives blessings to the land and to his children (Jub.14:18–28, 15:1–4).[85] The author asserts that the Lord blesses Abraham with descendants in order to establish a further covenant with them (15:4, 15:9–10). Here, the descendants of Abraham become

82. Shani Tzoref, "Covenantal Election in 4Q252 and Jubilees' Heavenly Tablets," 74–89.

83. Segal, *The Book of Jubilees*, 10; Bautch, *Glory and Power*, 132–33.

84. In Jub. 16:28 and Lev 23:40–42, it can be seen that the author employed the theme of feasts from Leviticus into Jubilees by adding expressions in order to make the text sacred.

85. Van Ruiten, "Land and Covenant in *Jubilees* 14," 259–76.

significant. But Jacob's son Levi is also very important,[86] for he is considered to be a person who maintains and renews all the laws he received from his ancestors. Levi becomes the priest of the Most High God (32:1), tithes are given to him (32:8), and all the books of the ancestors are given to Levi (45:15). The author of Jubilees describes Levi as having responsibility to preserve the laws in the books and renew them for his children until this day (Jub. 45:15). To achieve this command, Leviticus should be taken seriously as a guideline.[87]

Echoes of Levitic cultic images from Lev 2:2–5 are also found in various places in Jubilees, for instance, a pleasing aroma being one of the main cultic images in Leviticus evident in the book of Jubilees.[88] The following example is based upon my own use of electronic search instruments and seems to confirm that the use of Leviticus is more widespread than most scholars have previously thought.

Lev 2:2

And bring it to Aaron's sons the priests. After taking from it a handful of the choice flour and oil, with all its frankincense, the priest shall turn this token portion into smoke on the altar, an offering by fire of **pleasing odour [aroma] to the Lord**

Jub. 6:3

. . . and he offered up *a sweet* **aroma** *which was* **pleasing before the Lord**

Jub. 21:7

You will offer it all together on the altar (as) a burnt offering, *(as) a sweet* **aroma before the Lord**.

Jub. 32:4

. . . well pleasing for *a sweet-smelling* **aroma before God**.

Jubilees 6:3–4 emphasizes that Noah offers not only sacrifices but also a sweet aroma, "a food offering with a pleasing aroma to the LORD" (Lev 2:2). The author of Jubilees expands this concept from Lev 2:2, confirming that the Lord made a covenant that there would be no more judgement by a flood when He smelled the sweet aroma.

86. According to Jubilees, Moses' covenant was not just written by Moses himself but it was handed down to Moses from Noah and Abraham's generation (cf. Jub. 6:17–38; 15:25–34; 27:22–24; 32:2–9, 18–19, 21–24).

87. Davenport says, "the blessing will be upon Levi's children, that it will last throughout the ages, and that it is spoken under the influence of the spirit of prophecy means that A understood it to characterize the situation of the entire Levitical tribe as it should be in his own day as in the future (Jub. 13b–17)." See Davenport, *Eschatology of The Book of Jubilees*, 60.

88. Van Ruiten, "The Covenant of Noah in *Jubilees* 6. 1–38," 168–90.

CONCLUSION

In this chapter I have argued that the book of Jubilees is strongly influenced by Leviticus in two ways. The first of these has not been commented upon extensively by scholars who have worked on Jubilees. It is striking that, in addition to the obvious control of the narrative of Genesis and Exodus, Leviticus, especially chapter 26, has played a significant role in the structure of the opening and closing sections of the final edition of Jubilees, which begins and ends with the theme of Sabbaths from Leviticus and narrates the texts in relation to the Sabbath theme. The warning from Lev 26 is restated in Jub. 1:10 and the theme of Sabbaths, sanctification, and covenant in Lev 26 control the structure and content of the beginning and end of Jubilees (Jub. 2:19; 50:2–3).

In addition Jubilees adopts the term *jubilee* from Lev 25 and 27 to provide its chronological system. This term is found only in Leviticus. The entire book of Jubilees is based on a chronological system from Lev 25–27, and the calendrical system in Jubilees is adopted from Leviticus to inform the description of the appointed festival times, especially Sabbath observance. There is other evidence of the direct and indirect influence of Leviticus. For instance, Lev 26:1–13, 14–46 includes both God's promises of blessing and judgement, according to whether or not Israel obeyed the commands. These two themes, blessing and judgement, in terms of God's covenant and His plan of restoration for His chosen people, are prominent at the beginning of Jubilees.

Second, beyond the structural framing significance of Leviticus 25–27, Jubilees echoes several important themes, most of which are derived from Lev 16–27, that scholars have subsequently identified as the Holiness Code. Chief among these is the Sabbath: Jubilees insists that the Sabbath belongs to the Lord and that the Sabbath's regulations should be applied to the land as well as to the people of Israel. The authors of Jubilees employed other themes derived from the laws, chronology, covenant, and priestly ideology of Leviticus in significant ways.

Cumulatively, Leviticus influenced the book of Jubilees in terms of structure and contents, not just partially or in selected sections, but in the entire process of its composition.

IV

Leviticus in the Temple Scroll

INTRODUCTION

In this chapter, I will discuss some of the ways that Leviticus has influenced the Temple Scroll with respect to its structure, content, ideology, and expressions. Although the compilers of the Temple Scroll have relied on many biblical passages to compose new laws, my main focus will be on the use of Leviticus in this composition.

The two principal copies of the Temple Scroll were discovered in 1956. 11Q19 (11QT[a]) is well preserved except for the loss of the opening columns and damage to the tops of the columns throughout the scroll, damage thought to have been caused by the way Kando stored the scroll between 1956 and 1967. In 11Q20 (11QT[b]),[1] nine or ten columns are missing before the first preserved column and eight columns are missing at the end of the manuscript. 11QT[a] is the longest scroll to survive from the eleven caves at Qumran, for it unwinds to a full twenty-eight and a half feet.[2] The compiler(s)[3] seems to have collected laws from many parts of

1. Schiffman, "The Temple Scroll," in *ABD* 6:349. It seems to have been written by two hands, one scribe writing cols. 1–5 and another (with some overlap of text) writing the remainder of the scroll. See García Martínez, "Cave 11 in Context," 199–209; Stökl Ben Ezra, "Further Reflections Caves 1 and 11."

2. Levinson, "Refining the Reconstruction," 1–26.

3. The principal copies of the Temple Scroll seem to have been compiled or edited by a "compiler" or "author" from several sources, which might indeed have had

the Pentateuch, especially Exodus and Deuteronomy, but interestingly, the name Moses is omitted in this scroll. This omission seems to be intended to demonstrate that the scroll contains a direct revelation from God, without Moses as an intermediary, thereby presenting a new law for the new age.[4]

The compiler collected various documents from different times and sources to compose the Temple Scroll. In the section on purity laws, many of its purity regulations are similar to those found in other Qumran documents (D/CD).[5] The opening sentence describes the building of the temple, its courts, and other temple regulations with the purpose of describing the temple that Solomon should have built, but never did. The text implies that the contemporary Jerusalem Temple is inadequate and polluted. Finally, the text reworks a large part of Deuteronomy and, by expanding Deut 17, provides ways to defend the nation from its enemies and describes the ideal king for the nation of Israel.[6]

The law in the Temple Scroll is based on Exodus, Leviticus, Numbers, and Deuteronomy, all of which have been reworked.[7] The date of the compilation of the Temple Scroll is broadly agreed. Yadin has proposed that the text was composed in the late second or early first century BCE[8], and Hengel, Charlesworth, and Mendels support a slightly later date in the early first century BCE date because they see the King's Law as written against Alexander Jannaeus (103–76 BCE).[9]

As to the style of the Temple Scroll, God speaks in the first person singular.[10] He is not referred to in the third person singular in order to emphasize that God directly addresses God's people. As Alex Samely has commented, "only the Temple Scroll represents a substantial, standalone text that transposes what, in the 'biblical' books, are divine

"authors." In this chapter I will generally refer only to the composition itself to avoid confusion about authors or editors. This is an ongoing scholarly discussion about the social affiliation of the compiler/author of the composition. As with the book of Jubilees, the Temple Scroll was found in more than one copy in the Qumran Caves—it is widely acknowledged to be consistent with sectarian ideology but is not necessarily a sectarian composition itself (oral communication with George Brooke, May, 2017).

4. Wise et al., *The Dead Sea Scrolls*, 593.

5. Milgrom, "The Scriptural Foundations and Deviations," 83–100.

6. Much of the contents are also reflected in 4Q524.

7. Lawrence H. Schiffman, "The Temple Scroll (11Q19)," 6–20.

8. Yadin, ed., *The Temple Scroll*, 1:18.

9. Hengel et al., "The Polemical Character," 28–38; Schiffman, "Temple Scroll," 3036–107.

10. According to Yadin, the replacement of third person with the first person for God is normal in the scrolls. See Yadin, *Temple Scroll* 1, 71–73.

commandments—reported as speech, but from a third-person perspective—into continuous first-person divine speech."[11]

Representing God's divine speech provides corresponding authority to encourage the people to strictly follow the law since God himself is the lawgiver. It is also notable that the first person singular is used more than fifty times in Leviticus. In the Temple Scroll, the third person singular is replaced mostly by the first person singular.[12] Similar direct speech has been used in the Torah, such as in Exodus, but the form of the first person singular is especially dominant in Leviticus. In fact, God personally purifies the sanctuary, land, and other objects in Leviticus, which suggests the influence of Leviticus on the Temple Scroll.[13]

The parallel examples below show first person singular in Leviticus in reference to the Lord, as does the Temple Scroll.

Lev 11:44	11QT[a] 29:8
כִּי אֲנִי יְהוָה֮ אֱלֹהֵיכֶם	ואקדשה [את מ]קֿדשי בכבודי אשר אשכין
For I am the Lord your God	I shall sanctify my [te]mple with my glory, for I shall make my glory reside
Lev 20:24	11QT[a] 53:8
תִּירְשׁוּ אֶת־אַדְמָתָם֒ וַאֲנִ֞י אֶתְּנֶנָּה לָכֶם֙ לָרֶשֶׁת . . . אֲנִי֙ יְהוָה אֱלֹהֵיכֶם	לפני אני יהוה אלוהיכה
You shall inherit their land, and I will give it to you to possess . . . **I am the Lord your God.**	In my sight, **I am YHWH, your God**
	11QT[a] 60:16
	כי תבוא אל הארץ אשר אנוכי נותן לכה לוא תלמד לעשות
	When you enter the land which I am going to give you, you shall not learn to do

11. Samely, "Observations on the Structure," 233–77, esp. 234.

12. In the Temple Scroll the Lord is presented as speaking in the first person singular. See Wilson and Wills, "Literary Sources of the Temple Scroll," 275–88; Yadin, *The Temple Scroll: The Hidden Law of the Dead Sea Sect*, 64.

13. To show how the Temple Scroll depended on Leviticus, I have presented examples from the Scroll and the MT in parallel. Throughout the examples in this chapter, I have used an underline with bold for verbal overlaps, underline with italics for similar phrasing and ideas, and italics without underlining for compatible ideas.

Lev 25:38

אֲנִי יְהוָה אֱלֹהֵיכֶם אֲשֶׁר־הוֹצֵאתִי אֶתְכֶם מֵאֶרֶץ מִצְרָיִם לָתֵת לָכֶם אֶת־אֶרֶץ כְּנָעַן לִהְיוֹת לָכֶם לֵאלֹהִים

<u>**I am the Lord your God**</u>, who brought you out of the land of Egypt *to give you the land of Canaan*, and to be your God.

11QT[b] 12:7

[כי אני יהוה שוכן בתוך בני ישראל לעולם ועד]

[<u>**for I, YHWH**</u>, *dwell in the midst of the Israelites forever and always*].

In the following sections, I will present ideas reflecting the influence of Leviticus on the Temple Scroll in three main ways: First, I will show how the compiler of the Temple Scroll relied heavily upon Leviticus when formulating his theological agenda. Second, I propose that many of the motifs used in the Temple Scroll are heavily dependent upon Leviticus. And finally I will suggest that Leviticus serves as the base text for several sections of the Temple Scroll.

THE THEOLOGICAL AGENDA OF THE TEMPLE SCROLL

11QT[a] 29:2–9 is a key editorial section of the Temple Scroll. In this section, the Temple Scroll mentions the plan for the eschatological age. From this passage, we learn that God will come to build his Temple with his own hands (col. 29:9–10).[14]

Regarding the covenant with Jacob in col. 29:9–10, the text preserves only the name of Jacob and then it breaks off:

11QT[a] 29:9–10

עליו את כבודי עד יום הבריה אשר אברא אני את מקדשי
להכינו לי כול הימים כברית אשר כרתי עם יעקוב בבית אל

(29:9) for I will cause My glory to dwell upon it until the Day of Creation, when I Myself will create My temple; (29:10) <u>*I will establish it for Myself for everlasting in fulfilment of* **the covenant that I made with Jacob** *at Bethel*</u>

14. This reference might refer to God having made known his covenant to Jacob at Bethel. See Yadin, *Temple Scroll* 2, 129. Close parallels are found in Jub. 1:15–17 and 26–29. Schiffman suggests that that scroll is not a description of an eschatological Temple and its ritual; it is pre-eschatological. See Schiffman, *The Courtyards of the House of the Lord*, 46; Angel, *Otherworldly and Eschatological Priesthood*, 203–4.

Lev 26:42

וְזָכַרְתִּ֖י אֶת־בְּרִיתִ֣י יַעֲק֑וֹב וְאַף֩ אֶת־בְּרִיתִ֨י יִצְחָ֜ק וְאַ֨ף אֶת־בְּרִיתִ֧י אַבְרָהָ֛ם
אֶזְכֹּ֖ר וְהָאָ֥רֶץ אֶזְכֹּֽר

Then will I remember **my covenant with Jacob**; I will remember also my covenant with Isaac and also my covenant with Abraham, and I will remember the land.

There is no doubt that Lev 26:42[15] has a key influence on col. 29:9–10, but there are at least two different ways of understanding this covenant. First, some scholars argue that Lev 26 has extensive effect on the Temple Scroll and the compiler read into that chapter all three patriarchs' names, Jacob, Isaac, and Abraham for the composition of the Temple Scroll. Michael Wise suggests that Lev 26 was influential in the compiler's thoughts in three ways: 1) Lev 26:9–12 reiterates the terms of the promises made to Jacob at Bethel; 2) Lev 26:3–15 elaborates on the conditional element of the promises God makes in Gen 28:15, a concept which the Temple Scroll adopts, thus initiating the promises that follow in 29:7b–10; 3) taken as a whole, the primary theme of Lev 26 concerns life in the land and whether that life will be one of blessings or curses.[16] Wise also points out that Lev 26:42 is the only text that juxtaposes the name of Jacob with the term "covenant," thus showing its clear influence on the composition of col. 29.[17]

Second, other scholars argue that the Temple Scroll assumed only the person Jacob from Lev 26, since only Jacob is mentioned in the surviving text. In addition, Isaac and Abraham do not fit into the narrative of the Temple Scroll, whereas Jacob and Levi reasonably fit into its narrative.[18] At

15. This is the only place where Jacob is mentioned in direct relationship to the covenant in biblical tradition (Lev 26:40–45); Maier, *The Temple Scroll*, 86. Also, Chang suggests, "The Damascus Document's use of Deuteronomy and Lev 26 is possibly reminiscent of the Temple Scroll, which seems to be related to a development of a priestly sub-plot of Qumran covenant, especially for the Levitical priestly covenantal ideology." See Chang, *Phinehas, the Sons of Zadok, and Melchizedek*, 100; in addition, John Kessler suggests, "the concept of covenant is mentioned explicitly in Lev 26 and occupies a central place, occurring in Lev 26:9, 15, 25, 42(x3), 44–45." See Kessler, "Patterns of Descriptive Curse Formulae," 943–84, esp. 969.

16. See Wise, "The Covenant of Temple Scroll XXIX," 56–57. Leviticus 26 heavily influences the use of similar concepts and reference to the covenant with a promise in Jubilees and the Temple Scroll, which show similarities of language, vocabulary, doctrine, and law; cross references elaborate on passages (cf. 11QT[a] 29:10; Jub. 31:1–32:9, and Jub. 1:4 and 26). See Wentling, "11QT Eschatological Temple and the Qumran Community," 61–74, esp. 65–66; Swanson, "A Covenant Just Like Jacob's," 273–86; Elledge, *The Statutes of the King*, 211–13.

17. Wise, *A Critical Study of the Temple Scroll*, 159–61.

18. Cf. Jub. 1:10; Gen 28:10–22; 35:1–15. In Jub. 3 the installation of Levi as priest is linked with Jacob's stay at Bethel. See Maier, *Temple Scroll*, 86.

this point, I am not choosing either position since we have a lack of textual evidence; however, on both sides of the argument scholars agree that Lev 26:42 is one of the most significant passages for the composition of the covenant with Jacob at Bethel, a position I will argue in the following sections of this chapter.

The compiler of the Temple Scroll used Lev 26 as a basic source, though other texts such as Ezek 37 are used in col. 29 as secondary texts. The following discussion considers four issues related to the use of Lev 26 in the Temple Scroll.

First, the covenant with Jacob in Lev 26:42 is the base text for col. 29:9–10. It is not found in the book of Genesis, but only in Lev 26:42. Brooke suggests it is clear that Lev 26:42 must be the base text that explicitly refers to the covenant with Jacob in the Temple Scroll.[19] This covenant with reference to all three patriarchs is found in Exod 2:24, "God remembered his covenant with Abraham, Isaac, and Jacob," and 2 Kgs 13:23, "covenant with Abraham, Isaac, and Jacob," whereas in Lev 26:42 the covenant is connected with Jacob distinctively, "then I will remember my covenant with Jacob . . . ." These examples clearly indicate that col. 29:10 repeated the order found in Lev 26:42, namely that Jacob occurs first in the Temple Scroll and last in other texts.[20] Burgmann suggests that contemporary apocalyptic tendencies influenced the insertion of col. 29:7–10 between the feasts and the section on the building of the temple.[21] This suggests the compiler composed the texts with the belief that the Lord would establish the temple by himself to prove that he has kept the covenant with Jacob at Bethel (col. 29:8–10). The significant role of the covenant with Jacob in Lev 26:42 exemplifies the use of Lev 26 in the composition of the text.

Second, in addition to the use of Lev 26 as base text, Ezek 37 is used as a secondary text in col. 29. The compiler of the Temple Scroll recalls the

19. According to Brooke, "He [Jacob] is also associated with matters to do with the cult, with the temple and its sacrificial practices, and particularly with its priesthood that comes through his fatherhood of Levi." See Brooke, "Jacob and His House," 171–88, esp. 177–79.

20. This area is still under debate between those scholars who think that Jacob is mentioned first of three, and those who think that only Jacob is mentioned, since the rest of the scroll has to be restored; however, the scholarly consensus is that col. 29:10 depends on Lev 26:42.

21. Burgmann, "11QT: The Sadducean Torah," 257–63, esp. 258. Column 29:10 leads to three biblical passages, Gen 28:13–29; 35:1–15, and Lev 26:42. Leviticus 26:42 is the only passage in the Hebrew Bible that contains both the name Jacob and the term "covenant" without the inclusion of Abraham and Isaac as the recipient of the covenant. It is very clear that at 29:10 the compiler has Lev 26:42 specifically in mind. See Wise, "Covenant of Temple Scroll XXIX," 54–55.

covenant in col. 29:7 and 10, which references Ezek 37:23 and Lev 26:12, 42, 45.

11QT[a] 29:7
ורצית̊י̊ם̊ ו̊ה̊י̊ו̊ לי לעם ואנוכי אהיה להם לעולם

I will accept them, **<u>and they shall be my people, and I will be theirs</u>** forever.

Lev 26:12
וְהָיִיתִי לָכֶם לֵאלֹהִים וְאַתֶּם תִּהְיוּ־לִי לְעָם

<u>And will be your God and you shall be my people</u>

Lev 26:42
וְזָכַרְתִּי אֶת־בְּרִיתִי יַעֲקוֹב וְאַף אֶת־בְּרִיתִי יִצְחָק וְאַף אֶת־בְּרִיתִי אַבְרָהָם
אֶזְכֹּר וְהָאָרֶץ אֶזְכֹּר

Then will I remember my covenant with Jacob; I will remember also my covenant with Isaac and also my covenant with Abraham, and I will remember the land.

Ezek 37:23
וְהָיוּ־לִי לְעָם וַאֲנִי אֶהְיֶה לָהֶם לֵאלֹהִים

<u>They shall be my people, and I will be their God</u>

Ezek 37:26
וְכָרַתִּי לָהֶם בְּרִית שָׁלוֹם בְּרִית עוֹלָם יִהְיֶה אוֹתָם

I will make a covenant of peace with them. It shall be an everlasting covenant with them.

In Col 29:7, the compiler depends on Ezek 37:23 for its word order; it is possible Ezek 37:23 may also have been used as a secondary text in terms of the specific covenant with Jacob in col. 29:10, which clearly uses Lev 26:42. Though the compiler also seems to echo language from Ezek 37, col. 29:7 and 10 clearly depend on Lev 26:12 and 42:

Lev 26:12	11QT[a] 29:7
וְהָיִיתִי לָכֶם לֵאלֹהִים וְאַתֶּם תִּהְיוּ־לִי לְעָם	ורצית̊י̊ם̊ ו̊ה̊י̊ו̊ לי לעם ואנוכי אהיה להם לעולם
And **<u>will be your God, and you shall be my people</u>**.	And find favor they shall; **<u>they shall be My people, and I will be theirs</u>**, forever

Lev 26:42	11QT[a] 29:10
וְזָכַרְתִּי אֶת־בְּרִיתִי יַעֲקוֹב וְאַף אֶת־בְּרִיתִי יִצְחָק וְאַף אֶת־בְּרִיתִי אַבְרָהָם אֶזְכֹּר וְהָאָרֶץ אֶזְכֹּר	להכינו לי כול הימים כברית אשר כרתי עם יעקוב בבית אל
Then **will I remember my covenant with Jacob**; I will remember also my covenant with Isaac and also my covenant with Abraham, and I will remember the land.	And establish it for myself for all times, **according to the covenant which I have made with Jacob** at Bethel.

The above example contains verbal overlaps. Leviticus 26:42 lies behind col. 29:10, which is a stronger connection than with Ezek 37:26, which states "I will make a covenant with them" without specifying the recipient. The editor makes an eschatological point because the purpose of the temple is to fulfil the covenant that God had formed with Jacob (11QT[a] 29:10; Lev 26:42; cf. Jer 31:32). The temple is to be a part of the new creation at the end of days.[22] Brooke has clearly distinguished between the temple described in the plans for the Temple Scroll and the eschatological temple in col. 29,[23] the divinely created sanctuary that God promised Jacob at Bethel.[24]

Third, in addition to the use of Lev 26 as a base text, the compiler uses Exod 15:17–18 and 4Q174 1 2i:3 as secondary texts. The Temple Scroll adds the expression: "I will establish it for myself" (להכינו לי col. 29:10), which echoes "the sanctuary, O Lord, that your hands have established" (מִקְּדָשׁ אֲדֹנָי כּוֹנְנוּ יָדֶיךָ Exod 15:17), and "[— A temple of] the Lord are you to prepare with your hands . . ." ([—מקדש אדני כ]וננו ידיכה 4Q174 1 2i:3). The compiler clearly describes the man-made earthly temple that God had commanded to be built; nevertheless, eventually God himself would "create my temple . . . all times" in accordance "with Jacob at Bethel."[25] Thus col. 29:10 echoes Exod 15:17–18 and 4Q174 1 2i:3 in terms of God's plan to build the eschatological temple, but this text is still based on the covenant made with Jacob in Lev 26:42. It is clear that Exodus 15:17–18 and 4Q174 1 2i:3 are supplementary texts.

22. Yadin, *Temple Scroll*, 1:184.

23. Brooke, "The Ten Temples in the Dead Sea Scrolls," 417–34.

24. Column 29 is based on at least two biblical sources: Ezek 37 and Lev 26, with Lev 26 being dominant. See Swanson, "A Covenant Just Like Jacob's," 273–86, esp. 276–80. Schiffman and Eshel argue that the ideal plan, according to 11QT[a] 29:2–10 was intended for the present age, not for the eschatological future, but we do not have enough evidence to hold a firm position from the texts of the Temple Scroll. See Schiffman, *Courtyards*, 7, 46, 281; Eshel, *Exploring the Dead Sea Scrolls*, 200–201.

25. Yadin, *Temple Scroll*, 1:113.

Fourth, the covenant with Jacob in col. 29:9–10 is linked to Lev 26 in terms of Sabbath and creation.[26] In col. 29:9 the day of blessing is the day of new creation (יום הבריה) that is "at the End of Days," fulfilling the covenant.[27] Antoinette Collins suggests "the 'day of blessing' יום הבריה could also be identified with the only day recorded that God has blessed—that is, the Sabbath" (Gen 2:3).[28] The Temple Scroll deals with blessing and covenant, closely linked to Lev 26, and with God's glory, which is linked to Lev 9:6 and 23. In col. 29:9–10, the covenant with Jacob still controls the ideology in terms of the Sabbath. Tov suggests "the allusion to Sabbath and the indwelling of God in the people and the entire land conform to the characteristic of the covenant with Jacob. This seems to be a text of particular holiness—a mini 'holiness code' as in the Book of Leviticus."[29] Thus, it appears that the compiler of the Temple Scroll in col. 29:9–10 borrows the ideology of Sabbath and holiness from Lev 26 in the composition of the Temple Scroll.

To bring these ideas together, Lev 26 significantly influences 11QT[a] 29. The unique expression of the covenant with Jacob in Lev 26:42 controls the ideology of col. 29. The compiler of the Temple Scroll used other texts, such as Exodus and Ezekiel, but the examples in this section clearly show that Lev 26 is the base text controlling the Temple Scroll in col. 29.

MOTIFS FROM LEVITICUS

Beyond simply focusing on the construction of a building, the Temple Scroll includes several themes related to cultic practices. More than half of the Temple Scroll concerns the structure of the temple and its courts.[30] These passages include a discussion of the temple, courts, festivals, sacrifice, and purity laws and are all rewritten from various parts of the Pentateuch. While not much material is employed from Gen 1 through Exod 15 in the

26. Cf. Jub. 1:17 and 4QFlor 1–2.

27. Yadin, *Temple Scroll*, 1:177. Jub. 1:16, "and they will be a blessing . . . and I shall build my sanctuary in their midst." The possessive form of writing in Jubilees is closely related to the eschatological view from Lev 26. Yadin suggests that יום הבריה indicates the end of days, therefore implying an eschatological meaning. He provides two suggestions—day of blessing (יום הבריה i.e, the End of Days) or the day of (new) creation (יום הבריה). According to Yadin, the compiler believed in the earthly temple "on which I will settle my glory" (11QT[a] 29:8) and a possible eschatological (future) temple that God would build on "the day of blessing/day of creation." See Yadin, *Temple Scroll*, 1:113 and 2:125.

28. Antoinette Collins, "The Temple Scroll," 361–74, esp. 371.

29. Tov, *Collected Essays*, 3:372. See Baumgarten, *Studies in Qumran Law*, 51–54.

30. 11QT[a] 19 3:1–13:8, 30:3–45:7, 45:7–47:18.

development of the Temple Scroll,[31] Leviticus has heavily influenced the compiler in relation to those themes.

The next section builds on the previous argument and presents three examples of how Leviticus is used most prominently in the Temple Scroll: first, as general cultic practice, second, as light and lamps, and third, as sacrifice and land.[32]

General Cultic Practices

Two instances show the use of Leviticus with respect to cultic practices in the Temple Scroll. First, col. 34:7b–14b is strikingly dependent on Lev 1:5b–12b for its structure, content, and ideology. This column deals primarily with the process of the burnt offering, echoing Lev 1:5–12. Column 34:7b–14b copies the order of Lev 1:5b–12b with minor changes and borrows its ideology from Lev 1. Second, the priestly role from Leviticus has influenced col. 22:5–8. The following example contains verbal overlaps and similar phrasing and ideas that is based upon my own use of electronic search instruments and provides new information to the discussion of the use of Leviticus in the Scrolls.

Lev 1:5b	11QT[a] 34:7b–8a
וְזָרְקוּ אֶת־הַדָּם עַל־הַמִּזְבֵּחַ סָבִיב	7b כונסים א[ת הדם] במזרקות 8a וזורקים אותו על יסוד המזבח סביב
Dashing the blood against the sides of the altar	(7b) Gather *[all the blood] in bowls* (8a) *to sprinkle on the foundation of the altar, all around*
Lev 1:6	11QT[a] 34:9–10a
וְהִפְשִׁיט אֶת־הָעֹלָה וְנִתַּח אֹתָהּ לִנְתָחֶיהָ	9 את הגלגלים ופושטים את עורות הפרים מעל לבשרמה ומנתחים 10a אותמה לנתחיהמה
The burnt-offering shall be flayed and **cut up into its parts**	(9) The wheels and flay the bulls' skins from their flesh; next, **they shall cut them up** (10a) **into pieces**

31. The Book of Jubilees elaborates on Gen 1 to Exod 15 and the Temple Scroll elaborates on Exod 25 to Deut 34. Both texts freely adjusted what the compiler disagreed with or disliked from the biblical passage.

32. In this section, I have provided parallel examples of the Temple Scroll and Leviticus but not all of them are explict examples; however, these examples prove the use of Leviticus in the Temple Scroll in one way or the other.

Lev	11QT^{a}
Lev 1:9a (cf. 2:13a)	11QT^{a} 34:10b–11a
וְקִרְבּוֹ וּכְרָעָיו יִרְחַץ בַּמָּיִם	10b ומרחצים את 11a הקרבים ואת הכרעי
But its **entrails and its legs he shall washed with water**	(10b) **And washing** (11a) **the entrails and legs**,
Lev 1:7a	11QT^{a} 34:11b–12a
וְנָתְנוּ בְּנֵי אַהֲרֹן הַכֹּהֵן אֵשׁ עַל־הַמִּזְבֵּחַ	11b ומקטירים אותמה על 12a האש אשר על המזבח
The sons of the priest Aaron shall **put fire on the altar**	(11b) *Afterward they may burn them* (12a) *in the* **fire upon the altar**
Lev 1:13	11QT^{a} 34:13a–14
וְהַקֶּרֶב וְהַכְּרָעַיִם יִרְחַץ בַּמָּיִם וְהִקְרִיב הַכֹּהֵן אֶת־הַכֹּל וְהִקְטִיר הַמִּזְבֵּחָה עֹלָה הוּא אִשֵּׁה רֵיחַ נִיחֹחַ לַיהוָה	13a והקטירו הכוהנים בני אהרון את הכול 14 על המזבח אשה ריח ניחוח לפני יהוה
But *the entrails and the legs shall be washed with water*. *Then the priest shall offer the whole and turn it into smoke on the altar; it is a burnt-offering, an offering by fire of* **pleasing odour to the Lord**.	(13a) *The priests, the sons of Aaron, are to burn the entirety* (14) *upon the altar as an offering by fire,* **a pleasing odor before the LORD**.

In this example, it is apparent that Lev 1:5b–13 controls the structure and content in col. 34:7b–14b as follows: First, 11QT^{a} 34:7b–14 (cf. col. 52:19–21 and Lev 17:3–6)[33] is dependent upon the structure and order of Lev 1:5b–13. Column 34:7b–14 does not follow the order with explicit words or expressions; however, the order in col. 34:7b–14 is very similar to Lev 1:5b–13: sprinkle blood (Lev 1:5b // col. 34:7b–8a), cutting in pieces (Lev 1:6 // col. 34:10a), washing the entrails and legs (Lev 1:9a // col. 34:10b–11a),[34] fire upon the altar (Lev 1:7a // col. 34:11b–12a), priestly role, and pleasing aroma to the Lord (Lev 1:13 // 34:13a–14).

There are minor additions and omissions; col. 34:13a–14 does not include the expression "the entrails and the legs he shall wash with water" since it was mentioned in col. 34:10b–11a. In this example, the Temple

33. This purity law also seems to be dependent on Lev 17:3–6; Schiffman, "Temple Scroll," 3036–3107, esp. 3064–66.

34. Yadin suggests that as strangers or non-priests it was possible to slaughter a holy thing. And the compiler uses the idea of salting in col. 34:10 from Lev 2:13: "with all your offerings you shall offer salt." See Ezek 43:24, "and the priests shall sprinkle salt on them and offer them up as a burnt offering to the Lord." The compiler's emphasis on the fact that all offerings need to be salted links to Lev 2:13, "you shall season all your grain offerings with salt."

Scroll uses Lev 1, which might indicate the compiler used the whole book of Leviticus given evidence that Lev 26 has been used in a significant way in col. 29.

The connections between the two texts are shown in the following brief summary. Column 34:7b–8a, "gather [all the blood] in bowls to sprinkle on the foundation of altar" uses similar ideology; col. 34:8a echoes Lev 1:5b: "and throw the blood against the sides of the altar".[35] The expression על יסוד is rather close to a verbal overlap.[36] The expression "at the base or foundation of the altar" (אֶל־יְסוֹד מִזְבַּח) is used eight times in Lev 4–9. Column 34:8a, "and throw it around against the base or foundation of the altar," echoes the Levitical expression.[37] Also, "cut them up into pieces" (ומנתחים אותמה לנתחיהמה)[38] in col. 34:9b–10a echoes "cut into pieces" (וְנִתַּח אֹתָהּ לִנְתָחֶיהָ) in Lev 1:6; "washing the entrails and legs" (ומרחצים את הכרעים ואת הקרבים) in col. 34:10b–11a echoes "its entrails and its legs he shall wash with water" (וְהַקֶּרֶב וְהַכְּרָעַיִם יִרְחַץ בַּמָּיִם) in Lev 1:13; and col. 34:13a–14[39] depends on Lev 1:7a and 9b in terms of the priestly role and pleasing aroma to the Lord. "Pleasing aroma to the Lord" (רֵיחַ נִיחֹחַ לַיהוָה) is used in Leviticus from Lev 1 through Lev 26. This use of similar expressions provide evidence that col. 34:7b–14 depends upon Lev 1 for its structure and ideas.

Second, the Temple Scroll in 11QT[a] 22:5–8a is also influenced by the Levitical sacrificial process listed in Lev 3:2–11, which also contains verbal overlaps and similar use of phrasing and ideas. The following example is based upon my electronic instruments and seems to provide close relationship how Lev 3:2–11 influenced 11QT[a] 22:5–8a:

35. Yadin, *Temple Scroll*, 2:147.

36. Riska, *The House of the Lord*, 146.

37. Yadin considered that the compiler of the scroll borrowed from Lev 1:5 and added יְסוֹד, which is also from Leviticus. See Yadin, *Temple Scroll*, 2:145.

38. Column 34:9–10 uses the plural ומנתחים ("they shall cut them up"), which is also in the plural in the LXX at Lev 1:6; however, the Hebrew text of Lev 1:6 uses the singular וְנִתַּח ("Then he shall cut in pieces"). The scroll systematically put pronouns in the plural so that the content is close to the approach of the LXX. See Riska, *House of the Lord*, 146.

39. In col. 34:13 והקטירו הכוהנים בני אהרון but only the priest is mentioned in Lev 1:9, and Yadin suggests that the text of the scroll follows "and Aaron's sons the priests shall offer" (וְהִקְרִיבוּ בְּנֵי אַהֲרֹן הַכֹּהֲנִים, Lev 1:5). See Yadin, *Temple Scroll*, 2:147.

Lev 3:2	11QT^{a} 22:5
וְזָרְקוּ בְּנֵי אַהֲרֹן הַכֹּהֲנִים אֶת־הַדָּם עַל־הַמִּזְבֵּחַ סָבִיב	וזר]קֺו [הכוהנים בני] אֺהֺרֺוֺן את דמם [על המזבח סביב]
And *Aaron's sons the priests* shall **dash the blood against the sides of the altar**.	[and *the priests, the sons of] Aaron*, [are to **spri]nkle their blood [all around on the altar** . . .]
Lev 3:9	11QT^{a} 22:6
וְהִקְרִיב מִזֶּבַח הַשְּׁלָמִים אִשֶּׁה לַיהוָה חֶלְבּוֹ	ואת [בשרמה ו]חלבמה יקטירו על מזבח הֺ[עולה פט[כמש ואת]
You shall present its fat from the sacrifice of well-being, as an offering by fire to the Lord (cf. Num 18:17)	*and they shall burn [their flesh and] their fat on the altar of the burnt-[offering according to the re[gulation and].*
Lev 3:11	11QT^{a} 22:7
וְהִקְטִירוֹ הַכֹּהֵן הַמִּזְבֵּחָה לֶחֶם אִשֶּׁה לַיהוָה	[ומנחתמה]ונסכמה יקטירו
Then the priest shall turn these into smoke on the altar as a food-offering by fire to the Lord.	*They shall burn [their offering*] and libation.
	11QT^{a} 22:8
	[ל]יהוה וירימו מ[ן האילים ומן הכבשים תרומה]
	[To] the Lord. And they shall set aside an offering fr[om the rams and from the lambs]

The phrase "throw the blood on the side of the altar"[40] from Lev 3:2 is repeated in col. 22:5. The Temple Scroll did not display all the listed regulations from Lev 3, but in col. 22:6 the reconstructed expression, "the usual re[gulations]," is found and could refer to regulations in Lev 3, since col. 22:7–8 echoes Lev 3:11. 11QT^{a} 15:5–9 concerns the "ram of ordination"[41] and the expression "the fat tail near its spine" [האלי[ה תמימה לעומת עציהה 11QT^{a} 15:8) is based on "which shall be removed close to the backbone, the

40. The book of Leviticus deals with this subject twenty-three times from Lev 1 through 17. Other biblical books, like Exodus and Numbers, mention this same procedure but the Temple Scroll follows the structure of Lev 3 to explain the sacrifice. Leviticus 17:11 concludes "for the life of the flesh is in the blood, and I have given it for you on the altar to make atonement for your souls, for it is the blood that makes atonement by the life."

41. Leviticus 8:31 is reused by mentioning "the bread that is in the basket of ordination" in 11QT^{a} 15:3–4. See Schiffman, "*Milluim* Ceremony," 255–72, esp. 260–61.

fat that covers the entrails" (לְעֻמַּת הֶעָצֶה יְסִירֶנָּה וְאֶת־הַחֵלֶב הַמְכַסֶּה אֶת־הַקֶּרֶב, Lev 3:9).[42]

The Temple Scroll uses the list from Lev 3 in both 11QT[a] 15:5–9 and 22:5–8, with minor changes. Leviticus 3:2 is reflected in 11QT[a] 22:5 that Aaron's sons sprinkle (throw) the blood against the side of the altar. 11QT[a] 22:6–7 and Lev 3:9, 11 use the term "fat" on the altar and subsequently refer to burning the offering. Column 22:5–8a does not include the same words from Lev 3:2–11 but follows the order from Lev 3:2–11, making the texts very similar.

Lamp and Light

In 11QT[a] 9:12–14, the lamp and light are considered as a "statute forever throughout generations," which seems to be linked to Exodus and Leviticus;[43] however, Lev 24:3–4 appears to be the particular source for the motif of lamp and light in col. 9:12–14. In this section, it is clear that the compiler borrows the ideology rather than the structure or content from Leviticus. Column 9 is very fragmentary and it is not easy to ascertain accurate data. Though col. 9 employs the process of harmonization[44] with Exodus, the use of Leviticus is still dominant in col. 9:12–14. One of the reasons for this development may be that Exodus does not provide a detailed process of sacrifice while Leviticus does. The reconstructed text in 11QT[b] 7:21–22 states, "[. . . according to the re]gulation; it shall be a burnt-offering, a fire-sacrifice of a fragrance [appeasing to yhwh. . . .] they shall burn this oil in the lamps."[45] By comparing Lev 24:2–4 and Exod 27:1, we can see that the texts from Leviticus provide a more detailed process of keeping the light and lamp as an eternal statute. The following example contains verbal overlaps and compatible ideas.

42. Schiffman, "*Milluim* Ceremony," 260–61.

43. Both Exodus and Leviticus describe the covenant with an emphasis that the law of the Lord is forever and the generation shall keep it forever. See Exod 3:15; 12:14, 17; 27:21; 30:21; 31:16, Lev 3:17; 6:18; 10:9; 17:7; 23:14, 21, 31, 41; 24:3.

44. Yadin has already pointed out that harmonization is one of the main organizing features of the scroll. See Yadin, *Temple Scroll* 1, 74–77.

45. García Martínez and Tigchelaar, *The Dead Sea Scrolls Study Edition*, 1:1322.

Lev 24:2	11QT^{a} 9:12
צַו אֶת־בְּנֵי יִשְׂרָאֵל וְיִקְחוּ אֵלֶיךָ שֶׁמֶן זַיִת זָךְ כָּתִית לַמָּאוֹר לְהַעֲלֹת נֵר תָּמִיד	[. . . י]אִירו כול נרותיה ונתתה
Command the people of Israel to bring you pure oil of beaten olives *for the lamp, that a light may be kept burning regularly.*	*all its lamp [shall] give light you shall put*
Lev 24:3–4	11QT^{a} 9:13
3 מִחוּץ לְפָרֹכֶת הָעֵדֻת בְּאֹהֶל מוֹעֵד יַעֲרֹךְ אֹתוֹ אַהֲרֹן מֵעֶרֶב עַד־בֹּקֶר לִפְנֵי יְהוָה תָּמִיד חֻקַּת עוֹלָם לְדֹרֹתֵיכֶם 4 עַל הַמְּנֹרָה הַטְּהֹרָה יַעֲרֹךְ אֶת־הַנֵּרוֹת לִפְנֵי יְהוָה תָּמִיד	וערׄכו הׄכוהנים בני and *the priests, the sons of shall set*
(3) *Aaron shall set it up in the tent of meeting*, outside the curtain of the covenant, to burn from evening to morning before the Lord regularly; **it shall be a statute for ever throughout your generations**. (4) *He shall set up the lamps on the lampstand* of pure gold before the Lord regularly.	11QT^{a} 9:14 חוקות עׄול[ם לדורו]תׄמה **it shall be statutes for eve[r throughout] their [generation]***s*
Exod 27:21	
חֻקַּת עוֹלָם לְדֹרֹתָם מֵאֵת בְּנֵי יִשְׂרָאֵל	
It shall be a perpetual ordinance to be observed throughout their generations by the Israelites.	

In this example, the Temple Scroll suggests that Aaron and his sons, who were priests, will prepare this eternal statute for the next generation. 11QT^{a} 9:12 states, "all its lamps [shall] give light [toward its front]" (אׄירו כול נרותיה). The beginning of col. 9:12 was restored by Yadin, according to Exod 25:37 and Num 8:2,[46] and he also suggests that the texts were interpreted literally—namely, that all the lamps were turned to the front of the lampstand.[47] The compiler interprets other biblical passages literally; however, Lev 24:2–3 influences the contents of col. 9:12–24 in asserting that Aaron shall arrange the lampstands from evening to morning. Numbers 8:2 commands Aaron to set up the lamps, but the context of Lev 24:3 is closer to col. 9:12–14. Column 9:13 echoes Exod 27:21 and Lev 24:3, but the compiler's

46. Exodus 25:37, "you shall make seven lamps for it," Num 8:2, "the seven lamps shall give light in front of the lampstand." Cf. Exod 37:23; Num 8:2; Zech 4:2.

47. Yadin, *Temple Scroll*, 1:184.

reference to Aaron's role and its eternal statute for the generations has the contents of Lev 24 in mind.

Leviticus 24:3 distinctively declares that the lamp should be arranged before the Lord as a statute forever (חֻקַּת עוֹלָם, 11QT[a] 9:14; Lev 24:3). Both Exod 27:21 and Lev 24:3 use the expression "the statute forever" in relation to light; later the Temple Scroll connects it to the expression of pleasing aroma, which is dominant in Leviticus.[48] It seems that col. 9:12–14 (cf. 11QT[b] 7:21–22) harmonizes texts from Exodus, Numbers, and Leviticus; nevertheless, Levitical texts are still dominant in their use of similar expressions and regulations.[49]

Land and Idolatry

The themes of land and sacrifice in Leviticus are prominent. The land was an inheritance from the Lord (Lev 20:24) and was owned by the Lord. The land of Israel in Leviticus is also related to honouring God; the land would be defiled if people did not honour God (Lev 26:33) and His commandments (Lev 18:25). The theme of land is significant in Numbers and Exodus as well; however, Leviticus controls the ideology of the theme of the land in the Temple Scroll. The following section compares the vocabulary in col. 51:16 with vocabulary in Leviticus. It also surveys the ideology of land in Leviticus that appears in the Temple Scroll. The next example has uses of phrasing and ideas that are compatible with Leviticus. The following example is based upon my own use of electronic instruments and seems to confirm that the use of Leviticus is closely related to constructing ideas in this part of the Temple Scroll.

Lev 20:24a	11QT[a] 51:16
וָאֹמַר לָכֶם אַתֶּם תִּירְשׁוּ אֶת־אַדְמָתָם וַאֲנִי אֶתְּנֶנָּה לָכֶם לָרֶשֶׁת	את הארץ אשר אנוכי נותן לכמה לרשתה כול הימים
But I have said to you: *You shall inherit their land, and I will give it to you to possess.*	*The land that I am about to give you as an inheritance* (cf. 11QT[a] 56:12) forever

48. Seventeen times from Lev 1 through 26, whereas Exodus uses the expression three times.

49. The Levitical text seems to provide more accurate information about this forever statute in terms of light and lamp (cf. Lev. 24:3).

Lev 26:1	11QT[a] 51:19–21
לֹא־תַעֲשׂוּ לָכֶם אֱלִילִם וּפֶסֶל וּמַצֵּבָה לֹא־תָקִימוּ לָכֶם וְאֶבֶן מַשְׂכִּית לֹא תִתְּנוּ בְּאַרְצְכֶם לְהִשְׁתַּחֲוֺת עָלֶיהָ כִּי אֲנִי יְהוָה אֱלֹהֵיכֶם	19 לוא תעשו בארצכמה כאשר הגואים עושים בכול מקום המה 20 זובחים ונוטעים להמה אשרות ומקימים להמה מצבות 21 ונותנים אבני משכיות להשתחות עליהמה ובונים להמה
You shall make for yourselves no idols and erect no carved images or pillars, and you shall not place figured stones in your land, to worship at them; for I am the Lord your God (cf. Deut 16:22)	(19)*You shall not do in your land as the nations do. They sacrifice here, there,* (20) *and everywhere; they plant Asheroth, erect sacred stelae* (21) *set up carved stones to worship, and build themselves*

Lev 26:9	11QT[a] 59:11b–12a
וּפָנִיתִי אֲלֵיכֶם וְהִפְרֵיתִי אֶתְכֶם וְהִרְבֵּיתִי אֶתְכֶם וַהֲקִימֹתִי אֶת־בְּרִיתִי אִתְּכֶם	11b והושעתים 12a לארץ אבותיהמה ופדיתים והרביתים
I will look with favour upon you and make you fruitful and multiply you; and I will maintain my covenant with you.	(11b) *I will save them* (12a) *to the land of their fathers. So I will redeem them and multiply them*

First, though the compiler deals with the inheritance of the land in col. 51:16, found in various places in Torah, various aspects of the vocabulary are relevant. Exodus, Numbers, and Deuteronomy use the word נָחַל, while Lev 20:24 uses יָרַשׁ in examples shown above, meaning "inherit or possess." Column 51:16 uses יָרַשׁ instead of נָחַל. This is not a unique word in Lev 20:24, since other instances of יָרַשׁ can be found in other biblical texts such as Ps 25:13; 37:9 and Deut 16:20; however, the book of Leviticus uses the word יָרַשׁ in 20:24 twice. Column 51:16 uses the same word, יָרַשׁ, which means "to be an heir to someone"[50] while the meaning of נָחַל is "to maintain as a possession."[51] The land in Lev 20:24 is focused on the land as God's inheritance to be given to the Israelites as heirs to possess, an influence indicated by the addition of the word *forever* in col. 51:16.

Second, the ideology of the land in Lev 26:1, 9, the Lord's command to the Israelites to protect the land from moral uncleanness (Lev 18:25), influenced col. 51:19–21 and 59:11b–12a. Column 51:19–21 maintains that the ritual cleanliness of the land is God's command and is linked to the promise and covenant in col. 59:11b–12a.[52] The land of Israel is to be given

50. Koehler and Baumgartner, "יָרַשׁ," *HALOT,* 2:441–42.

51. Koehler and Baumgartner, "נָחַל," *HALOT,* 2:686

52. Molly M. Zahn sees col. 52:2–3 as a combination of Deut 16:22 and Lev 26:1 because of the phrase "do not erect for yourself a standing stone" in Deut 16:22; however, Lev 26:1 also contains this phrase. See Zahn, *Rethinking Rewritten Scripture*, 186.

by God to Israel as part of a covenant requiring separation from the nations and from their idolatrous practices (11QT[a] 51:19–21; 60:9–16),[53] which is also emphasized in Lev 26. Column 51:15, 19–21 and 52:2–3 closely follow the concepts from Lev 20:24 and 26:1 to protect the land the Lord gave them as an inheritance. Once the Temple Scroll moves to the passage in Deut 16:22, it takes advantage of a parallel formulation in order to include related material from Lev 26:1.[54]

In sum, the Temple Scroll borrows motifs such as cultic practices, lamps and light, and land and idolatry from other texts, particularly Leviticus. The compiler begins with the commandment to build a temple (Exod 28) and then proceeds through the temple plan, which includes the process of sacrifices and purity laws relevant to the various temple structures.[55] Much of the content, ideology, structure, and laws from Leviticus influence sections of the Temple Scroll to varying degrees.[56] The compiler of the Temple Scroll not only reuses the biblical passages, but also extends the ideology by adding words to emphasise certain aspects.

LEVITICUS AS A BASE TEXT FOR PURITY LAWS

Leviticus is used in some sections of the Temple Scroll as a base text to compose certain laws, especially purity laws[57] that are central to both Leviticus and the Temple Scroll in order to make the rules clearer and stricter. In cols. 48:1–51:10, the concern for purity continues, but the subject shifts from the temple to the land, that is, to people and objects in the towns.[58] This shift of the purity laws from the temple to the people and objects in the

53. Schiffman, *Courtyards*, 25, 282; Collins, *Scripture and Sectarianism*, 31–34, 47–50. Also see Deut 18:14.

54. Zahn, *Rethinking Rewritten Scripture*, 186.

55. Schiffman, *Courtyards*, 445.

56. In Leviticus, the regulations apply to the Levitical camp in the wilderness. The Temple Scroll extends the regulations to apply to all Israelite cities, a significant intensification. See Japhet, "The Prohibition of the Habitation of Women," 69–87. It is clear that the Temple Scroll moves in the direction of expanded (or maximum) holiness for the temple, land, objects, and inhabitants, which depends upon Leviticus. See Harrington, "Holiness and Law in Dead Sea Scrolls," 124–35.

57. Wilson and Wills suggest that the purity law in the Temple Scroll might have been added later by the compiler. See Wilson and Wills, "Literary Sources of the Temple Scroll," 275–88; Schiffman, "The Unfinished Scroll," 67–78.

58. Swanson, *The Temple Scroll and The Bible*, 175. Schiffman suggests that the compiler of the Temple Scroll extended the rules from the Levitical camp and the Temple Mount to the entire sanctuary, thus expanding the purity laws along with its architectural plan for an expanded *temenos (the Temple City)*. See Schiffman, *Courtyards*, 17.

Temple Scroll echoes the Levitical approach to considering holiness from God to animals (sacrifices), space (sanctuary), people (including priests), and land.[59] The concept of holiness originated from God and was expanded to include human beings and objects, including the sanctuary and the land.[60]

In this segment, I will discuss three substantial sections: the purity laws (11QT[a] 48:3–5a; 50:20–51:2), sacrifices and festivals (11QT[a] 18:2–12; 19:3), and grain offerings (11QT[a] 20:9–14).

The Purity Laws

Purity laws in the Temple Scroll are used extensively in cols. 45–51:1a. I will focus on 11QT[a] 48:3–51:2[61] and 11QT[a] 45:15–17 in this section.[62] These two passages significantly depend on Lev 11:21–31 and Lev 15:13 in terms of words and expressions, as well as in terms of their meaning. The following example contains verbal overlaps and similar use of phrasing and ideas.

59. Choi, "Exegetical Interpretation of Leviticus 19:1–18," 10. The Temple Scroll not only prefers the more stringent of the possibilities the Torah offers, but also expands the purview of the stringency to the law. Cf. Lev 15 and Num 5:2. See Himmelfarb, *Kingdom of Priests*, 94.

60. The Temple Scroll articulates its notion of sanctity and the presence of sanctity spread from the temple to the land of Israel (col. 47:3–6). This concept is the way Leviticus is described in terms of expanding the nature of holiness from God to human beings and from human beings to nature or objects. Likewise, the Temple Scroll considers the entire land as sacred space. See Schiffman, *Courtyards*, xxvii–xxviii; Werrett, *Ritual Purity and the Dead Sea Scrolls*, 125.

61. The purity laws in cols. 48–51 focus specifically on the holiness of the people, which reflects the Levitical theme of holiness (cf. Lev 19 and col. 51:8 "holy"). See Kratz, "Law and Narrative," 109–21, esp. 113–14.

62. Wise suggests that the redactor of the Temple Scroll drew from one or more collections of purity regulations and inserted them in the end of one section of the Temple Scroll (cols. 45-47), and that he has continued to construct his section in cols. 48-51. See Wise, *Critical Study*, 133–34. See also 11QT[a] 45:18 and Lev 14:1–8; 9–32. The Temple Scroll relies heavily on the purity laws from Leviticus, but I have chosen certain sections of the Temple Scroll that seem to be influenced heavily by Leviticus.

Lev 11:21

אַךְ אֶת־זֶה תֹּאכְלוּ מִכֹּל שֶׁרֶץ הָעוֹף הַהֹלֵךְ עַל־אַרְבַּע אֲשֶׁר־לֹא [לוֹ] כְרָעַיִם מִמַּעַל לְרַגְלָיו לְנַתֵּר בָּהֵן עַל־הָאָרֶץ

But among the winged insects that walk on all fours you may eat those that have jointed legs above their feet, with which to leap on the ground.

11QT[a] 48:4b–5a

4b אלה משרץ העוף תואכלו ההולכים על ארבע אשר
5a יש לו כרעים מעל רגליו לנתור בהמה על הארץ

(4b) **Also, among the winged insects that go about on four feet you may eat** (5a) **those that have jointed legs above their feet, which both leap on the ground**"

Lev 11:22

אֶת־אֵלֶּה מֵהֶם תֹּאכֵלוּ אֶת־הָאַרְבֶּה לְמִינוֹ וְאֶת־הַסָּלְעָם לְמִינֵהוּ וְאֶת־הַחַרְגֹּל לְמִינֵהוּ וְאֶת־הֶחָגָב לְמִינֵהוּ

Of them **you may eat: the locust according to its kind, the bald locust according to its kind, the cricket according to its kind, and the grasshopper according to its kind**.

11QT[a] 48:3–4a

3 [את אלה משרץ]העוף תוכלו הארבה למינו
והס[ל]עם למינו והחורגול
4a למינו והחגב למינו

(3) [The following are the] winged [insects] **you may eat**: "**the locust according to its kind, the ba[ld] locust according to its kind, the cricket** (4a) **and its kind, the grasshopper and its kind**.

Lev 11:29

וְזֶה לָכֶם הַטָּמֵא בַּשֶּׁרֶץ הַשֹּׁרֵץ עַל־הָאָרֶץ הַחֹלֶד וְהָעַכְבָּר וְהַצָּב לְמִינֵהוּ

These are **unclean** for you among the creatures that **swarm upon the ground**: **the weasel, the mouse, the great lizard according to its kind**

11QT[a] 50:20

כול שרץ הארץ תטמאו החולד והעכבר והצב
למינו והלטאה

Everything which **swarms upon the ground** will be **unclean**: **the weasel, the mouse, the great lizard according to its kind, and the gecko**

Lev 11:30

וְהָאֲנָקָה וְהַכֹּחַ וְהַלְּטָאָה וְהַחֹמֶט וְהַתִּנְשָׁמֶת

the gecko, the great lizard, the sand-lizard, and the chameleon.

11QT[a] 50:21

והכח והחמט והתנשמת כול איש אשר יגע בהמה
במותמה

The great lizard, the sand lizard, and the chameleon. *Anyone who comes in contact with them after they dead*

Lev 11:31

אֵלֶּה הַטְּמֵאִים לָכֶם בְּכָל־הַשָּׁרֶץ כָּל־הַנֹּגֵעַ בָּהֶם בְּמֹתָם יִטְמָא עַד־הָעָרֶב

These are unclean for you among all that swarm; *whoever touches one of them when they are dead shall be unclean until the evening*.

11QT[a] 51:1

[-..וכול היו]צא מהמ[ה במותמה ?.. — יהי]ו
טמאים

[As for everything that co]mes out of them, *[if a man touches it, he becomes unclean]*, for they are unclean.

11QT[a] 51:2

[ולוא] תׄטמאו בהמׄ[ה וכול הנוגע בהמה ב]
מותמה יטמא

You are [not] to defile yourselves with the[m. *"But anyone who does touch] a dead [creeping thing] becomes impure*

Lev 15:13

וְכִי־יִטְהַר הַזָּב מִזּוֹבוֹ וְסָפַר לוֹ שִׁבְעַת יָמִים לְטָהֳרָתוֹ וְכִבֶּס בְּגָדָיו וְרָחַץ בְּשָׂרוֹ בְּמַיִם חַיִּים וְטָהֵר

When the one with a discharge is cleansed of his discharge, *he shall count seven days for his cleansing; he shall wash his clothes and bathe his body in fresh water, and he shall be clean*.

11QT[a] 45:15–17

15 וכול איש אשר יטהר מזובו וספר לו שבעת
ימים לטהרתו ויכבס ביום
16 השביעי בגדיו ורחץ את כול בשרו במים חיים.
אחר יבוא אל עיר
17 המקדש

(15) Any man who wishes to purify himself from a genital emission *must count seven days as a cleansing period. On the seventh* (16) *day he must launder his clothes and bathe his entire body in running water. Afterwards he may enter the city of* (17) *the temple*.

Three observations can be made regarding 11QT[a] 48:3–51:2: First, this passage uses Lev 11:21–22 in terms of order and contents. Second, this passage, along with 11QT[a] 45:15–17, relies upon Lev 11:29–30 and 15:13 (cf. Lev 14:8)[63] in its use of words. Third, this passage uses the ideology of not touching the dead from Lev 11:31.

The first observation is that 11QT[a] 48:3—51:2 uses Lev 11:21–31 as a base text.[64] Column 47 does not continue in col. 48 and the beginning of

63. 11QTa 45:15–17 relies heavily on passages from Leviticus. According to the Temple Scroll, the impure person is allowed to enter the Temple City on the seventh day, which is found in Leviticus. See Jacobs, *The Biblical Masorah and The Temple Scroll:*, 43–51; Holtz, "Temple and Purification Rituals," 197–215, esp. 199; Berkovitz, "Some Temple Scroll Restorations" 445–50.

64. In 11QT[a] 48–51, Deut 14 has been used as a secondary text. Deuteronomy 14 seems to have only partially influenced col. 48 while Lev 11:22–31 seems to have broadly influenced the purity law, Lev 11:21 (48:3–5a), 11:22 (48:3–4a), 11:29a (50:20–21), 11:29b (50:20–21), 11:31b (50:20–21; 51:1b–3a), 11:32a (49:16a), 11:33 (49:8b–9; 50:17b–19a), 11:34 (49:7b–8a), 11:35b (51:1b–3a, 6b–7a), and sexual laws in Lev 18–20 (66:11–17). See Wise, *Critical Study*, 236. Deuteronomy 14 seems to have partially influenced the purity law (e.g., 48:7–10) as a base text while Lev 11 influenced the whole as a base. The Temple Scroll uses Deut 14:18, 21 and Lev 11:21–22 regarding animals that the Israelites may or may not eat in col. 48:3–7. Prohibitions from Lev 21:5 and 19:28 are related to col. 48:8–10. Both of these implicit usages of Leviticus conclude with a reference to the holiness of God's people. See Callaway, "Extending

col. 48 does not include all the laws on clean and unclean animals from Lev 11:22–31 and Deut 14. This implies there might be additions to the beginning of col. 48[65] because these two columns are not connected naturally and the beginning part of col. 48 is missing. The compiler combines two texts from Lev 11:21–31 and Deut 14 at the beginning of col. 48 before using Lev 11:22–31. Though the author harmonizes these two texts,[66] Lev 11:21–22 can be considered the controlling text in terms of words and expressions.[67] The Temple Scroll follows the process of ritual cleanliness from Lev 15:13 in 11QT[a] 45:15–17, such as by counting seven days, washing one's clothing and bathing one's flesh in living water, but as Werrett points out, the Temple Scroll in this section ignores some rules, such as providing two turtledoves or two pigeons for atonement (Lev 15:14–15).[68]

The Temple Scroll adapts Lev 11:21–22 in col. 48:3–5a and adds the term שרץ העוף. Yadin considers this to be the most ingenious piece of editing. The author uses the word from Leviticus, rather than Deut 1:8, and he uses לְמִינֹו, instead of לְמִינָהּ with the objective of harmonizing the text—"locusts of any kind" (הָאַרְבֶּה לְמִינֹו)—with Leviticus.[69] The author, in this case, is trying to combine two texts from Leviticus with Deut 14:19–20. Yadin suggests that Lev 14:20 has been used rather than Deut 14:19–20 because the compiler of the Temple Scroll fills the space at the beginning of col. 48;[70] however, cols. 48–52 closely follow the structure and contents in Lev 11:22–31, which implies that Lev 11 is controlling the section in 11QT[a] 48:3—51:2, not Deut 14.

In addition, col. 48:4b–5a echoes, with a slight variation, line 4b–5a: "That go about on four feet you may eat" (תואכלו ההולכים על ארבע) is very similar to the expression "to go on all fours you may eat" (תֹּאכְלוּ הַהֹלֵךְ עַל־אַרְבַּע, Lev 11:21). The author also follows Lev 11:21, rather than Deut 14:20, because the definition of "you may eat any clean

Divine Revelation: Micro-Compositional Strategies in the Temple Scroll," 149–62, esp. 154; Crawford, "The Use of the Pentateuch," 301–18, esp. 309–10.

65. Yadin, *Temple Scroll*, 2:206.

66. The compiler finishes the first sentence according to the shorter Lev. 11:20 "All winged insects that crawl upon all fours are detestable to you," since the space appears to be too short for the longer version found in Deut 14:19 and Deut 14:20, "you may eat any clean winged creature." See Yadin, *Temple Scroll*, 2:206–7.

67. 11QT[a] 48:1–2 also depends on Lev 11:20 that all winged insects that walk on all fours are detestable. See de Troyer, "The Legs and the Wings of the Grasshopper," 153–63.

68. Werret, *Ritual Purity and the Dead Sea Scrolls*, 155.

69. Yadin, *Temple Scroll*, 2:207.

70. Yadin, *Temple Scroll*, 2:206–7.

winged creature" (כָּל־עוֹף טָהוֹר תֹּאכֵלוּ Deut 14:20) is explained in Leviticus and reduces the contradiction presented by these two texts.[71] Thus, it is apparent that Lev 11:22–31 is the base text for cols. 48:3–5a; 50:20–21; 51:1, with omissions and additions.

The second observation concerns the heavy reliance of the author of 11QT[a] 50:20–21 on Lev 11:29–30. This section of the Temple Scroll begins by "loosely quoting the list of eight unclean swarming animals (שֶׁרֶץ) from Lev 11:29–30."[72] The lists of the unclean things are Levitical words that can be found only in Lev 11. Column 50:20–21 does not include all the names from Lev 11; however, col. 50:20–21 echoes Lev 11:29–30 in expressions such as "unclean, on the ground" before the list names.

Finally, the Temple Scroll borrowed the prohibition on touching a carcass from Lev 11:31 in col. 51:1–2, with small changes. The expression "you are not to defile yourself with them" (ולוא] תטמאו בהמ[ה] col. 51:2) is heavily influenced by Lev 11:31, which explains the meaning of defiling "dead shall be unclean" (מֵתָם יִטְמָא). This seems to have influenced the expression "a dead [creeping thing] becomes impure" (ב]מותמה יטמא col. 51:2). The idea that touching carcasses makes one unclean is clearly a concept derived from Leviticus. Deuteronomy 14:18 warns the people not to touch carcasses, but the text does not explain how one may become pure again.

Touching carcasses is strongly discouraged in Lev 11,[73] and those who touch carcasses are commanded to wash their clothes (11:25, 28, 40). However, the author of the scroll chooses to expand this purity law by harmonizing Lev 11 with "wash his clothes and bathe himself in water" (וְכִבֶּס בְּגָדָיו וְרָחַץ בַּמַּיִם Num 19:19), even though Num 19 does not limit the prohibition to carcasses (i.e., it includes human bones or a grave [Num 19:16]). The author expands the text of Lev 11:25, 28, 40 by using Num 19:16 to include bones, skin, and nails.

In summary, with respect to purity laws, 11QT[a] 48:3–5a depends heavily on Lev 11:21–22. 11QT[a] 20–21 adopts words or expressions from Lev 11:29–30. 11QT[a] 51:1–2 borrows the ideology from Lev 11:31. Thus,

71. The purity laws from Leviticus (17:15–16; 5:2–3, 5) are applied and a life of holiness is required of those who live in the land of Israel, for priests and community members alike. The command from Lev 19:2 "be you holy" could have influenced the ideology of the Temple Scroll in this section of purity laws. See Milgrom, "The Qumran Cult," 165–80, esp. 167.

72. Werrett, *Ritual Purity,* 127. The compiler of the Temple Scroll seemed to apply the priestly rules from Lev 22:4–7 in terms of the call to bathe. See Yadin, *The Temple Scroll,* 1:340; Harrington, "Leniency in the Temple Scroll's Purity Law?," 35–49.

73. Cf. 11:24, 25, 27, 28, 31, 32, 39, 40.

Lev 11 highly influences the structure and content of 11QT[a] 48:3–51:2 in the Temple Scroll.

Sacrifices and Festivals

In general, the list of festivals in the Temple Scroll corresponds to those given in Lev 23 and Num 28–29. First-fruits festivals in cols. 18:10–23:9 are closely related to Lev 23[74] in terms of the number and calculation of dates for its nonbiblical first-fruit festivals.[75] Leviticus 23:12–19 controls the structure and word order of 11QT[a] 18:1–12; 19:3, with minor changes. As Leviticus defines the Sabbath as an eternal statute, the Temple Scroll strongly relies on the Sabbath as a statute forever.[76] My argument is based on two observations: First, the Temple Scroll uses the same or similar words with minor changes, and second, the Temple Scroll's understanding of the Sabbath is based on the Levitical understanding of the Sabbath.[77]

Lev 23:12–19	11QT[a] 18:1–12; 19:12–13	Num 28:26–31
12 a lamb a year old	1 [-]ה אׄ[—] [. . . lambs a ye]ar old	
12 כֶּבֶשׂ Male lamb	2 לׄאיל הזה for this ram	אַיִל 28:27; 11:15 ram
14 עַד־עֶצֶם הַיּוֹם הַזֶּה until that very day	3 היום הזה on this day	

74. Leviticus 23 is used in the scroll from cols. 17–23, in various places. Leviticus 23 is dominant in the cultic legislations in the scroll, a text which the compiler adopted mainly from Leviticus and uses Numbers as supplementary texts: cf. col. 25:2–10 and Lev 23:23–25; cols. 25:10–27:10 and Lev 23:26–32, Num 29:7–11, and Lev 16. See Levine, "A Further Look at the *Mo'adim*," 53–65, esp. 54–55; Ginsburskaya, "Leviticus in the Light of the Dead Sea Scrolls," 263–77. 11QT[a] 17:6–16 also depends upon Lev 23:5–8. See Pakkala, "The Temple Scroll as Evidence for Editorial Processes of the Pentateuch," 101–27, esp. 118; Yadin, *Temple Scroll*, 1:89–90.

75. Callaway, "Extending Divine Revelation," 151–52. The Temple Scroll does not base its calendar on the lunar year, which means that it is based on the fixed solar year of 364 days reflected in other Qumran texts. Leviticus 23 heavily influences the Temple Scroll to interpret the dates for each festival. See Beckwith, "Temple Scroll and Its Calendar," 17–19. Leviticus 23 deals with Passover sacrifices, which influences both Jub. 49:1–23 and 11QT[a] 17:6–16; 18:2–12; 19:3 exclusively.

76. Due to space, I have provided only key words or expressions to show how Lev 23 controls the structure of 11QTa 18:1–12; 19:12–13.

77. The reconstructions follow the suggestions by Yadin, *Temple Scroll*, 2:75.

19 שְׂעִיר־עִזִּים אֶחָד לְחַטָּאת with one male goat for a sin offering (Lev 23:12)	4 שעיר]עזים לחטאת One male goat for sin offering	28:30 שְׂעִיר עִזִּים אֶחָד with one male goat
13 מִנְחָת . . . וְנִסְכֹּה grain offering and drink offering	5 מנחתו ונ]סכו grain offering and drink offering	28:31 וּמִנְחָתוֹ . . . וְנִסְכֵּיהֶם grain offering . . . and their drink offering
13 יַיִן רְבִיעִת הַהִין Wine, one-fourth of a hin.	6 ו]יין לנסך רביעית ההין a quarter of hin of wine for drink offering	15:5 וְיַיִן לַנֶּסֶךְ רְבִיעִית one-fourth of hin of wine as a drink offering
14 חֻקַּת עוֹלָם Statute forever[78]	8 חו]קות עולם Statute forever	15:15 חֻקַּת עוֹלָם a perpetual statute
12 בְּיוֹם הֲנִיפְכֶם אֶת־הָעֹמֶר On the day when you wave the sheaf (cf. Lev 23:11)	10 ביום הניפת העומר On the day when you wave the sheaf	
15 שֶׁבַע שַׁבָּתוֹת Seven Sabbaths	11–12 השבת השביעית Seven(?) full Sabbaths 19:13 השבת השביעית Seven(?) full Sabbaths	
16 עַד מִמָּחֳרַת הַשַּׁבָּת הַשְּׁבִיעִת תִּסְפְּרוּ חֲמִשִּׁים יוֹם You shall count until the day of seventh Sabbath, fifty days.	19:13 (cf 18:13) ממוחרת השבת השביעית תספורו חמשים יום The day after the seventh Sabbath. You are to count fifty days	
20 עַל לֶחֶם הַבִּכּוּרִים The bread of the firstfruits	19:12 את] לחם הבכורים The bread of the firstfruits	

First, the above example clearly shows that 11QT[a] 18:1–12; 19:12–13 depends extensively on Lev 23:12–19, even though 11QT[a] 18:1–12;

78. Cf. Lev 16:34; 17:7.

19:12–13 does not follow the order of Lev 23. The texts in the Temple Scroll emphasize and extend the notion that the sin offering is to include the wave offering, accompanied by a grain offering and libation.[79] In this section, the compiler of the Temple Scroll borrows most of the words or expressions from Lev 23 and applies them with minor changes to the order.

Second, the compiler of the Temple Scroll uses words, expressions, and ideology from Leviticus. In col. 18:2–10, the Temple Scroll echoes each of the sin offering regulations from Lev 23:12–19.[80] The Temple Scroll depends on concepts from Leviticus texts such as "a year old ram," "on this day," "male goat," "cereal offering," and "drink offering." The compiler also adds certain words. The added הזה in line 2 and the repetition of the term in line 9 ("the one ram") emphasizes the addition of a ram to the Leviticus provision for the offering.[81] In line 3, "on this day" (היום הזה), some space is left between ה and זה due to a flaw in the skin or an erasure,[82] and it is very clear that Lev 23:14 "until that very day" (עַד־עֶצֶם הַיּוֹם הַזֶּה) influences the Temple Scroll as a base text. Yadin suggests that Num 28:27 and 30, "with one male goat" (שְׂעִיר עִזִּים אֶחָד), are the base text for this line because of the similar phrase found in line 4, "a male goat for a sin offering" (שעיר [עזים לחטאת),[83] but Num 28:30 does not explain the addition of "sin offering"(לחטאת). Line 4 describes the importance of the sin offering, which is discussed in Leviticus more than fifty times. For example, the phrase "One male goat for a sin-offering" (שְׂעִיר־עִזִּים אֶחָד לְחַטָּאת) clearly bears a similarity to line 4.[84] In col.18:2–12, the author uses both Num 28 and Lev 23 in order to reconstruct the texts.

79. Swanson, *Temple Scroll*, 21. Lev 14:10. Lev 14–18 also describes the process of the sin offering of the male goat, which Jub. 7:2–3 describes. Yadin suggests that the Temple Scroll relied upon most of these concepts from the book of Leviticus. See Yadin, *Temple Scroll*, 1:146–8.

80. The application of Lev 23 in cols. 21:12–23:1 is very strong; therefore, it is reasonable to assume that the compiler of the Temple Scroll depends on Lev 23 to compose a new law, with some modification of the biblical passages. See Zahn, *Rethinking Rewritten Scripture*, 206–9; Zahn, "Identifying Reuse of Scripture in the Temple Scroll," 341–58.

81. Yadin, *Temple Scroll*, 2:77.

82. Yadin, *Temple Scroll*, 2:77. He suggested a partial restoration [מקרא קודש יהיה להמה] היום הזה according to Lev 23:21: וּקְרָאתֶם בְּעֶצֶם | הַיּוֹם הַזֶּה מִקְרָא־קֹדֶשׁ יִהְיֶה לָכֶם.

83. Yadin, *Temple Scroll*, 1:102–3.

84. In line 4, Num 28:30 שְׂעִיר עִזִּים אֶחָד לְכַפֵּר is reflected in line 4b–5a "[. . . and a male] goat for a sin offering to [atone]" [. . . ושעיר]עזים לחטאת ל[כפר] The author here harmonizes texts from Leviticus and Numbers to reduce the conflict by producing a festival law including sin offerings from Lev 23:19 and atonement from Num 28:30. Yadin suggests that according to the scroll, sacrificing the male goat for the sin offering is also to be accompanied by a cereal offering and a drink offering. See Yadin, *Temple*

Regarding the Sabbath law in 11QT[a] 18:11–12; 19:13, the Temple Scroll expands Lev 23:15–16 to make the law stricter. Milgrom suggests that "the fifty-day interval that Scripture mandates between the New Barley and New Wheat festival (Lev 23:15–16) is expanded by the Temple Scroll to the New Wine, New Oil, and Wood Offering festivals (cols. 19-25)."[85]

In 11QT[a] 18:10–13, the word שבת means literally "Sabbath," and "perfect Sabbath" (שׁבֹתוֹת תמימות col. 18:11) refers to the weeks terminating on the Sabbath day, a concept based on "full Sabbath" (שַׁבָּתוֹת תְּמִימֹת Lev 23:11, 15).[86] And all of the first-fruit festivals were to be celebrated on Sabbaths.[87] 11QT[a] 19:7–8 depends upon the assertion in Lev 23:21 that the Sabbath is to be a holy convocation as a statute forever, another implication that Lev 23:21 might influence col. 19:7–8. The Sabbath regulations are found in CD 10:14—11:18a and Jub. 1:10. Leviticus 16:31 declares that the Sabbath is a statute forever (חֻקַּת עוֹלָם). Though Exodus and Leviticus both share this expression, Lev 16:31 has very clear instructions that the statute lasts forever (חֻקַּת עוֹלָם). The following example contains similar use of phrasing and ideas and it is based upon my own use of electronic search facilities.

Lev 23:21	11QT[a] 19:7b–8 (cf. 17:3)
וּקְרָאתֶם בְּעֶצֶם ׀ הַיּוֹם הַזֶּה מִקְרָא־קֹדֶשׁ יִהְיֶה לָכֶם כָּל־מְלֶאכֶת עֲבֹדָה לֹא תַעֲשׂוּ חֻקַּת עוֹלָם בְּכָל־מוֹשְׁבֹתֵיכֶם לְדֹרֹתֵיכֶם	7b [הזה ם]ויה היהו 8 [מקרא קודש חוקות עו]לם לדורותם כול מלאכת עבו[דה לוא]
On that same day you shall make a proclamation; *you shall hold a holy convocation; you shall not work at your occupations. This is a statute for ever in all your settlements throughout your generations.*	(7b) *[That] day is to be* (8) *[a holy convocation, and these statutes are ete]rnal, for generation after generation. They shall do no work.*

Scroll, 2:75.

85. Milgrom, "The Qumran Cult," 172–73. Milgrom comments that this concept is found again in connection with the biblical tithe (cf. Deut. 14:23; Neh. 13:5, 12). See Beckwith, "The Temple Scroll and Its Calenda," 3–19, esp. 16.

86. Milgrom, "'Sabbath' and 'Temple City,'" 25–27. See also Lev 23:16b–17a and Temple Scroll 21:14–15, the Temple Scroll depended on the source from Lev 23:15–17 in col. 21:12–16. "The first fruits before YHWH" in col. 21 corresponds to Lev 23:17b "first-fruits for YHWH" see Zahn, *Rethinking Rewritten Scripture*, 208. See Wilson and Wills, "Literary Sources of the Temple Scroll," 275–88; Beckwith, "Temple Scroll and Its Calendar," 3–19, esp. 17; Elior, "From the Covenant," 74–113. Various texts from Qumran rely on the interpretation of Lev 23:11 as referring to the Sheaf that was to be offered on the Sunday of the week after the week of Unleavened Bread.

87. VanderKam, "The Temple Scroll and The Book of Jubilees," 216.

11QT[a] 19:7b–8 paraphrases Lev 23:21 to describe regulations on the Sabbath. The structure and contents of Lev 23:12–19[88] heavily influence cols. 18:2–12; 19:13, with a few changes.[89] In lines 10–13, no direct biblical passages explicitly link the day of the Waving of the Sheaf that is to take place fifty days earlier than the sin offering with any produce of the field. However, the redactor of the Temple Scroll prescribes a scale of sacrifices for the sheaf—waving to be commensurate with a major feast.[90] A wave-offering (תְּנוּפָה), which is mentioned in col. 18:12, is often used in one of two ways: Leviticus refers to an animal or a harvest offering, and Numbers refers to the Levites (Num 8:11). In addition, the author of the Temple Scroll echoes the Sabbath regulations "seven weeks, seven full weeks" (שבעה שבועות שבע שבתות תמימות col. 19:12; cf. cols. 18:11–12; 19:12–13) from Lev 23:15. The expression "and from the day after the Sabbath, seven weeks" (שֶׁבַע שַׁבָּתוֹת תְּמִימֹת תִּהְיֶינָה) is found only in Lev 23:15.

These examples show that the Temple Scroll uses biblical passages from Leviticus in several ways: in verbal overlaps (for certain laws), in paragraphs (for structure), or in ideology (for what is implicit in the text).

Grain Offering

The passage on the grain offering in cols. 20:9–14 follows Lev 2:1a–13 with respect to its purpose and procedure. Exodus, Leviticus, and Numbers describe grain offerings, but Lev 2:1a–13 is the base text for col. 20:9–14 because the author of the Temple Scroll closely follows the order of the grain offering from this text. Numbers 5:15 does not agree with Lev 2:1b–2 because Num 5:15 states that the participant should not pour oil and frankincense on the offering, while Lev 2:1b–2 encourages pouring oil and frankincense; the author of the Temple Scroll follows Lev 2:1b–2 in col. 20:10–11.

88. Yadin also observes that Lev 23:12–14 seems to influence the author of the Temple Scroll, at least the imagery of: a) waving the sheaf from the first fruit of the harvest (without designating the type), b) sacrificing a male lamb without blemish, c) the ban on eating either bread or parched or fresh grain "until this same day," and d) it is a statute forever. See Yadin, *The Temple Scroll*, 1:101.

89. Leviticus 23 seems to influence cols. 17–29. 11QT[a] 17:6 echoes Lev 23:5 that they keep the Passover to the Lord. The offering from Lev 23:38 also influences 11QT 29:5–6. The Law for Atonement in the Temple Scroll (25:10–27:10) is influenced by Lev 16, 23 and Num 29.

90. Yadin, *Temple Scroll*, 1:89.

Lev 2:1a

וְנֶ֗פֶשׁ כִּֽי־תַקְרִ֞יב קָרְבַּ֤ן מִנְחָה֙ לַֽיהוָ֔ה

When anyone presents a **grain-offering** to the Lord

11QT[a] 20:9

והקרׄיבו כול מנחה אשר קרב עמה נסך
כ[משפט]

Any **grain offering** that is accompanied by a drink offering is to be offered following [the usual regulations.]

Lev 2:1b–2a

1b וְיָצַ֤ק עָלֶ֙יהָ֙ שֶׁ֔מֶן וְנָתַ֥ן עָלֶ֖יהָ לְבֹנָֽה
2a וֶֽהֱבִיאָ֗הּ אֶל־בְּנֵ֣י אַהֲרֹן֮ הַכֹּהֲנִים֒ וְקָמַ֨ץ מִשָּׁ֜ם
מְלֹ֣א קֻמְצ֗וֹ מִסָּלְתָּהּ֙ וּמִשַּׁמְנָ֔הּ עַ֖ל כָּל־לְבֹנָתָ֑הּ
וְהִקְטִ֨יר הַכֹּהֵ֜ן אֶת־אַזְכָּרָתָהּ֙ הַמִּזְבֵּ֔חָה

(1b) *the worshipper shall pour oil on it, and put frankincense on it*, (2) *and bring it to Aaron's sons the priests. After taking from it a handful of the choice flour and oil, with all its frankincense, the priest shall turn this token portion into smoke on the altar* (cf. Lev 6:8, 9–10; 9:17)

11QT[a] 20:10–11

10 [וכול מנחה א]שר קרב עליה לבונה או
חרבה יקמוצו ממנה את
11a [אזכר]תׄהׄ ויקטירו על המזבח

(10) From [every grain offering th]at is accompanied by *frankincense, or else offered dry, they are to take a handful*— (11a) *the [memor]ial portion*—*and burn it on the altar*.

Lev 2:13b

וְלֹ֣א תַשְׁבִּ֗ית מֶ֚לַח בְּרִ֣ית אֱלֹהֶ֔יךָ מֵעַ֖ל מִנְחָתֶ֑ךָ

You shall not omit from your grain-offerings the salt of the covenant with your God

11QT[a] 20:13b–14a

13b ועל כול קורבנכמה תתנו מלח ולוא
תשב[י]ת
14a [ברית מלח לעולם]

(13b) *You are to put salt on all your offerings, never relaxing* (14a) *[the covenant to use salt, forever.]*

The author of the Temple Scroll in col. 20:9–14 selects passages from and follows the order of Lev 2:1–13. Columns 20:9b with its inclusion of "regulations [כ[משפט]" suggests that the author of the Temple Scroll follows the rules from Lev 2:1–13. "from [every grain offering th]at is accompanied by frankincense" in col. 20:10–11 agrees with Lev 2:1b–2a, which Lev 2 describes in detail. In col. 20:13–14, the author of the Temple Scroll follows the adding of salt in every offering from Lev 2:13, which is only found in Leviticus. Salt mentioned in Exod 30:35 is defined as "pure and holy" and in Num 18:19 it is referred to as a covenant. Thus, the author of the Temple Scroll follows the procedure for grain offerings only from Lev 2:13.

CONCLUSION

In this chapter, I have attempted to show how the book of Leviticus extensively influenced the structure, content, and ideology of the Temple Scroll. I have arranged my argument in three sections which have (1) set out the theological agenda of the Temple Scroll, especially as that is evident in col. 29, (2) described the significant motifs from Leviticus that occur in various places in the scroll, and (3) shown how Leviticus sometimes forms the base text in the composition.

Based on examples and parallels in my discussion above, four conclusions can be drawn. First, the use of the first person singular in Leviticus seems to heavily influence the whole rewriting strategy of the Temple Scroll where the Lord is presented as speaking in the first person singular. "I am YHWH your God" is found frequently in Leviticus, whereas Exodus uses this construction only three times.[91] Thus it is reasonable to assume that the compiler of the Temple Scroll has Leviticus in mind.

Second, Lev 26:42 heavily influences 11QT[a] 29:2–10, a key editorial section of the Temple Scroll. This is made clear when the compiler of the Temple Scroll adapts the covenant with Jacob at Bethel from Lev 26:42 in col.29:9–10, since this covenant with Jacob is found only in Lev 26:42. Though there are two different scholarly views about this covenant, both sides strongly agree that the Temple Scroll borrowed this key passage from Leviticus. The theology of the reestablishment of the covenant in Lev 26:42 seems to influence the covenant in col. 29:9–10. Inasmuch as the Temple Scroll presents the content of a renewed covenant, Lev 26 plays a key role in naming that covenant. Consequently, the theology of the book of Leviticus may be assumed to play a significant, controlling role in the construction and presentation of the ideology and structure of the Temple Scroll.

Third, the Temple Scroll uses motifs from the book of Leviticus, such as cultic practices (11QT[a] 34:7–15; Lev 1:5–9), placement of lamp and lights (11QT[a] 9:12–14; Lev 24:2–4), and themes of land and sacrifice (11QT[a] 51:15, 19–21; Lev 20:24 and 26:1, 11QT[a] 2:5–8; Lev 3:2–11). These examples show that the author of the Temple Scroll borrows motifs from the book of Leviticus to compose a new text for ritual practices in a pre-eschatological period. For example, col. 34:7b–14 clearly follows the structure and order of Lev 1:5b–9b with minor changes. 11QT[a] 9:12–14 ("lamps and light") borrows the concepts of arranging the lamps and the statement that it should be a statute forever from Lev 24:2–4, again clearly showing the influence of the strict law from Lev 24:2–4.

91. Exodus 6:7; 16:12; 20:2.

Finally, I have attempted to show how some passages from Leviticus serve as a base text for the Temple Scroll. One section of the purity laws in 11QT[a] 48:3–51:2, that is col. 48:3–5a, heavily depends on Lev 11:21–22, and other passages in col. 48:3–51:2 follow the structure, words, or expressions of Leviticus very closely. The purity laws from Leviticus and its emphasis on the theme of holiness (Lev 19:2) are especially evident in the Temple Scroll, even though the compiler had a choice of concepts from other Pentateuchal books. The many passages from Leviticus imply that the compilers of some of the sources and the final editors of the Temple Scroll may have had the complete book of Leviticus in mind.

V

Leviticus in the Damascus Document

INTRODUCTION

IN THIS CHAPTER, I will attempt to establish that the book of Leviticus influences the composition of the Damascus Document (D). The laws and regulations in Leviticus are reflected frequently and consistently throughout D.[1] My arguments are organized as follows: In section A, I will briefly describe the basic information presented in D; I will discuss the use of Leviticus in the structure of D; and I will discuss parallel passages from D and Leviticus in order to argue that Levitical themes influence the Damascus Document.

The Cairo Genizah copies of the Damascus Document (CD) have drawn worldwide scholarly attention before and after the discovery of the Dead Sea Scrolls in the 1940s and 1950s. The two mediaeval manuscripts from Cairo are usually referred to as manuscripts A and B. These two manuscripts are divided into Admonitions (CD 1–8 [19–20]) and Laws (CD 9–16).[2] Manuscript A is the older (tenth century CE) and longer of the two

1. Davies, "The Textual Growth," 319–33, esp. 319–20.

2. CD 1–8 and 19–20 are often called the Admonition or Exhortation and CD 9–16 refers to laws or statutes. While CD 19–20 in manuscript B appears to be a continuation of CD 1–8, a part of pages 7–8 overlaps manuscript B. The discovery of fragments of CD in caves 4, 5, and 6 of Qumran proved that the mediaeval manuscripts were based on a much older original. See Hempel, *The Damascus Texts*, 16; Angel, "Damascus

manuscripts, while MS B dates from the twelfth century CE.[3] There is a partial overlap between the two texts; however, there are also significant differences between the two (e.g., major differences can be found between MS A 7:4–8:2 and MS B 19:1–14).[4] Brooke suggests that the text was motivated over the years by differences in messianic beliefs manifested in each of the versions and that MS B, in which only one messianic figure is mentioned, is more original ("the Messiah of Aaron and Israel").[5]

The laws in D can be divided into legal rulings for all Israel and regulations governing life in the specific community, which is different from the Temple Scroll in which the text does not refer to a specific community or group.[6] Maxine Grossman states, "They have conflicts with certain other Jewish groups, who fail to understand scripture appropriately, and whose standing in God's world is problematic. And they are in expectation of a significant and immediate change in the state of the world."[7] In support of Grossman's position, it appears that the author of D reuses the Torah to create the New Covenant community in the land of Damascus (CD 6:19), and there is evidence that this author uses Leviticus significantly to write part of the composition, especially some of the legal materials.[8]

After the legal section, D continues with the community rules (CD 12:22–14:19) and the penal code (CD 14:18b–22; 4QD). According to Hempel, this penal code was influenced by the community of the Yahad from the beginning.[9] Schiffman suggests that the penal code was intended to be read to potential candidates as part of the training for their membership in the

Document," 3:2975–3035.

3. Hempel, *Damascus Texts*, 19–20.

4. Kister, "The Development of the Early Recensions," 61–76, esp. 61–62.

5. Brooke, "The Amos–Numbers Midrash," 397–404; Brooke, "The Messiah of Aaron," 215–30.

6. Hempel, *The Laws of the Damascus Document*, 29.

7. Grossman, *Reading for History*, 2.

8. Schiffman, "The Relationship of the Zadokite Fragments to the Temple Scroll," 133–45, esp. 133–35; Abegg, "The Covenant of the Qumran Sectarians," 81–97; Wise, "The Concept of a New Covenant," 99–128. The compiler of D uses Leviticus to compose concepts concerning the covenant and uses Jeremiah to internalize a New Covenant to help the Israelites keep the law in their hearts. However, that New Covenant is still one. Hultgren says, "God recalls this covenant at different times in history and even 'expands' upon it by giving it a new configuration in order to fulfill God's purpose." See Hultgren, *From the Damascus Covenant*, 474; Hogeterp, "Eschatological Identities," 111–30.

9. Hempel, *Laws of The Damascus Document*, 141–48; Steudel, "The Damascus Document," 605–20.

community so that new members would understand its significance when they were being sworn in.[10]

It is clear that the full publication of the 4QD fragments must be used to analyse the literary construction of D as a whole.[11] In this chapter, I will include 4QD, 5QD, and 6QD manuscripts, but the main focus will be on CD, since CD closely reflects the other three documents. Before going into more detail, I will introduce three examples from Leviticus that the compiler uses in significant ways throughout the composition of D.

First, several expressions suggest that D uses Leviticus to develop a particular view of its community. For example, the expression womC htow, used three times in CD (1:1, 2:2 and 2:14 and also in 4QD[a]),[12] occurs in the Hebrew Bible in the singular.[13] However, D uses the plural imperative form of womC htow to refer to certain groups instead of to an individual. The following example contains similar use of phrasing and ideas, based upon my own use of electronic search search instruments, showing how Lev 26 is reminiscent of the conditional commands in CD 1:1; 2:2, 14; 20:32b–33a.

Lev 26:14	CD 1:1
וְאִם־לֹ֥א תִשְׁמְע֖וּ לִ֑י וְלֹ֣א תַעֲשׂ֔וּ אֵ֥ת כָּל־הַמִּצְוֺ֖ת הָאֵֽלֶּה	⟦ ⟧ ועתה שמעו כל יודעי צדק ובינו במעשי
But *if you will not obey me*, and do not observe all these commandments,	*So listen*, all you who recognize righteousness, and consider the deeds of
Lev 26:18a	CD 2:2
וְאִ֨ם־עַד־אֵ֔לֶּה לֹ֥א תִשְׁמְע֖וּ לִ֑י	⟦ ⟧ ועתה שמעו אלי כל באי ברי
And *if in spite of this you will not obey me*	*So now listen to me*, all members of the covenant
Lev 26:21a	CD 2:14
וְאִם־תֵּלְכ֤וּ עִמִּי֙ קֶ֔רִי וְלֹ֥א תאב֖וּ לִשְׁמֹ֣עַ לִ֑י	⟦ ⟧ ועתה בנים שמעו לי
If you continue hostile to me, and will not obey me	So now, my children, *listen to me*

10. Schiffman, *Sectarian Law*, 157. Cf. CD 19:33.

11. Baumgarten, *DJD* XVIII, 6–7.

12. In CD, three exhortations are found: description of the covenant (1:1–24), uncovering the path of the wicked (2:2), and the deeds of God (2:14) by recounting forefathers' history. See Loader, *The Dead Sea Scrolls on Sexuality*, 95–96; van Beek, "A Temple Built of Words," 319–31, esp. 324–25.

13. Cf. 1 Sam 8:9; Isa 44:1; Amos 7:16; Jer 37:20; Dan 9:17. Even Exodus uses only the imperative of שמע in the singular form.

Lev 26:27a	CD 20:32b–33a
וְאִם־בְּזֹאת לֹא תִשְׁמְעוּ לִי	32b והאזינו לקול מורה צדק ⟦ ⟧ ולא יעזבו 33a אֹתֹ חֻקי הצדק בשמעם אתם
<u>*But if, despite this, you disobey me*</u>	(32b) and <u>*listen attentively to the voice of a Teacher of Righteousness*</u>, not abandoning (33a) the correct laws when they hear them

The warning from Lev 26 has been applied to the beginning and ending of CD with a command to listen to the New Covenant (CD 1:1; 20:32b–33a).[14] Though the compiler of D does not use exact expressions from Lev 26, passages in CD 1:1, 2:2, 2:14 truly echo the warning in Lev 26. It seems that the author of D keeps Lev 26 in mind to compose its text since D begins with a command to listen to all the new laws. The use of שמע strongly echoes the threatening language of Lev 26:18a, 21a, 27a, where omC is used in the plural. This shows clearly that the language of warning in Lev 26 influences D.

A second example of D's use of Leviticus can be seen in the regulations concerning the period for purification. In 4QD[a] 6ii. 5, there is mention of "on the eighth day" (ביום השמיני) and "on the eighth day" (יום השמיני). These time periods are similar to Lev 15:14, which employs the expression "on the eighth day" (ביום השמיני). In 4QD[a], the authors use a seven-day time period for becoming clean, found in Lev 15:14. It is on the eighth day that the priests are considered to be clean and then able to enter the sanctuary and the tent in D. Thus, we see that the D fragments depend upon Leviticus' time period to be clean.[15]

A third example is the well-known influence of Leviticus on the legal passages in the 4QD fragments. In particular, Lev 19:17–18 is found in the 4QD fragments, as is shown below (cf. CD 9:2–8b). Aharon Shemesh suggests "this particular ordering of the laws in CD 9:2–8 is due to the dual source of the law of the talebearer: Lev 19:16 and 27:29."[16] The example below shows how 4QD[a] 8ii:10 and 4QD[e] 6iii:17 (CD 9:2–8) significantly uses Lev 19:17–18 which contains verbal overlaps and similar use of phrasing and ideas.

14. CD 1:1, 4QDa 2 i 6, and 4QDc f 1:8–9, see Wassen, *Women in the Damascus Document*, 93; Ruzer, *Mapping the New Testament*, 215–17; Brooke, "Zedekiah, Covenant, and the Scrolls from Qumran," 95–109.

15. See Baumgarten, *DJD* XVIII, 8; Harrington, "The Rabbinic Reception of Leviticus," 381–402.

16. Shemesh, "The Scriptural Background," 191–224; Shemesh, "Qumran Polemic on Marital Law," 147–75, esp. 174–75.

Lev 19:18a	4QD^{a} 8ii:10
18a לֹא־תִקֹּם וְלֹא־תִטֹּר אֶת־בְּנֵי עַמֶּךָ	לו תקום ולו תטור את בני עמך
You shall **not take vengeance or bear a grudge against** any of your people	**Take no vengeance and bear no grudge against** your kin folk
	4QD^{e} 6iii:17
	[לא תקום ולא] תטור את בני עמך כל [א]יש מבאי הבْ[רית אשר י]ביא על רעהוْ [דבר אש]ר
	Take no vengeance and] bear [no] grudge against your kin folk (Lev 19:18) [a]ny co[venant] member [(CD 9:3) who b]rings against his fellow [an accusation]
Lev 19:17	4QD^{b} 9i:3
לֹא־תִשְׂנָא אֶת־אָחִיךָ בִּלְבָבֶךָ הוֹכֵחַ תּוֹכִיחַ אֶת־עֲמִיתֶךָ וְלֹא־תִשָּׂא עָלָיו חֵטְא	[הוכח תוכיח את רעכה ולוא תשא עליו]חטא
You shall not hate in your heart anyone of your kin; *you shall reprove your neighbour, or you will incur guilt yourself.*	*[You (CD 9:8) shall reprove your fellow and not bear] the sin [yourself]*

As has been shown, 4QD^{a} 8ii:10 and 4QD^{e} 6iii:17, reflect Lev 19:18 in its ideology, order, and content. In this example, we see that because God knows the actual problem that exists, God can therefore avenge. However, it is not permitted for human beings to retaliate.[17] These examples lead to a discussion of the use of Leviticus in D in greater detail.

THE USE OF LEVITICUS IN D

Structure of D and Lev 26

Preliminary Comments

I have developed my view of the structure and contents of D by considering Joseph Fitzmyer's proposed outline of the Damascus Document (CD, 4QD, 5QD, and 6QD)[18] and the material subsequently published by Joseph Baumgarten in DJD XVIII.[19] Both Fitzmyer and Baumgarten identified

17. Wacholder, *The New Damascus Document*, 32; Angel, "Damascus Document," 3015–17.

18. Fitzmyer, *A Guide to the Dead Sea Scrolls*, 132–33.

19. Baumgarten, *DJD* XVIII, 1–199. I have especially refered to the outline for all

several uses of Leviticus in D. In addition, I have used electronic search facilities to identify further phraseology from Leviticus that seems to indicate that the Damascus Document as a whole was widely influenced by the book.[20] That influence can be seen in the overall structure of D, particularly in the way in which there are allusions to Lev 26 in several key passages of the composition. However, the influence is also strong in the choice of topics in the various sections of D and in how the discussion of these topics is phrased.

I have not included all allusions to Leviticus in the outline below because many are insignificant and do not directly affect the findings of this chapter. The outline below is not an attempt at providing a definitive structure of some notionally reconstructed Damascus Document, but is a tentative list of the key uses of Levitical words, expressions, and ideology in D, arranged under headings suggested by the running content of D. The result is not a definitive structural outline but is a useful tool for seeing the richness of the use of selected passages from Leviticus in parts of D and the overall influence of Leviticus on D's ideology. Maxine Grossman asserts:

> But the evidence of Damascus Document cannot be taken as a straight-forward or transparent reflection of historical reality. Rather, the text reflects an ideological stance—a selective reading of scripture, a specific understanding of communal identity, and a programmatic view of history—and the righteous covenant community of the text must be recognized, similarly, as an *ideological construct.*[21]

Various texts in D rely upon Levitical passages, which indicate the author was dependent upon and engaged with Leviticus and its ideology. The outline illustrates the significant number of passages in Leviticus that influence D. Some of the uses of Leviticus are clear verbal overlaps, while others are similar uses of phrasing and ideas. The important point is that D uses most of Lev 26, which will become evident in my argument below; allusions to Lev 26 are indicated in bold in the following structural outline.

Structural Outline (4QD$^{a\text{-}b}$; 5QD; 6QD; CD A-B)

I. Introductory Columns in 4QD texts (not in CD)

---

the D manuscripts on pp. 3–5.

20. I have used word search in Accordance Bible software for one word, two words, and three or more words that can be found in Leviticus and D.

21. Grossman, "Reading for Gender," 212–39, esp. 212.

II. God's Saving Plan in History: the Admonition (based mainly on CD)

A. Introduction

1. Meditation on the Lessons from History (CD 1:1–2:1)

CD 1:1; 2:2; 2:14 / **Lev 26:14, 18, 21, 27**

CD 1:3 / **Lev 26:40**

CD 1:4, 17; 7:13; 19:10, 13 / **Lev 26:25, 45**

CD 1:4, 17–18; 3:10; 4:9; 6:2; 7:6; 9:2; 12:11; 19:13, 31; 20:25–26 / Lev 24:8; **26:9, 25, 42, 45**

CD 1:8 / Lev 20:24; **26:39** [4QD[a] 2i:12 / Lev 20:24; 25:46]

CD 1:18 / **Lev 26:25** [4QD[a] 2i:21]

2. Predestination of the Upright and the Wicked (2:2–13)

CD 2:6 / Lev 19:31

CD 2:18, 21 / **Lev 26:3**

3. Second Meditation on the Lesson from History (2:14—4:12a)

CD 3:7–15 / Lev 18:5; **26:14, 18, 27, 33**

CD 3:7 / Lev 20:24

CD 3:10, 13 / **Lev 26:32, 33–34**

B. The Three Nets of Belial (4:12b–6:11 [6QD15 1:1–3=CD 4:19–21; 6QD 15])

2:1–2=CD 5:13–14; 6QD15 3:1–5a= CD 5:18; 6:2a])

1. CD 4:17 / Lev 20–21.

2. CD 4:17 / Lev 25:37

3. CD 4:18 / Lev 20:3; **26:2.**

C. The Community of the New Covenant (6:12–7:9a [6Q15 3:5=CD 6:2b; 6Q15 4:1–4=CD 6:20–7:1. CD 19:1–5a=7:5b–9a])

1. The Expected Life to Enter the Sect and Marriage (6:12–7:9) CD 6:2 / **Lev 26:45**

CD 6:5 / **Lev 26:43** [4QD[a] 3ii:12; 4QD[b] 2:7 / **Lev 26:42, 43, 45**]

CD 6:18 / Lev 23:11; 23:15, 16; 24:8

CD 6:19 / Lev 23:11, 15, 16; 24:8 [4QD[a] 3ii.23]

CD 6:20 / Lev 16:20; 22:14

CD 6:20 / Lev 19: 18

2. Diverse Fates of those Who are Faithful to the Covenant and of those Who are Apostates (7:9b–8:21 [= (ms. B) 19:5b–34])

CD 7:9 / **Lev 26:15**

CD 8:2, 5–6; 9:1; 19:18 / Lev 19:17–18; **26:46; 27:29**

3. Conclusion (CD 19:35–20:34)

CD 19:4–6, 13/ **Lev 26:14–15, 25, 40**; 27:16

CD 20:12 / **Lev 26**. Cf. Jer 31:31

CD 20:18 / Lev 25:14 [4QD[b] 3:3 / Lev 17:10; 20:3, 6, 18]

CD 20:29 / **Lev 26:45**

III. 4QD Prescriptions (not in CD)

4QD[a] 6i:9 / Lev 13:33

4QD[a] 6i:13 / Lev 13:12; 13:13; 14:3, 7, 54, 57

4QD[a] 6ii:4 / Lev 15:14, 29; 23:36, 39

4QD[a] 6ii:9 / Lev 22:10

4QD[a] 8ii:10 / Lev 19:18

4QD[e] 8iii:9 / Lev 14:8; 16:26, 28

IV. 15:1–16:20; 9:1–14:22 Constitution: Life in the New Covenant (based mainly on CD)

A. Rules for Entrance into the Covenant and for Oaths (15:1–16:16)

1. Oaths

2. Regulations within the Community (9:1–10:10a; 5QD)

CD 9:1 / Lev 20:23; CD 9:1 / Lev 27:28–29

CD 9:2–8 / Lev 19:17, 17–18; 22:9 [4QD[b] 9i:3]

CD 9:8b–16a [5Q12 1:3–5=CD 9:8b–10]

CD 9:16b–10:3

CD 10:4–10a)

3. Rites to be Observed in the Community (10:10b–12:18)

CD 10:10b–13

CD 10:14–11:18a [4QD[a] 3ii:24 /Lev 23:3]

CD 11:15–18; 12:6–7 / Lev 10:10; 23:38

CD 11:17–18 / Lev 23:38

CD 11:18b–12:11a [cf. 6Q15 5:1–5]

CD 12:11–18 / Lev 20:25

CD 12:15b–17a / Lev 22:4–6

B. The Organization of the Community (12:19–14:19)

1. Community

CD 12:20 / Lev 10:10; 11:47; 20:25 [4QD[a] 9ii:6]

2. The Penal Code (14:20–22)

CD 14:4–6, 13–15 / Lev 19:9, 33

3. Liturgy for the Feast of the Renewal of the Covenant [4Q columns]

V. Conclusion (not in CD)

4QD[a] 11:3–4, 5 / **Lev 26:15, 31, 43**

4QD^{a} 11:7 / **Lev 26:11, 15, 30, 43.**

Analysis of the Structural Outline

General Comments

The majority of Levitical passages are found in the Admonition section, CD 1–8 and 19–20; some of the allusions are found in the Law section, 15–16, 9–14.[22] The above structural outline illustrates D's dependence upon Leviticus, especially Lev 17–26, which dominates its contents.[23] As Eibert Tigchelaar says, "the influence of Leviticus 26 on the Damascus Documents is apparent in quotations, all allusions, and use of the same vocabulary."[24]

The influence of Lev 26 on D is evident in its structure, as illustrated in the outline, and in its themes. Leviticus 26 has particularly influenced the historical section of D (CD 1:1–2:1). It seems the author of D already has Leviticus in mind while constructing the various sections of D. Leviticus 26 is shown in the historical section (CD 1:1–2:1; 3:7), the community of the new covenant (CD 6:2), covenantal life (4QD^{a} 4 2i:21, 4QD^{a} 11.4), and the conclusion (CD 19:3).

As section II.A.1 shows, the warning with the "sword" in Lev 26:25 heavily influences the beginning and ending of CD A–B. The compiler of D seems to take this expression and uses it throughout the composition to remind the reader of the warning from Lev 26. Bilhah Nitzan notes, "Qumran writings deal not only with the theoretical idea of repentance, but also with those activities in which the men of the Community are to realize repentance in daily life."[25] The ideology of repentance and judgement of Lev 26:25 is applied in D.

As sections II.C.3 shows, the covenant from Lev 26 was probably part of the basis for developing the New Covenant idea in D (CD 20:12. Cf. Jer 31:31), namely, that the purposes of the religious elite are to exegete the meaning of the laws and encourage the laws to be written on the hearts of

22. Tigchelaar, "The Cave 4 Damascus Document Manuscripts," 93–109.

23. According to Philip Davies, the structure of CD has not been understood due to the lack of "the boundaries of source-material or redactional sub-divisions in the Admonition, or explain how it grew into its present form." However, the structural outline in this section should be able at least to help see the influence of the structural formation of Leviticus in D. See Davies, *The Damascus Covenant*, 49; Campbell, *The Use of Scripture*, 138; Norton, "Composite Quotations in the Damascus Document," 92–118.

24. Tigchelaar, "Cave 4 Damascus Document Manuscripts," 93–109, esp. 107.

25. Nitzan, "Repentance in the Dead Sea Scrolls," 144–70, esp. 146; Langille, "Old Memories, New Identities," 57–85.

the members of their community.[26] The ideology of the covenant in Lev 26 was developed to become the New Covenant. Dwight Swanson argues, "Even in CD the term 'new covenant' should not be limited in reference to a narrow frame of reference, i.e., internal fractions in the Damascus Document, but be seen to be part of a larger difference of opinion within Judaism regarding covenant renewal."[27]

Second, various themes from Leviticus seem to contribute to the composition of D. Levitical themes such as the patriarchs, Sabbath, land, and three Nets of Belial are found in D. Not all of these examples are discussed with verbal overlaps, but the compiler of D seems to use Levitical words, expressions, or ideology throughout the composition. In the examples which I will discuss below, there are instances of verbal overlaps but also examples that reflect the ideology of Leviticus. The frequent mention of the theme of the patriarchs is evident in II.A.1. The expression "the covenant of forefathers" in CD 1:4 is found in Lev 26:45 and Jer 11:10.[28]

Sections II.A, IV.A.3, and IV.B describe Sabbath regulations (also extant in 4QD[a]). The regulations about the Sabbath in D depend on the explanation provided in Leviticus. For example, Lev 23:38 mentions a specific time period for the Sabbath, which seems to influence 4QD[a] 3ii:24, "the Sabbath day according to specification and holidays" and CD 10:14, "About the Sa[bb]ath, how to keep it properly."

Leviticus describes the land as inherited from God and as desolate. D relies on the Levitical understanding of land and its blessing and fruits shown in section II.A.1 (CD 1:8) and as desolate due to disobedience of the Lord's commands in section II.A.3 (CD 3:10).

The Three Nets of Belial (CD 4:12–5:15) in the Admonition Section (II.B) are fornication, wealth, and polluting the sanctuary, concepts that are explained according to the interpretation of Leviticus.[29] Cumulatively, the book of Leviticus heavily controls and influences the compiler of D.

26. The New Covenant urges all Israelites to obey the commands but only people who enter the group with an oath would have an opportunity to learn the covenant. Once they entered the group, they were required to learn it with all their heart and soul (CD 15:7–9). See Hultgren, *From the Damascus Covenant*, 77–140; Eisenman, "An Esoteric Relation," 439–56.

27. Swanson, "A Covenant Just like Jacob's," 273–86, esp. 284.

28. Jeremiah 11:10, "They have turned their back to the iniquities of their forefathers, who refused to hear my words . . ." In Jer 11:10, however, it is not related to the covenant of the forefathers that the Lord remembered.

29. Compare Lev 18:3 and CD 6:14b–7:4a; Grossman, "Reading for Gender," 212–39, esp. 220–21.

Leviticus 26 as a Major Influence in D

Leviticus 26 is important to the overall structure of D in addition to themes concerning covenant, holiness, and other topics, and it borrows from Lev 26 both at the beginning and the end of the account. The language of warning of Lev 26 is reflected in CD 1:1–3; 2:2; 2:14.[30] George Brooke notes, "in CD 1, 3–4 there are allusions both to Lev 26:40 with its characteristic use of M'L, 'to be unfaithful,' and to Lev 26:42 and 45 with their highly distinctive language of ZKR BRYT, 'remembering the covenant' (cf. CD VI, 2)."[31] Warning, disobedience, and punishment from Lev 26 are also reflected in 19–20.[32] John Kessler suggests, "Leviticus 26 presents a very conflicted view of the nation's capacity to respond. Its heart is described as proud, uncircumcised and in need of radical change."[33] The basis for the composition of D may have been the warning and consequences presented in Lev 26. I find Stephen Hultgren's opinion persuasive:

> This chapter of Leviticus ends the so-called Holiness Code (Lev 17–26), the laws of which feature prominently in the precepts of D . . . Thus it is not a surprise that allusions to Lev 26, the chapter that stands at the very end of the Holiness Code and outlines the consequences of obedience and disobedience to the covenant, should give structure to CD VII:9–VIII:12 (and XIX:5b-25a), which follows closely on VI:1:1b-VII: 4a and also stands at the end of its document (or rather its part of the document, the admonition), outlining the consequences of obedience and disobedience to the covenant.[34]

However, as my structural outline shows, Lev 26 influences not only particular sections of D but also the entire structure of D.

In this section, I will look more closely at the use of Lev 26 and its influence on the structure of D.[35] The section on punishment in Lev 26:14–45 is twice as long as the section on reward in Lev 26:3–13, also evident in the

30. Evans, "Covenant in the Qumran Literature," 55–80.

31. Brooke, "Messiah of Aaron," 215–30, esp. 219.

32. See section II and IV in the structural outline. CD begins with, "now listen" in CD 1:1 and ends with disobedience in CD 20:29, and restoration in CD 20:34.

33. Kessler, "Patterns of Descriptive Curse Formulae," 943–84; Lyons, "How Have We Changed?,"1055–73; Ganzel and Levitt Kohn, "Ezekiel's Prophetic Message," 1075–84.

34. Hultgren, "A New Literary Analysis," 549–78, esp. 553–54; Collins, *The Use of Sobriquets*, 31–36.

35. See section I. B, II. A. 1. and section IV in the structural outline.

structure of CD in its beginning and ending.[36] The themes of warning and references to the forefathers in Lev 26 also seem to heavily influence the structure of D.[37]

First, D relies upon the theme of sword and enemy from Lev 26:25 throughout the document.[38] In Lev 26:25, God is the one who will bring a sword when the Israelites disobey the command and the punishment will be to deliver them into the hand of the enemy. D does not use the term "enemy" but does use "sword," a term related to forsaking the covenant, throughout the text.[39]

Lev 26:25	CD 1:3–4a (4QD[a] 2i:9; 4QD[c] 1:11)
וְהֵבֵאתִ֨י עֲלֵיכֶ֜ם חֶ֗רֶב נֹקֶ֙מֶת֙ נְקַם־בְּרִ֔ית וְנֶאֱסַפְתֶּ֖ם אֶל־עָרֵיכֶ֑ם וְשִׁלַּ֤חְתִּי דֶ֙בֶר֙ בְּת֣וֹכְכֶ֔ם וְנִתַּתֶּ֖ם בְּיַד־אוֹיֵֽב	3 כי במועלם אשר עזבוהו הסתיר פניו מישראל וממקדשו 4a ויתנם לחרב
I will bring the sword against you, executing vengeance for the covenant; and if you withdraw within your cities, I will send pestilence among you, *and you shall be delivered into enemy hands*.	For when Israel abandoned Him by being faithless, He turned away from Israel and from His sanctuary and *gave them up to the sword*.
	CD 1:17 (4QD[a] 2i:21)
	הדבק בהם את אלות בריתו להסגירם לחרב
	For the curse of his covenant took hold on them, because of this *they were handed over to the sword*.
	CD 3:10b–11a
	ויסגרו לחרב בעזבם את ברית אל
	And so *were handed over to the sword* because they abandoned the covenant of God,
	CD 7:13
	וכל הנסוגים הוסגרו לחרב
	All who backslid were *handed over to the sword* (cf. CD 8:1)

36. Cf. CD 1:3–4, 3:7–8, 6:2, 7:13 // Lev 26:14, 18, 21, 27.

37. See section II. A. 1. in the structural outline.

38. Harkins, "The Emotional Re-Experiencing," 285–308, esp. 302.

39. Lied, "Another Look at the Land of Damascus," 101–25; VanderKam, "The Pre-History of the Qumran Community," 59–76.

CD 19:10

והנשארים ימסרו לחרב

But all the rest <u>*will be handed over to the sword*</u>

CD 19:13

והנשארים הסגרו לחרב נוקמת נקם ברית

But the rest <u>*were given to the sword*</u> that makes retaliation for covenant violations

The warning and punishment for not honouring God's covenant in Lev 26:25 is reflected in the structure of D in the use of the term "sword" in CD 1 and CD 19. CD 20 goes on to assert that the disobedience to the covenant is a consequence of not heeding the warning in Lev 26. Hultgren notes:

> Lev 26:14–15 and 26:25 . . . speak of the consequences of the breach of the covenant (see Lev 26:15). That speaks for the fundamental and original unity of the whole of the section VII, 9–VIII, 12 (with XIX, 5b–25a). I contend that Lev 26:25 is the primary source for the motif of the "sword" that features so prominently in the midrash.[40]

The phrase in CD 1:4, "and gave them up to the sword" (ויתנם לחרב) is similar to Lev 26:7–8, which states "and they shall fall before you by the sword" (וְנָפְל֥וּ לִפְנֵיכֶ֖ם לֶחָֽרֶב), "and your enemies shall fall before you by the sword" (וְנָפְל֧וּ אֹיְבֵיכֶ֛ם לִפְנֵיכֶ֖ם לֶחָֽרֶב).

Second, the compiler of D adapted the ideology of the Israelites' unfaithfulness to the covenant from Lev 26 in the composition of D, shown in CD 1:4b–5a; 6:2 and 20:29.

Lev 26:9

וּפָנִ֣יתִי אֲלֵיכֶ֔ם וְהִפְרֵיתִ֣י אֶתְכֶ֔ם וְהִרְבֵּיתִ֖י אֶתְכֶ֑ם
וַהֲקִימֹתִ֥י אֶת־בְּרִיתִ֖י אִתְּכֶֽם

I will look with favour upon you and make you fruitful and multiply you; <u>*and I will maintain my covenant with you*</u>.

CD 1:4b–5a

4b ובזכרו ברית ראשנים השאיר שאירית
5a לישראל ולא נתנם לכלה

(4b) <u>*But when He called to mind the covenant He made with their forefathers, He left a remnant*</u> (5a) *for Israel and did not allow them to be exterminated*

40. Hultgren, *From the Damascus Covenant*, 32.

Lev	CD
Lev 26:40	CD 3:13
וְהִתְוַדּ֤וּ אֶת־עֲוֺנָם֙ וְאֶת־עֲוֺ֣ן אֲבֹתָ֔ם בְּמַעֲלָ֖ם אֲשֶׁ֣ר מָֽעֲלוּ־בִ֑י וְאַ֕ף אֲשֶׁר־הָלְכ֥וּ עִמִּ֖י בְּקֶֽרִי	אשר נותרו מהם הקים אל את בריתו לישראל עד עולם
But *if they confess their iniquity and the iniquity of their ancestors, in that they committed treachery against me and, moreover, that they continued hostile to me*	*With those who were left from among them, God established his covenant with Israel forever*
Lev 26:44	CD 6:2
וְאַף־גַּם־זֹ֗את בִּֽהְיוֹתָ֞ם בְּאֶ֣רֶץ אֹיְבֵיהֶ֗ם לֹֽא־מְאַסְתִּ֤ים וְלֹֽא־גְעַלְתִּים֙ לְכַלֹּתָ֔ם לְהָפֵ֥ר בְּרִיתִ֖י אִתָּ֑ם כִּ֛י אֲנִ֥י יְהוָ֖ה אֱלֹהֵיהֶֽם	ויזכר אל ברית ראשנים ⟦ ⟧ ויקם מאהרן נבונים ומישראל חכמים
Yet for all that, *when they are in the land of their enemies, I will not spurn them, or abhor them so as to destroy them utterly and break my covenant with them; for I am the Lord their God*	But *God called to mind the covenant of the forefathers*; and He raised up from Aaron insghful men and from Israel wise men
Lev 26:45	CD 20:29b
וְזָכַרְתִּ֥י לָהֶ֖ם בְּרִ֣ית רִאשֹׁנִ֑ים אֲשֶׁ֣ר הוֹצֵֽאתִי־אֹתָם֩ מֵאֶ֨רֶץ מִצְרַ֜יִם לְעֵינֵ֣י הַגּוֹיִ֗ם לִהְי֥וֹת לָהֶ֛ם לֵאלֹהִ֖ים אֲנִ֥י יְהוָֽה	גֹּם אנחנו גם אבותינו בלכתנו קרי בחקי הברׄית
but *I will remember in their favour the covenant with their forefathers* whom I brought out of the land of Egypt in the sight of the nations, to be their God: I am the Lord.	*We and our ancestors by living contrary to the covenant laws*

The covenant with the patriarch in Lev 26:9, 42 is reflected in CD 1:4; the will of the Lord for the remnant in Lev 26:44 is reflected in CD 1:5a (cf. 2:11–12; 3:12f). God left the remnant and "with this remnant He made his Covenant with Israel forever, revealing to them the hidden things in which all Israel had gone astray."[41] Remembering the covenant by God in Lev 26:42 is a key passage for the ideology of the remnant in CD 1:4 that implies God is the one who established the covenant with Israel forever (CD 3:13). CD 1:4 simply mentions that he remembered the covenant without including detailed information that can be found in Lev 26:42, 45.[42] In addition, Lev 26:40 is reflected in CD 20:29.

41. Pfann, "Historical Implications," 172–86; Lichtenberger, "Historiography in the Damascus Document," 231–37.

42. Grossman, *Reading for History*, 105–6, 111–12.

The unfaithfulness of the forefathers to the covenant from Lev 26[43] is apparent in both CD 1 and CD 19. This example contains similar use of phrasing and ideas.

Lev 26:15	CD 1:20 (4QD^{a} 2i:23)
וְאִם־בְּחֻקֹּתַי תִּמְאָסוּ וְאִם אֶת־מִשְׁפָּטַי תִּגְעַל נַפְשְׁכֶם לְבִלְתִּי עֲשׂוֹת אֶת־כָּל־מִצְוֺתַי לְהַפְרְכֶם אֶת־בְּרִיתִי	ויעבירו ברית ויפירו חוק ויגודו על נפש צדיק ובכל הולכי
if you spurn my statutes, and abhor my ordinances, so that you will not observe all my commandments, and you break my covenant	*Violated the covenant, broke the precept, banded together against the life of the just man,* their soul abominated all those who walk
Lev 26:25	CD 19:13a
וְהֵבֵאתִי עֲלֵיכֶם חֶרֶב נֹקֶמֶת נְקַם־בְּרִית וְנֶאֱסַפְתֶּם אֶל־עָרֵיכֶם וְשִׁלַּחְתִּי דֶבֶר בְּתוֹכְכֶם וְנִתַּתֶּם בְּיַד־אוֹיֵב	והנשארים הסגרו לחרב נוקמת נקם ברית
I will bring the sword against you, executing vengeance for the covenant; and if you withdraw within your cities, I will send pestilence among you, and you shall be delivered into enemy hands	But *those who remained were delivered up to the sword, which carries out the vengeance of the covenant*.

The warning of future violation of the covenant in Lev 26:15 and 25 is reflected in CD 1:20 and 19:13a. The cursing in CD 19:5–6 echoes the cursing in Lev 26 and relies upon its description of the result of disobedience to the covenant.[44] Jonathan Campbell asserts that "we can be sure that allusion to Lev 26 informs CD at this point, because that scriptural passage reappears as the source of numerous other phrases in CD, as well as of a more general story-line important for our author."[45] It is clear that Lev 26 is reflected in CD 1:1–21.[46] All of these examples indicate that Lev 26 influences more than merely the beginning section of CD; it is the key text for the structure, content, and ideology of D.

43. Rabin, *The Zadokite Document*, 42.
44. Hultgren, *From the Damascus Covenant*, 32, 402.
45. Campbell, *Use of Scripture*, 31.
46. Campbell, *Use of Scripture*, 58–59.

The Themes of Leviticus in D

The purpose of the Damascus Document is to provide a correct interpretation of the Torah to Israel, because D seems to understand that disobedience was not merely wilful but also partly caused by misunderstanding the Torah (CD 6:4–11). Its texts depend upon Levitical themes—patriarchs, Sabbath, land, and the Three Nets of Belial—for its composition. The use of these themes is shown in the structural outline above.

Patriarchs and Covenant

The theme of the patriarchs, which is described in Lev 26:42, is central to D.[47] The covenant with the forefathers, their disobedience, and repentance in Lev 26 are reflected in both the beginning and end in D. Hultgren notes that "in Lev 26:42–45 God promises that even if Israel should fall into disobedience and be scattered among nations, God will remember his covenant 'to be their God.'"[48] The next example contains verbal overlaps, based upon my use of electronic search instruments that show the use of Leviticus as highly influential with respect to the theme of covenant.

Lev 26:42	4QQD^{d} 4i:3 (4QQD^{e} 2:9)
וְזָכַרְתִּי אֶת־בְּרִיתִי יַעֲקוֹב וְאַף אֶת־בְּרִיתִי יִצְחָק וְאַף אֶת־בְּרִיתִי אַבְרָהָם אֶזְכֹּר וְהָאָרֶץ אֶזְכֹּר	יזכור אל ברית ראישונים
Then **will I remember my covenant with Jacob; I will remember also my covenant with Isaac and also my covenant with Abraham**, and I will remember the land.	But **God remembered the covenant of the forefathers**
	CD 1:4 (4QD^{a} 2i:9)
	ובזכרו ברית ראשנים
	But when **He called to mind the covenant He made with their forefathers**

47. Nitzan, "Repentance in the Dead Sea Scrolls," 83. (Cf. MMT C 26–30.)

48. Hultgren, *From the Damascus Covenant,* 472–74. (cf. The "Covenant of the Fathers" in CD 8:18 and 19:31, which echoes Deut 7:7–8; 9:5). See Devorah Dimant, "Sectarian and Non-Sectarian Texts from Qumran," 7–18.

Lev 26:45	CD 6:2a
וְזָכַרְתִּי לָהֶם בְּרִית רִאשֹׁנִים אֲשֶׁר הוֹצֵאתִי־אֹתָם מֵאֶרֶץ מִצְרַיִם לְעֵינֵי הַגּוֹיִם לִהְיֹת לָהֶם לֵאלֹהִים אֲנִי יְהוָה	ויזכר אל ברית ראשני
But **I will remember in their favour the covenant with their forefathers** whom I brought out of the land of Egypt in the sight of the nations, to be their God: I am the Lord.	But **God called to mind the covenant of the forefathers**
	CD 20:17
	מוכיח בצדק ושבי פשע יעקב שמרו ברית אל
	Reproaches in justices. But those who repent of the sin of **Jacob have kept God's covenant**.

Leviticus 26:42 and 45 are reflected in 4QD[d] 4i:3; CD 1:4, 6:2a, 20:17. In most biblical passages in the Torah, such as Lev 26:45 and Jer 11:10, רִאשֹׁנִים is understood as "forefathers." In these two examples of the use of the term "forefathers" in biblical passages, it is Lev 26:45 that uses the phrase, "the covenant of the forefathers," mirrored in several places in D. In addition to relying on Lev 26, D develops the patriarchal theme from Abraham to the sons of Jacob, as shown below:

CD 3:3b וימסור לישחק וליעקב וישמרו ויכתבו אוהבים
CD3:4a לאל ובעלי ברית לעולם

> (3b) And he passed them on to Isaac and to Jacob and they too observed them. They too were recorded as friends (4a) of God and eternal partners in the covenant.

D describes patriarchs as those who kept the covenant according to the correct calendar, relying on the Levitical calculation.[49] The warning in Lev 26 simply implies not only God's covenant, but also a request to the Israelites to return to the Lord. CD 20 contains the themes of transgression, repentance, return, and restoration found in Lev 26 in relation to the covenant of patriarchs, which is constantly repeated throughout D. The covenant with patriarchs in Lev 26 controls the compiler of D to such an extent that CD assimilates the covenant with the patriarchs from beginning to end.

49. Hopkins, "Hebrew Patriarchs," 239–52; Schiffman, "The Patriarchs and Halakhah," 251–62.

Sabbath and Land

This section considers the themes of Sabbath and land together because proper observance of the Sabbath was considered necessary for the return to the land.[50] First, D relies on the Levitical understanding of how to keep the Sabbath properly (Lev 23:3, 32; 25:4) but seems to have included more detailed rules.[51]

Lev 23:3	CD 6:18a (4QD[a] 3ii:24)
שֵׁשֶׁת יָמִים תֵּעָשֶׂה מְלָאכָה וּבַיּוֹם הַשְּׁבִיעִי שַׁבַּת שַׁבָּתוֹן מִקְרָא־קֹדֶשׁ	ולשמור את̇ יום השבת כפרושה ואת המועדות
For six days shall work be done; but the seventh day is a Sabbath of complete rest, a holy convocation.	They must *keep the Sabbath day according to specification and the holy days*
Lev 23:32	CD 10:14a (4QD[e] 6v:1)
שַׁבַּת שַׁבָּתוֹן הוּא לָכֶם וְעִנִּיתֶם אֶת־נַפְשֹׁתֵיכֶם בְּתִשְׁעָה לַחֹדֶשׁ בָּעֶרֶב מֵעֶרֶב עַד־עֶרֶב תִּשְׁבְּתוּ שַׁבַּתְּכֶם	על הש[ב]ת לשמרה כמשפטה
It shall be to you a sabbath of complete rest, and you shall deny yourselves; *on the ninth day of the month at evening, from evening to evening you shall keep your sabbath.*	*About the Sa[bb]ath, how to keep it properly*

CD 6:18a (4QD[a] 3ii:24) makes a firm statement: "they must keep the Sabbath day according to specification and the holy days," without mentioning how. Leviticus 23:3 and 23:32 provide the information for calculating the right date for the Sabbath (cf. Lev 23:15–16, 23).[52] Wassen comments that the Sabbath Code provides a rigorous interpretation of the commandments to abstain from work on the seventh day (Exod 20:8; 31:12–17).[53]

50. Exodus 31:15 and Deut 5:14 mention that the seventh day is the Sabbath. However, Leviticus provides more information, calculating its date for the Sabbath, which seems to have influenced the Sabbath theme in D. See Werman, "CD XI:17," 201–12.

51. CD 10:18–23 describes the detailed rules for speaking, court proceedings, discussion, activity, travel, eating, and drinking on the Sabbath day. The rules of Sabbath in D are not related to polluting the altar by presenting an offering while being unclean (CD 11:19–20). See Weyde, *Appointed Festivals of YHWH,* 11–17.

52. Jubilees 6:20–22 and 11QT[a] 19:9 share a similar idea, which implies that these two texts might share a common source. The sectarian Halakah is used as a primary source of conceptual inspiration for these laws. See Henshke, "The Day after the Sabbath," 225–47, esp. 232.

53. Wassen, *Women in the Damascus Document*, 93. The theme of the Sabbath is

However, D seems to be more reliant on Leviticus when it comes to the detailed lists relating to the Sabbath.

Without Leviticus as a guide, it seems difficult to keep the Sabbath day, according to specification and the holy days. CD follows the injunction in Lev 23:3 that no one should work on the Sabbath, and it extends the ruling further with many lists to help Israel understand the precise way they were to keep it. CD seems to be stricter on the Sabbath laws because of a concern that the remnant may pollute their spirit once again.

Second, D fragments employ the ideology of land from Leviticus, particularly the theme that the Lord bequeathed his land (Lev 23:10; 25:2), which is reflected in CD 1:7–8. The laws in CD imply that the covenant of the forefathers brought the remnant back and allowed them to become the children of the Lord. Since the laws in D could be applied to everyone equally, they were required to follow the commandments, but the anger of the Lord would thus also be applied to all who disobeyed (CD 19:31–33).[54] The example below shows the devastation of their inheritance of God's land due to their disobedience. The next example shows both verbal overlaps and the similar use of phrasing and ideas.

Lev 20:24	CD 1:7–8a
אַתֶּם֮ תִּֽירְשׁ֣וּ אֶת־אַדְמָתָם֒ וַאֲנִ֞י אֶתְּנֶ֤נָּה לָכֶם֙ לָרֶ֣שֶׁת אֹתָ֔הּ אֶ֛רֶץ זָבַ֥ת חָלָ֖ב וּדְבָ֑שׁ	7 פקדם ויצמח מישראל ומאהרן שורש מטעת לירוש 8a את ארצו ולדשן בטוב אדמתו
You shall inherit their land, **and I will give it to you to possess, a land flowing with milk and honey**.	(7) He visited them and caused to grow from Israel and from Aaron a root of planting **to inherit** (8a) **His land and to grow fat on the good produce of His soil.**

significant in both Exodus and Leviticus. Exodus warns of death when speaking about the Sabbath, while Leviticus is concerned with land. D seems to be influenced by the Sabbath in Leviticus rather than Exodus because D does not include death when the Sabbath law is broken. D is more concerned with the detailed information about the Sabbath because the purpose of D is to interpret the laws correctly to help the people listen to and obey the laws in the D community.

54. Hempel comments that the bulk of this section recalls how past generations brought divine punishment upon themselves by following guilty thoughts and lustful eyes from the generation of the watchers of the exile. See Hempel, *Damascus Text*, 28.

Lev 26:32	CD 5:21 (4QD^b 2:5)
וַהֲשִׁמֹּתִי אֲנִי אֶת־הָאָרֶץ וְשָׁמְמוּ עָלֶיהָ אֹיְבֵיכֶם הַיֹּשְׁבִים בָּהּ	ותישם הארץ כי דברו סרה על מצות אל ביד משה
I will devastate the land, so that your enemies who come to settle in it shall be appalled at it (cf. 26:33, your land shall be desolated).	*And the land was devastated*, for they had spoken rebellion against the commandments of God through Moses

CD 1:7–8 employs the ideology from Leviticus, particularly that God owned the land and gave it to His people from the beginning. Leviticus 23:2 and 25:2 say that God gave His land to Israel with a covenant and that the land will produce good fruits if they keep the commands—concepts mirrored in CD 1:8. The ideology of God's judgement on the land for disobedience to the command and covenant in Lev 25 is reflected in CD 5:21, and also found in both CD 1 and 19.

Three Nets of Belial

The Damascus Document introduces the Three Nets of Belial in CD 4:15: fornication, wealth, and defiling the sanctuary, which are based on Isa 24:17 and Jer 5:26, 48:43–44.[55] D describes fornication and defilement of the temple in detail (CD 4:19–5:21), themes which are found in Leviticus. Regarding the three-sin pattern in MMT, Hanan notes that the word מעל (treachery or deceit or evil)[56] "with which lists of three cardinal sins opens in MMT, should be interpreted in accord with Lev 5:15–16."[57] Levitical texts provide detailed information in relation to fornication and defilement of the temple. Devorah Dimant notes: "'Fornication' refers to transgressing the Torah incest laws by unlawful marriages, 'wealth' concerns misuse of the temple dedicative gifts and other dues and possession of 'wicked wealth,' and 'defilement of the temple' is committed by unlawful intercourse with menstrual women.[58]

Forbidden unlawful marriage and defilement of the temple are mentioned in Leviticus in great detail, found mainly in Lev 18 and 21, and the

55. Tromp, "Damascus Document IV 10–12," 225–37; Eshel, "The Damascus Document's 'Three Nets of Belial,'" 243–55; Loader, *Dead Sea Scrolls on Sexuality*, 107–9.

56. MMT C 8–9; Qimron and Strugnell, *DJD* X, 58–59.

57. Eshel, *Exploring the Dead Sea Scrolls*, 38–39.

58. Dimant, "Between Qumran Sectarian and Non-Sectarian Texts," 235–56, esp. 243.

impurity of menstruation is found in various places in Leviticus.[59] As Grossmann notes, "all of human history is a period of wickedness, dominated by Belial and those who are sympathetic to or innocent victims of, his false standards of practice and behavior."[60]

D relies on the treatment of fornication and defilement of the temple in Leviticus to compose the Nets of Belial,[61] as shown in the comparisons below:

Lev 15:31	CD 4:17–18a
וְהִזַּרְתֶּם אֶת־בְּנֵי־יִשְׂרָאֵל מִטֻּמְאָתָם וְלֹא יָמֻתוּ בְּטֻמְאָתָם בְּטַמְּאָם אֶת־מִשְׁכָּנִי אֲשֶׁר בְּתוֹכָם	17 הראשונה היא הזנות השנית ההון השלישית 18a טמא המקדש
Thus you shall keep the people of Israel separate from their uncleanness, so that they do not die in their uncleanness by *defiling my tabernacle* that is in their midst.	(17) The first is *fornication*; the second is wealth; the third is (18) *defiling the sanctuary*
	CD 5:6b–7a
	6b וגם מטמאים הם את המקדש אשר אין הם 7a מבדיל כתורה ושוכבים עם הרואה את דם זובה
	(6b) *They also defile the sanctuary*, for they do not (7a) *separate clean from unclean according to the Law, and lie with a woman during her menstrual period.*
Lev 18:13	CD 5:9a
עֶרְוַת אֲחוֹת־אִמְּךָ לֹא תְגַלֵּה כִּי־שְׁאֵר אִמְּךָ הִוא	אחות אמך לא תקרב שאר אמך היא
You shall not uncover the nakedness of your mother's sister, for she is your mother's flesh.	**The sister of your mother you shall not draw near; she is the flesh of your mother**

59. Leviticus 15:19; 20:24–26, 33; 18:19; 20:18.

60. Grossman, *Reading for History,* 171; Wassen, *Women in the Damascus Document*, 114–15, 181–83.

61. Naudé, "Holiness in the Dead Sea Scrolls," 171–99; Wassen, *Women in the Damascus Document,* 80; Ginsburskaya, "Leviticus in the Light of the Dead Sea Scrolls," 1:263–77; Hultgren, *From the Damascus Covenant,* 267; Schiffman, *Courtyards,* 527–28.

Lev 18:20, 22–23	CD 11:20b
20 וְאֶל־אֵשֶׁת עֲמִיתְךָ לֹא־תִתֵּן שְׁכָבְתְּךָ לְזָרַע לְטָמְאָה־בָהּ	להרשותו לטמא את המזבח
22 וְאֶת־זָכָר לֹא תִשְׁכַּב מִשְׁכְּבֵי אִשָּׁה תּוֹעֵבָה הִוא	Thus allowing him to defile the altar
23 וּבְכָל־בְּהֵמָה לֹא־תִתֵּן שְׁכָבְתְּךָ לְטָמְאָה־בָהּ וְאִשָּׁה לֹא־תַעֲמֹד לִפְנֵי בְהֵמָה לְרִבְעָהּ תֶּבֶל הוּא	
(20) *You shall not have sexual relations with your kinsman's wife, and defile yourself with her.* (22) *You shall not lie with a male as with a woman*; it is an abomination. (23) *You shall not have sexual relations with any animal and defile yourself with it, nor shall any woman give herself to an animal to have sexual relations with it:* it is perversion.	

The purity law of Leviticus is adapted in D, enjoining its community to maintain purity and holiness. The Two Nets of Belial (defiling sanctuary and fornication in Lev 15:31 and 18:20, 22–23) are reflected in CD 4:17–18a and CD 5:6b–7a. Leviticus 15:31 warns against defiling the tabernacle to preserve purity, which had to be preserved.[62] Jacobus Naudé states, "such a concept of holiness is reflected in the community's daily life of keeping the biblical laws of purity, festivals, etc."[63] CD 5:8–9a reuses the language of Lev 18:13 concerning fornication. The compiler of D made a slight alteration in this example and CD applied the prohibition, "a man to marry his maternal aunt" in Lev 18:13, to apply equally to women.[64] D applies the ideology of holiness in Leviticus to the entire community.

The theme of holiness in Leviticus is not limited to the sanctuary itself; it is extended from the sanctuary to the city, also reflected in CD 4:16–17 and CD 12:1–2. In Leviticus, purity regulations, especially for priests, are expanded. Milgrom suggests the requirement for priestly purity and holiness

62. Hultgren, *From the Damascus Covenant*, 267; Wacholder, *The New Damascus Document*, 303–5; Himmelfarb, "The Purity Laws of 4QD," 155–69; Keady, *Vulnerability and Valour*, 110–27; Harrington, "How Does Intermarriage Defile the Sanctuary?" 177–95, esp. 181–89.

63. Naudé, "Holiness in the Dead Sea Scrolls," 170–99, esp. 184.

64. See Grossman, *Reading for History*, 51–52; Shemesh and Werman, "Halakhah at Qumran," 104–29, esp. 120; Wassen, "Women in the Damascus Document," 80 (cf. 4QDf 3 10b–12 and Lev 21:7–8a); Crawford, "Use of Pentateuch in the Temple Scroll," 314–15; Gruber, "Women in the Religious System of Qumran," 173–95.

in Lev 21:10–15 is "for the entire lifetime of the high priest and not just for the seven days of his consecration."[65]

In terms of fornication, CD 5:9a borrows the Law of Moses from Lev 18:13. Leviticus 18:6–18 provides detailed information about sexuality and warns that the land will be desolated if the community does not keep these commands. The understanding of fornication is ambiguous, due to use of the expression בחייהם.[66] Having two wives in a lifetime (בחייהם) is considered to be fornication as they understand Gen 1:27, but this is also one of the most disputed texts in the copies of CD.[67] The ideology of the Three Nets of Belial is dependent upon Leviticus, especially fornicating and defiling the sanctuary. Grossman notes: "For this special community, an understanding of collective identity is grounded in the priestly images of the text: from the Zadokite priesthood of Ezekiel (CD 4:3–4), to the Aaronites who are given certain authoritative roles in communal leadership and perhaps a more generalized Levitical priesthood, hinted at in the Levi quotation and the various references to a Levitical presence in the community."[68]

As shown in the outline above, D focuses generally on priestly images from various places in Lev 16–27, the chapters that modern scholarship associates with the Holiness Code (H).[69] Philip Davies notes, "the collection of laws in CD . . . cover matters of holiness, discipline, Sabbath observance and commerce."[70] The rules for sexuality in Lev 18:6–18 mainly concern men, but CD includes both men and women (CD 5:9–10). "This text utilizes a slight alteration of its normal gender construction as an exegetical tactic that ultimately confirms the passive and secondary role of women with respect to the normative male covenant," according to Grossman.[71]

CD 5:9a–10 adds the phrase, "But the law of consanguinity is written for males and females alike" (ומשפט העריות לזכרים הוא כתוב וכהם הנשים), directly from Lev 18:3, extending that law. Sidnie White Crawford argues

65. Jacob Milgrom, "Studies in the Temple Scroll," 501–23, esp. 510.

66. If this expression is correct, then a man should not remarry. However, many scholars insist that such interpretation is false. A man cannot have another wife while the first one is alive. See Fitzmyer, "Divorce among First-century Palestinian Jews," 106–10.

67. Schiffman, *Reclaiming the Dead Sea Scrolls*, 130.

68. Grossman, *Reading for History*, 188–89; Kugler, "Priesthood at Qumran," 93–114; Regev, *Sectarianism in Qumran*, 255–57.

69. CD texts clearly differentiate between two groups: those that try to be perfect in holiness and those that live according to the Torah with the community rule of the land. See Baumgarten, "The Laws of the Damascus Document," 17–26; Levine, "Leviticus," 11–23; Milgrom, "HR in Leviticus," 24–40; Hogeterp, "Relations to Gentiles," 217.

70. Davies, "The Judaism(s) of the Damascus Document," 27–43, esp. 33.

71. Grossman, *Reading for History*, 52.

that the importance of holiness and the purity of the land from Leviticus' Holiness Code influences CD's new composition of laws for all Israelites.[72]

In summation, D agrees with Leviticus that the Law of Moses should be obeyed and respected; however, fornication should be considered more seriously. It seems that the author of CD reads Leviticus very closely and applies it carefully to make sure the CD community understands the meaning of fornication well.[73] According to Wassen, the closer reading of Leviticus influences the way CD applies the law to both men and women equally.[74] It appears that D purposely includes men and women in terms of the fornication law because CD 5:10 asserts that fornication causes uncleanness to both men and women and also that it pollutes their spirit (CD 5:11). CD does not describe the second net of wealth but chooses to expand on fornication, which implies that the author of CD seems to have chosen particular laws from Leviticus in order to protect the CD community.

Disobedience in General

The instruction to observe and keep God's commandments in Leviticus appears frequently in D. Part of its purpose in doing so was to establish the New Covenant.[75] D uses the past tense in various places to remind the Israelites of their disobedience of the commands.

CD 1:1–2 commands all to listen to the deeds of God, CD 2:2–3 calls all members of the covenant to listen to the ways of the wicked, and CD 2:14 15 encourages the children to listen to the deeds of God, especially concerning what pleases God and what God rejects. The compiler of D points out Israelites' disobedience throughout, shown in the examples below. The following example is based upon my own use of electronic search instruments and offers something new to the discussion of the use of Leviticus in the Scrolls.

72. Crawford, "Use of Pentateuch in the Temple Scroll," 315; Collins, "Sectarian Consciousness in the Dead Sea Scrolls," 177–92.

73. See Wassen, *Women in the Damascus Document*, 121; Rabin, *The Zadokite Documents*, 19.

74. See Wassen, *Women in the Damascus Document*, 121.

75. Hempel points out that it lies in the nature of halakhic exposition, of course, that the interpretations arrived at often have different conclusions from the halakhic decisions taken in other groups. See Hempel, *Laws of the Damascus Document*, 72; Kapfer, "Attitude toward the Temple," 152–77.

Lev 18:4	CD 2:18b
אֶת־מִשְׁפָּטַי תַּעֲשׂוּ וְאֶת־חֻקֹּתַי תִּשְׁמְרוּ לָלֶכֶת בָּהֶם אֲנִי יְהוָה אֱלֹהֵיכֶם	אשר לא שמרו מצות אל
My ordinances you shall observe and *my statutes you shall keep, following them*: I am the Lord your God. (cf. 18:5).	For *they did not observe the commandments of God*.
Lev 19:37	CD 2:21
וּשְׁמַרְתֶּם אֶת־כָּל־חֻקֹּתַי וְאֶת־כָּל־מִשְׁפָּטַי וַעֲשִׂיתֶם אֹתָם אֲנִי יְהוָה	ולא שמרו את מצות עשיהם עד אשר חרה אפו בם
You shall keep all my statutes and all my ordinances, and observe them: I am the Lord.	And *did not keep the commandments of their Maker*, until finally His anger was aroused against them
Lev 23:24	CD 3:7b–8a
דַּבֵּר אֶל־בְּנֵי יִשְׂרָאֵל לֵאמֹר בַּחֹדֶשׁ הַשְּׁבִיעִי בְּאֶחָד לַחֹדֶשׁ יִהְיֶה לָכֶם שַׁבָּתוֹן זִכְרוֹן תְּרוּעָה מִקְרָא־קֹדֶשׁ	7b ולא שמעו 8a לקול עשיהם מצות יוריהם
Speak to the people of Israel, saying: In the seventh month, on the first day of the month, *you shall observe a day of complete rest*, a holy convocation commemorated with trumpet blasts.	(7b) and *they did not listen* (8a) to their Maker's voice or the commandments of their teacher
Lev 26:3	CD 19:20a
אִם־בְּחֻקֹּתַי תֵּלֵכוּ וְאֶת־מִצְוֹתַי תִּשְׁמְרוּ וַעֲשִׂיתֶם אֹתָם	איש הישר בעיניו ויבחרו איש בשרירות לבו
If you follow my statutes *and keep my commandments and observe them faithfully*.	*Each man did what was right in his eyes and each one has chosen the stubbonness of his heart* (cf. 3:2–3).

Even though the command to observe God's commandments is not limited to Leviticus, it is fair to note that the compiler of D kept the Levitical command with its warning in mind. Angela Kim Harkins notes:

> There are also spiritually elite individuals who possess a pre-eminence, a "perfect holiness" (תמים קדש, CD 7:5; 20:7). The complex stratification and internal diversity of the readers and hearers of D indicate scenarios in which individuals move constantly between states of inclusion and exclusion, with the most grievous offenses (via., flagrant crimes committed by long-standing members, CD 14:24) marked as especially deserving of expulsion.[76]

76. Harkins, "Emotional Re-Experiencing," 285–308, esp. 295.

According to CD, the Sabbath and covenant are not being kept as commanded in Lev 26. Placing these instances of general disobedience in the past tense ties them to themes from Leviticus.

It is true that this section recalls the past generation's disobedience and its result, but CD 2:14–3:14 more likely explains the past and God's divine punishment by using increasingly higher judgement. For example, His anger burns (CD 3:9), and then they were handed over to the sword (CD 3:11). We can observe God's anger (CD 3:8) and judgement (CD 7:9), and how God's burning anger was applied to the Israelites (CD 8:18b–19). The word "commandments" (מצות) first appears in CD 2:18 and mainly appears in the Admonition (CD 1–8, 19–20) section. CD 3 includes מצות four times and that word appears in Lev 4:2, 13, 22, 27; 5:17; 22:31, and 27:34. CD includes the same commandments as those found in Leviticus, but Leviticus uses a different writing style. The word twxm in Lev 4:2, 13, 22, 27; 5:17 is used with the conditional clause *if*. However, it does not refer to the past but is God's warning for the future generation, if they do not keep the commandments.

CONCLUSION

In this chapter I have argued that the compiler of the Damascus Document uses Leviticus extensively with respect to its structure and themes. In regard to structure as mentioned in the introduction, God's command to listen in Lev 26 is reflected in CD in both the beginning and the end of the document.

This warning in Lev 26 is consistent throughout the composition of D, as the structural outline shows. The influence of Lev 26 in D is significant in the repeated descriptions of the community's unfaithfulness and God's remembering the covenant, as in Lev 26:42. God's warning against unfaithfulness in Lev 26:26 is found in CD 1:3–4a, 17; 3:10–11; 7:13; 19:13. This confirms the persistent use of Lev 26 throughout D, reminding the readers how important it is to remember and keep the laws. The theme of God's faithfulness to the covenant in Lev 26 is also found throughout D (cf. CD 1:4b; 3:13; 6:2; 20:29), as is the community's unfaithfulness to the covenant (CD 1:20; 19:13; 20:29). The promise of God's restoration from Lev 26 is also found in CD 7:9–8:4a (19:5b-32a).

With regard to themes from Leviticus, I have shown that many passages of D are heavily influenced by Leviticus: patriarchs and covenant, Sabbath and land, Three Nets of Belial, and disobedience in general. Some of the references are verbal overlaps and some are implicit; however, cumulatively Leviticus seems to have been very influential in the composition of D.

The theme of the patriarchs and covenant with the forefathers, their obedience, and God's faithfulness in Lev 26:42 and 45 is reflected in CD 1:4, 6:2, 20:17. The ideology of Sabbath and land in Leviticus is also found in CD 6:18 and 10:14, as the compiler of D relies upon themes found in Leviticus, that the land was devastated by the Lord because of disobedience (CD 5:21). Levitical purity laws in relation to fornication and defilement of the temple are found in the Three Nets of Belial in CD 4:15, 4:19–5:21, as it is used in Leviticus. The particular nature of fornication and of defiling the sanctuary treated significantly in Leviticus is reflected in D. Leviticus contains many cultic laws and commands the people were required to keep but were not observing. This disobedience is pointed out in CD 2:18, 2:21; 3:7b–8a, and 19:20.

Overall, Leviticus is a major resource for compiling the Damascus Documents. Leviticus often controls the structure in several significant ways, and the use of its ideology is obvious in the composition of D. The data and research in this chapter, especially concerning Lev 26 and the Holiness Code, show that Leviticus is a major foundational text for D. Why might this be? Most probably, of all the places in the Torah, it was certain sections of Leviticus that provided the theological resources for addressing the overwhelming problem of Israel's ongoing disobedience in the Second Temple period.

VI

Leviticus in MMT

INTRODUCTION

I WILL ARGUE IN chapter VI that Leviticus is used both explicitly and implicitly in *Miqṣat Maʿaśe Ha-Torah* ("some works of the law"—MMT). This document has at least three distinct sections: calendric, halakhic,[1] and homiletic, represented as sections A, B, and C respectively.[2] Leviticus plays a significant role in ordering section B and influences ideology in section C. MMT is interpreted in several ways, but a majority of scholars suggest that it encapsulates a debate between sectarians and non-sectarians.

MMT is extant in six fragmentary manuscript copies (4Q394–399). Qimron and Strugnell estimate that the surviving text covers roughly two-thirds of the original. According to palaeographers, the oldest manuscript dates from about 75 BCE, the youngest from about 50 CE.[3] The copies come from Qumran but the composition of this text was almost certainly

1. I realize I have used this word in this chapter anachronistically; however, I have found no better term.

2. Qimron and Strugnell, *DJD* X, 109–11. Since Section A is only in one manuscript, it is likely that it did not form part of the composition as more generally understood in the community. See VanderKam, "The Calendar, 4Q327, and 4Q394," 179–94; Pérez Fernández, "4QMMT: Redactional Study," 191–205.

3. Qimron and Strugnell, *DJD* X, 1; Kampen, "4QMMT and New Testament Studies," 130–32; Doering, *Ancient Jewish Letters*, 194–95; Steudel, "4Q448–The Lost Beginning of MMT?" 247–64.

pre-Qumran. The majority of scholars consider the writing of this composition to have taken place in late second-century BCE.

Many scholars have considered MMT to be a Halakhic letter,[4] since it employs some elements of the letter form. In its original version, MMT was likely written to persuade opponents to adopt a particular view of the law (4Q397 14–21, 7–10). However, six fragmentary copies of MMT suggest that the original purpose of MMT changed from being a letter to something more like an educational tool in subsequent decades. The purpose of MMT may have been to persuade its intended recipient to think of the law in a certain way to educate them.[5] Brooke comments: "Although the composition might be construed as some kind of letter sent at some point probably in the second century BCE, the text was copied through the first century B.C.E., indicating that it was not a flash in the pan for a single readership, but understood as of didactic value or authority or as having some other significance for subsequence generations as well."[6]

Based upon Brooke's argument, the author of MMT might have used ideology from Lev 11 in terms of purity regulations with intentional educational purpose that provide clearer and stricter rules.

Subsequently, MMT was copied within the sectarian movement and probably used as a pedagogical tool to reinforce priestly identity. The role of Leviticus in this work highlights the significance of priestly issues in debates both within the sectarian movement and also in the wider Jewish community.

The legal aspects of MMT are influenced by the Pentateuch, especially Exodus, Leviticus, and Numbers, but I will focus on the contribution of Leviticus to its composition. I will examine passages in MMT that quote Leviticus almost exactly, similarly, or in terms of shared ideology. Because the manuscripts of MMT are very fragmentary and difficult to read, I have used the reconstruction of the whole composite text of MMT as presented in DJD X as a basic source for examples in this chapter.[7] In his recent edition of MMT, Elisha Qimron has republished the composite text in exactly the same order and arrangement as in DJD X but with some improved readings.

4. Eshel, "4QMMT and the History of the Hasmonean Period," 53–65, esp. 54–55.

5. It is still too ambiguous to determine the purpose (addressees) and its date. Steven Fraade argues that MMT was written for insiders rather than outsiders. See Fraade, "To Whom It May Concern," 507–26.

6. See Brooke, "Authority and the Authoritativeness of Scripture," 507–23. Fraade suggests that this letter was written to help the opponent understand the way to properly worship God and the right practices to be holy and clean. See Fraade, "To Whom It May Concern," 507–26.

7. Qimron and Strugnell, *DJD* X, 1–178.

He has shown that for all practical purposes it is still appropriate to work with DJD X.[8]

The rulings in MMT, especially in what is labelled as section B, are concerned with sacrifice, slaughtering, ritual purity, priestly marriages, and other boundary markers. There are explicit Levitical scriptural references in MMT B. In Section C the theme of cursing, blessings, and holiness is also influenced by Leviticus. Not only the contents of MMT but also its structure is controlled by Leviticus (sections B and C). Therefore, I will argue below that Leviticus significantly influences the entire structure of MMT.

The identity of the original addressees is debatable, but we can assume at least a certain purpose for MMT by looking at the texts, beginning with C 7:

> 4Q397 14–21, 7 [ואתם יודעים ש]פֿרשנו מרוב הע֯[ם ומכול טמאתם]
>
> (4Q397 14–21, 7) [But you know that] we have separated from the majority of the peo[ple and from all their uncleanness]

In addition to the above line, other lines in MMT seem to express the purpose of MMT separating and keeping clean recipients from the unclean. Nevertheless, without knowing the identity of the addressee, it remains a challenge to define the precise purpose of MMT. C 7 suggests an author and addressee(s), but it is still difficult to determine the relationship between "we" and "you."[9]

The sender was initially identified with the Teacher of Righteousness and the addressee with the Wicked Priest,[10] but such a view is only an assumption and is not confirmed explicitly in the text. Even though we do not have clear evidence concerning who the addressees were, we can still investigate how and why MMT uses Leviticus.[11]

8. Elisha Qimron, *The Dead Sea Scrolls*, 2:212. [Heb.]

9. Reinhartz, "We, You, They," 89–105, esp. 89. Reinhartz states on 89, "This line makes two clear points. First, it identifies an author or authors ('we') and an addressee or addressees ('you'). Second, it establishes a boundary line between 'us,' that is, the author(s)'group and 'the multitude of the people,' on account of impurity."

10. Qimron and Strugnell, *DJD* X, 1. See also Qimron and Strugnell, "An Unpublished Halakhic Letter from Qumran," 400–407.

11. For the various scholarly views on the addressee of MMT, see Brooke, "Luke–Acts and the Qumran Scrolls," 80–82; Kampen, "4QMMT and New Testament Studies,"130–32; Fraade, "To Whom It May Concern," 507–26. Based upon these articles, many laws and regulations in MMT could be seen as having a pedagogical purpose rather than a polemical one. Fraade says, "purposes of the 4QMMT: to instruct members, or prospective members, in the 'correct' understanding of Israel's sacred scriptures and history . . . 4QMMT was composed as a 'pseudo-letter,' that is, that it was composed with intramural study as it fiction, but in the form of a communication

Two scholars, Bernstein and Brooke, have discussed the way MMT uses biblical texts. Bernstein argues that MMT contains some biblical language and that much of its contents are the product of scriptural interpretation.[12] In relation to several legal issues in B, Brooke focuses on explicit citations where biblical texts influence either the content or the structure of MMT.[13] Brooke points to various influences of biblical citations and argues that certain formulaic words such as כתוב ("it is written") need to be seen as introducing explicit citations.[14] Though it is true there is no clear overall scriptural basis for the order of section B, certain sections in B are clearly controlled by Leviticus, as later discussion in this chapter will show. This discussion will consider the influence of Leviticus on the overall structure of MMT, what parts of Leviticus dominate MMT, and what might be its purpose.

USES OF LEVITICUS IN MMT SECTION B

I will begin my argument by exploring how MMT has used and worked with Leviticus.[15] Over a period of time (from the end of the second century BCE through the end of the first century BCE), the genre of MMT changed from a circular letter to a pedagogical manual. The use of Leviticus in MMT may have been one of the factors that kept MMT in circulation and in use in the sectarian movement. Section B reveals its purpose by beginning with the expression "these are some of our pronouncements (rulings)" (אלה֯ מקצת דב֯רינו B1).

between the leadership of the community and its extramural opponents." See Fraade, "To Whom It May Concern," 514–24. According to Grossman, "the purpose of this text—as articulated in its concluding section—is to rectify this misunderstanding and provide a source of proper edification for people outside the community who might be willing to reconsider their errors." See Grossman, *Reading for History*, 59; Brooke, "Authority and the Authoritativeness of Scripture," 507–23.

12. Bernstein, "The Employment and Interpretation of Scripture," 29–51, esp. 46.

13. Based upon Brooke's argument, MMT heavily depends upon Leviticus for its structure, content, and ideology. See Brooke, "Explicit Presentation," 67–88, esp. 83.

14. Brooke explains the difference between כתוב and אמר: "בותכ is nearly always associated with scripture explicitly or in summary form, whereas the opinions of the group behind MMT are expressed in terms of thinking or considering or saying." See Brooke, "Explicit Presentation," 71.

15. The legal section B in MMT is not just a list of laws or regulations, MMT actually shows the "structural analysis of text" which seems to depend upon the book of Leviticus. See Miller, *Performances of Ancient Jewish Letters*, 228.

Within the fragmentary opening statement, there is a reference to purity (טהרת), which is a concept chiefly found in Leviticus and Numbers;[16] issues of purity and impurity are the main focus of B. My discussion will highlight three important themes from Leviticus explicitly or implicitly adapted in MMT ideology. Though there are few explicit examples of the use of Leviticus in MMT, there are enough to conclude that Leviticus plays a substantial role in the formation of MMT, an assertion supported by the many implicit examples of the use of Leviticus to be discussed below.

The following sections will highlight and discuss important Levitical themes and how these Levitical themes are adapted and utilised by MMT.[17]

Slaughtering

Purity of Hides and Bones

The rules about purity of hides and bones are distinctive regulations covered in Leviticus. MMT depends on the ideology of Leviticus to compose the rule in B 21–24.[18] The Leviticus passages prohibit the handling of carcasses in several ways.[19] B 21–24 extends this prohibition with an addition not to make handles for vessels from their bones or their hides and not to "have access to the sacred food" (B 21–23). The ideology is clearly dependent on Lev 11:24–25, 27–28.[20] However, the author of MMT seems to have adjusted the law to align it with Lev 11:24–25, 27–28. The following example contains similar use of phrasing and ideas; based upon my own use of electronic search instruments that offers new insights to the discussion of the use of Leviticus in B 21–24.

16. Brooke, "Explicit Presentation," 72.

17. Some of the examples that follow are dependent on identifications made by Qimron and John Strugnell; others are my own, through my interpretations and interactions with the general comments in *DJD* X and elsewhere.

18. Cf. Lev 11:24–25, 27–28.

19. They prohibit touching (Lev 5:12), they prohibit touching and carrying (Lev 11:24–28), they prohibit touching, falling, and eating (Lev 11:35–40). This ideology is found in 11QT[a] 47:7–17 as well.

20. Qimron and Strugnell, *DJD* X, 1, 155; Yadin, *Temple Scroll*, 1:277 (cf. 11QT[a] 51:4–5 and 47:7–15); Schiffman, *Courtyards*, 131–32.

Lev 11:24–25, 27–28

24 וּלְאֵ֖לֶּה תִּטַּמָּ֑אוּ כָּל־הַנֹּגֵ֥עַ בְּנִבְלָתָ֖ם יִטְמָ֥א עַד־הָעָֽרֶב

25 וְכָל־הַנֹּשֵׂ֖א מִנִּבְלָתָ֑ם יְכַבֵּ֥ס בְּגָדָ֖יו וְטָמֵ֥א עַד־הָעָֽרֶב

27 וְכֹ֣ל ׀ הוֹלֵ֣ךְ עַל־כַּפָּ֗יו בְּכָל־הַֽחַיָּה֙ הַהֹלֶ֣כֶת עַל־אַרְבַּ֔ע טְמֵאִ֥ים הֵ֖ם לָכֶ֑ם כָּל־הַנֹּגֵ֥עַ בְּנִבְלָתָ֖ם יִטְמָ֥א עַד־הָעָֽרֶב

28 וְהַנֹּשֵׂא֙ אֶת־נִבְלָתָ֔ם יְכַבֵּ֥ס בְּגָדָ֖יו וְטָמֵ֣א עַד־הָעָ֑רֶב טְמֵאִ֥ים הֵ֖מָּה לָכֶֽם

(24) By these you shall become unclean; *whoever touches the carcass of any of them shall be unclean until the evening* (25) *and whoever carries any part of the carcass of any of them shall wash his clothes and be unclean until the evening*. (27) All that walk on their paws, among the animals that walk on all fours, are unclean for you; *whoever touches the carcass of any of them shall be unclean until the evening* (28) and *the one who carries the carcass shall wash his clothes and be unclean until the evening; they are unclean for you*.

B 21–24

21 ואף על עוֺרֿ[ות ועצמות הבהמה הטמאה אין לעשות]
22 [מן עצמותמה] ומן עֹ[ו]ר֯[ות]מה ידות כ֯[לים ואף על עור נבלת]
23 [הבהמה] הטהורה [הנוש]א א[ו]ת[ה] נבלתה [לוא יג֯ש לטהרת ה֯קודש]
24 [-- וא]ף על הע[]ת שהמ [ה -מ -- ים

(21) Concerning the hid[es and bones of unclean animals, one is not allowed to make] (22) handles for v[essels from their bones] or their h[ides.] [Concerning the hi]de from the carcass (23) of a clean [animal]: *he who carries such a carcass [shall not] have access to the sacred food* . . . . (24) [. . .] and concerning the [. . . . .] that they [use to . . . .]

The impurity level of slaughtered animals' skins (עור) declared to be equal to that of its flesh (בשר) in B 21–22 provokes a practical issue. The animals' hides were material for vessels that carry many kinds of offerings, so the author of MMT believed that unclean animals' skins or leather for vessels could contaminate its contents. Thus, MMT specifically prohibits the manufacturing of handles from bones and vessels from hides (B21–22). In addition, MMT protects the sacred pure food by creating a strict boundary without mentioning the time period of cleansing stated in Lev 11:39 (until evening). The focus in MMT, not only on the one who touched or carried the objects, but also on the things that were touched, implies that the laws became stricter. In this case, MMT depends on the ideology of Leviticus and its rules about purity of hides and bones with additions and omissions.

Place for the Slaughter of Animals

In the halakhic section, cultic and purity regulations are largely based on Leviticus and Numbers. The sanctity of various places is discussed in two passages in MMT: in a halakha dealing with slaughter in the camp

(B 27–33), and the entry of dogs into Jerusalem (B 58-62).[21] B 27–33 echoes Lev 17:1–9, especially 17:3 and in B 27–33, as can be seen by the author's use of the expressions "outside the camp" (מֹחוץ לסֹחֹנה) and "an ox or a lamb or a goat" (שור וכשב ועז), which are taken verbatim from Lev 17:3. The word "lamb" (כשב) appears seven times in Leviticus, and it is collocated with goat (עז), which appears in B 28 as well. It is not a paraphrase but an explicit restatement of Leviticus in MMT.

Lev 17:3	B 27b–28a
אִישׁ אִישׁ מִבֵּית יִשְׂרָאֵל אֲשֶׁר יִשְׁחַט שׁוֹר אוֹ־כֶשֶׂב אוֹ־עֵז בַּמַּחֲנֶה אוֹ אֲשֶׁר יִשְׁחַט מִחוּץ לַמַּחֲנֶה	[ועל] שא כתוב [איש כי ישחט במחנה או ישחט] מֹחוץ לסֹחֹנה שֹור וכשב ועז
If anyone of the house of Israel *slaughters an ox or a lamb or a goat in the camp, or slaughters it* **outside the camp**	[and re]garding that which is written [should an individual slaughter in the camp or slaughter] **outside the camp** ox, sheep or goat

B 27–28 is based on Lev 17:3–4, as noted by Qimron (cf. 11QT[a] 52:13–16).[22] The term "camp" (מַחֲנֶה) is used seventeen times in Leviticus; the camp was separated from the inside to the outside. Leviticus 17:3–4 states that anyone who does not slaughter an ox, lamb, or goat in front of the Tent of Meeting shall be cut off, a concept that indicates Leviticus influences the author of MMT.[23]

The Levitical idea that the camp is a place where holiness should be maintained and all uncleanness kept outside of the camp (Lev 14:8) is evident in MMT, which considered Jerusalem as a holy camp (4Q394 8iv: 10). The author of MMT follows detailed instructions from Leviticus to maintain its holiness.[24] In MMT, God commands not only His people but also the physical space around his people to be holy.

21. Maintaining sanctity in the sanctuary in Leviticus is very significant, and MMT considered Jerusalem as a holy camp (4Q394 f8iv:10) that needed to be pure. See Hempel, "The Laws of the Damascus Document and 4QMMT," 69–84; von Weissenberg, "The Centrality of the Temple in 4QMMT," 293–305, esp. 297–98.

22. Qimron and Strugnell, *DJD X*, 156–57. For a discussion of scriptural background, see Bernstein, "Employment and Interpretation," 39–40. Brooke suggests that Lev 17:3 has been reordered in MMT rather than paraphrased. See Brooke, "Explicit Presentation," 72; Rothstein, "The Laws of Immolation and Second Tithe," 334–53; Brooke, "Luke–Acts and the Qumran Scrolls," 72–90, esp. 79. See also 11QT[a] 52:13–53:4 where this material has been represented. B 27–28 employs Leviticus to support this particular view. See Miller, *Performances of Ancient Jewish Letters*, 233.

23. Werrett, "The Reconstruction of 4QMMT," 210.

24. MMT depends upon Leviticus and its emphasis on holiness in terms of humans and objects. Harrington says, "MMT provides explicit and implicit data on these issues

MMT does not mention the biblical text when the word "it is written" (כתוב) is used in MMT, but this expression sometimes precedes a description or a paraphrase of a biblical text. Leviticus 17:3 is paraphrased, according to Qimron and Strugnell;[25] however, with a slight change.[26] B 27b–28a does not paraphrase Lev 17:3 to deliver the same idea, but rather the author copies expressions from Lev 17:3 and adds more words to make it clearer, thus an explicit use of scripture in MMT. Apparently the author of MMT has Leviticus in mind either as a base or as a secondary source to compose this manuscript.

Since MMT has been preserved very poorly, it is not easy to interpret the text, but it is not difficult to discover the text's overarching theme: animal slaughter, both profane and sacred, at the temple (B27–35).[27] Its purpose is to protect the people from guilt and punishment and to make readers aware that the priests are responsible for caring for all these matters (B26b–28a). It therefore reconstructs biblical texts to explain these concepts. The combination of Lev 17:1–9 and Deut 12:20–28 (two contradictory laws) produces a stricter rule for the people to avoid punishment by forbidding any kind of slaughtering outside the Jerusalem temple.[28] Clearly, the significant themes of purity and holiness in Leviticus are adapted in B 27b–28a and influenced by Lev 17:3.

---

in all three socio-anthropological areas: space, persons, and food," which Leviticus describes. See Harrington, "Holiness in the Laws of 4QMMT," 109–28, esp. 110. Cf. Lev 11:1–47; 20:24–26; and Lev 17–26 in terms of the theme of holiness in Leviticus. The author of MMT expanded the nature of holiness from one place to a larger place, i.e., sanctuary, Jerusalem, and encampment (B 29–31), a gradation that seems to follow Leviticus.

25. Qimron and Strugnell, *DJD X*, 140–41, write of the use of כתוב, "This word is known in MH as a technical term introducing scriptural citations. In MMT it never introduces biblical verses . . . it would therefore seem that כתוב is not intended to introduce a verbatim quotation from Scripture, but rather to introduce the statement which was derived from such a verse" like Lev 17:3 in MMT.

26. Brooke defines paraphrase as the use of alternative words to express the same or a similar idea. Here in B 27–28, there is not a single major word that does not come from the scriptural source in Lev 17. See Brooke, "Explicit Presentation," 72.

27. Qimron and Strugnell, *DJD* X, 112.

28. Kratz, "The Place Which He Has Chosen," 57–80, esp. 61–62. These two texts (Lev 17:1–9 and Deut 12:20–28) contradict the laws regarding slaughter. According to Lev 17:1–9, the law is intended to remove all sacrifice outside the central sanctuary while Deut 12:20-28 allows slaughter outside the cultic space into the sanctuary. The editor of MMT seems to resolve this conflict that "Leviticus meant to indicate only that it was permitted to sacrifice as many *shelamim* as desired, and that non-sacral slaughter was permitted anywhere." See Schiffman, *Courtyards*, 134–35; Weissenberg, "Centrality of the Temple in 4QMMT," 293–305." The passage of 4QMMT can be compared with 11QT 52:13–53:8, as the same law in Lev 17:3 is linked with Deut 12:6 and 12:13–15.

The Slaughter of Animals

According to Qimron and Strugnell's reconstruction in *DJD* X, B 36–38 is based on Lev 22:28. A biblical background to the law of B 36–38 is found in Deut 22:6–7 and Lev 22:28, though Deut 22:6–7 is not related to sacrificial killing or sacred rituals but is a more general rule about mothers and eggs.[29] B 36–38 refers to Lev 22:28 and its command not to kill both an ox or sheep and their young in one day.[30]

Lev 22:28

וְשׁ֕וֹר אוֹ־שֶׂ֖ה אֹת֣וֹ וְאֶת־בְּנ֑וֹ לֹ֥א תִשְׁחֲט֖וּ בְּי֥וֹם אֶחָֽד

But *<u>you shall not slaughter, from the herd or the flock, an animal with its young on the same day</u>*

B 36–38

36 [ועל העברות אנחנו חושבים שאין לזבוח א]ת
האם ואת הולד ביום אחד
37 [ועל האוכל אנח]נו חושבים שאיאכל את
הולד
38 [שבמעי אמו לאחר שחיטתו ואתם יודעים
שהו]אׄ כן והׄדבר כתוב עברה

(36) [Concerning pregnant animals, w]e have de[termined that *<u>one must not sacrifice] the mother and the fetus on the same day</u>*. [. . .] (37) [Concerning] one who eats [of the fetus, w]e have determined that a person might eat the fetus (38) [which is found in the womb of its mother after it has been sacrificed. You know that thi]s is correct, for the matter is written: a pregnant animal.

Leviticus 22:28 introduces rules about killing (שְׁחָטְ) pregnant animals (שְׁוֹר אוֹ־שֶׂה) and their offspring (בְּנוֹ) on the same day (בְּיוֹם אֶחָד), which is reflected in B 36–38, with slight reconstruction.[31] The author of 4QMMT has written at B36, "one must not sacrifice] the mother and the fetus on the same day" (חושבים שאין לזבוח א[ת האם ואת הולד ביום אחד), and replaced שְׁחָטְ with זבוח; B36 clearly echoes "But you shall not kill an ox or a sheep and her young in one day" (וְשׁ֕וֹר אוֹ־שֶׂ֖ה אֹת֣וֹ וְאֶת־בְּנ֑וֹ לֹ֥א תִשְׁחֲט֖וּ בְּי֥וֹם אֶחָֽד Lev 22:28). It appears that MMT applies this biblical law to pregnant animals.[32]

29. Schiffman, *Courtyards*, 138; See Schiffman, "The Place of 4QMMT," 81–98, esp. 88–89.

30. Qimron points to two things regarding this ruling: "it is forbidden to slaughter pregnant animals and a fetus found alive within a (dead) pregnant animal must be ritually slaughtered before it may be consumed." See Qimron and Strugnell, *DJD* X, 157.

31. "According to the restoration it is possible that this law only refers to sacrifice, not to "non-sacral" slaughter" See Schiffman, *Courtyards*, 137–39; Bernstein, "Employment and Interpretation of Scripture," 40.

32. Qimron and Strugnell, *DJD* X, 156–57. Brooke suggests that B 36 seems to echo

The editor of MMT uses Lev 22:28 to provide the specific reason for which the offering of pregnant animals is forbidden.[33] 4Q396 1–2 i 4 uses the citation of the formula כתוב, which implies that the author(s) of MMT interpret the basis of this ruling as scripture.[34] The law not to sacrifice pregnant animals is parallel with the law not to sacrifice a parent and child on the same day in 11QT[b] 52:5–7.

Leviticus 22:28 says mother and calf should not be killed on the same day, a ruling written not only for economic reasons but also for religious reasons. This verse also makes it clear that killing can happen unintentionally or unexpectedly, but it does not speak directly to the case of pregnant livestock. Instead, the emphasis is on religious obligations and their observance.[35] Kugler suggests whatever one thinks of the quality of the author's logic, its foundation is clear: it depends on "relexicalizing" the Leviticus passage and on claiming that fresh vocabulary as the rule translation of Leviticus' meaning.[36] B36–38 clearly adapts the information of the law about pregnant animals from Leviticus.

Sacrifice

The Cooking of Purification Offerings

The precepts of the Torah mentioned in MMT display various offerings described in Leviticus.[37] B 5b–8a, which is fragmentary, depends on the ideology and expressions of Lev 6:28; this example contains similar use of phrasing and ideas.

Lev 22:28 and MMT seems to summarise scriptural passages. See Brooke, "Explicit Presentation," 73.

33. Schiffman, *Courtyards*, 139.

34. Werrett, "Reconstruction of 4QMMT," 211.

35. Cf. 4Q270 2ii:15 and Lev 22:28.

36. Kugler, "Relexicalizing Leviticus in 4QMMT," 135.

37. In MMT B 5–8 the sin-offering, 9–13 the cereal-offering, 36–38 the ritual state of sacrificial animal, 55–58 liquid streams, and B 54 the purity of the temple.

Lev 6:28

וּכְלִי־חֶרֶשׂ אֲשֶׁר תְּבֻשַּׁל־בּוֹ יִשָּׁבֵר וְאִם־בִּכְלִי
נְחֹשֶׁת בֻּשָּׁלָה וּמֹרַק וְשֻׁטַּף בַּמָּיִם

An earthen vessel in which it was boiled shall be broken; *but if it is boiled in a bronze vessel, that shall be scoured and rinsed in water*.

B 5b–8a

5b [ועל זבח החטאת]
6 שהם מבשלים [אות]ה בכלי
[נחושט ומ. . .ים בה את]
7 בשר זבחיהם ומ֯[ ]ים בעזר[ה ומ... או֯ת֯ה]
8a במרק זבחם

(5b) [And concerning the sacrifice of the purification-offering] (6b) *that they cook in a [copper] vessel [and that they] . . . in it* (7) the flesh of their sacrifices and that they . . . in the Temple court [and that they . . .] it (8a) with broth of their sacrifice

The idea of cooking the purification offering echoes Levitical ideology, as seen in words from Lev 6:28, "to boil" (בֻּשַּׁל), "vessel" (כְּלִי), and "to scour" (מֹרַק) adapted in B 5b–8a.[38] MMT follows the process of preparing a sin offering from Lev 6:21; the purification offering, which is holy, could be boiled either in an earthenware or bronze vessel. The vessel should be broken if it were made with clay (חֶרֶשׂ), and the bronze vessel should be purified by boiling (בֻּשַּׁל), cleaning (מֹרַק), and rinsing (שֻׁטַּף).[39] MMT adapts the strict rules for cleaning a vessel with preparing a sin-offering from Lev 6:28. One possible explanation for using a bronze vessel and its treatment is to avoid "forbidden sacrificial remnants."[40] As Qimron mentions, MMT possibly either protests against violating the law of dealing with the remains of sacrifices (נותר) or against cooking other sacrifices in the vessels of the purification offerings.[41] Leviticus 6:22–23 says the priest from among Aaron's sons shall sacrifice an offering to the Lord, but all remains from the offering shall not be eaten and burned (כליל תקטר). The cooking of the purification offering in MMT comes from Leviticus since it is not found in other places in the Torah and uses the same words and ideology.

38. Qimron and Strugnell, *DJD* X, 149.

39. The word וּמֹרַק in biblical passages has a verb form that means "to polish" and which uses a pual form "to wash away" in Lev 6:21 (Lev 6:28 NRSV). The word מֹרַק as a noun form in MMT, which means "broth." The strict rule of purification from Lev 6:21 was applied to the laws of purification offering in MMT.

40. Qimron and Strugnell, *DJD* X, 149.

41. Qimron and Strugnell, *DJD* X, 149.

Remains of the Meal Offering

B 10–11 concerns consuming the last meal offered in the temple and protecting the holy things of the people of Israel. B 10b–11a borrows the rhetoric and content from Lev 7:15 and 19:6 to construct a law that deals with the remains of the meal offering.[42] Schiffman states, "it is significant that 4QMMT takes as a unit the meat, fat and meal offering, understanding them all to be required to be eaten on the very day the sacrifice is offered."[43] This requirement is found especially in Lev 7:15 and 16, though Lev 7:16 allows a participant to eat the remaining food if it is a freewill offering. In B 10b–11, MMT depends on Lev 7:15 with its rule to finish all the food on the same day.

Lev 7:15; 19:6

7:15 וּבְשַׂר זֶבַח תּוֹדַת שְׁלָמָיו בְּיוֹם קָרְבָּנוֹ יֵאָכֵל לֹא־יַנִּיחַ מִמֶּנּוּ עַד־בֹּקֶר

19:6 בְּיוֹם זִבְחֲכֶם יֵאָכֵל וּמִמָּחֳרָת וְהַנּוֹתָר עַד־יוֹם הַשְּׁלִישִׁי בָּאֵשׁ יִשָּׂרֵף

(7:15) And the flesh of your thanksgiving sacrifice of well-being shall be eaten **<u>on the day it is offered</u>**; you shall not leave any of it until morning. (19:6) <u>*It shall be eaten on the same day you offer it, or on the next day*</u>; and anything left over until the third day shall be consumed in fire.

B 10b–11a

10b ואף [כתוב --]
11 שהמנ[חה נאכלת] על החלבים והבשר ביומ
זוב[חם כי לבני]

(10b) As [it is written] (11a) that the offe[ring should be ea]ten after the fat and the flesh (are sacrificed), **<u>on the day when they are sacri[ficed</u>** <u>*(i.e. before sunset)*</u>. For the sons of]

Leviticus 7:15 and 19:6 need clarification. "On the day it is offered" (בְּיוֹם קָרְבָּנוֹ) in Lev 7:15 suggests that the offering must be consumed by the first sunset after it is offered, i.e., the end of the day, but "until morning" (עַד־בֹּקֶר) permits continued consumption through the night. But "on the day of your offering it shall be eaten, and on the next day" (בְּיוֹם זִבְחֲכֶם יֵאָכֵל וּמִמָּחֳרָת) in 19:6 requires interpretation.[44] MMT follows the end of Lev 7:15, "you shall not leave any of it until the morning," implying parts of the offering must be consumed before sundown. MMT respects the strict rule

42. Qimron and Strugnell, *DJD* X, 47, 51–52. Brooke, "Explicit Presentation," says, "instead of a quotation we have a combination of scriptural terminology being used to produce the desired halakic ruling that everything should be eaten before sunset," 71.

43. Schiffman, *Courtyards*, 124–26. (cf. Lev 22:29–30; 11QT[a] 20:11–13).

44. Kugler, "Rewriting Rubrics," 90–112, esp. 99. Kugler comments, "Echoing the ambiguous biblical passages Lev 17:15; 19:6, MMT solves their ambivalence with a strict interpretation of their language," 101.

and time period that Lev 7:15 allows for the leftover offering to last until the following dawn.[45] Qimron and Strugnell state, "[the] rabbis interpreted the word יוֹם as including also part of the following night. This is according to their general rule that in sacrificial matters night follows day, and in accordance with the second statement in this biblical source (לֹא־יַנִּיחַ מִמֶּנּוּ עַד־בֹּקֶר)."[46]

Since these two passages seem contradictory, the author of MMT combines the two and allows no room for misinterpretation. B 10b–11a intends the meal sacrifice to be consumed without providing the extra time that is found in Lev 17:5 and 19:6, ameliorating error in the matter. Thus, it makes the ruling stricter to avoid mistakes in applying this biblical law. MMT harmonizes and resolves the tension produced by ambiguous biblical witnesses.[47] B 11b–13a depends on Lev 22:15–16, warning priests to protect the people from causing guilt. Though it does not depend upon Lev 22:15–16 in terms of explicit examples of words or expressions, it is clear that its ideology, regarding the priest's responsibility is applied in B 11b–13a.

Lev 22:15–16	B 11b–13a
15 וְלֹא יְחַלְּלוּ אֶת־קָדְשֵׁי בְּנֵי יִשְׂרָאֵל אֵת אֲשֶׁר־יָרִימוּ לַיהוָה 16 וְהִשִּׂיאוּ אוֹתָם עֲוֺן אַשְׁמָה בְּאָכְלָם אֶת־קָדְשֵׁיהֶם כִּי אֲנִי יְהוָה מְקַדְּשָׁם	11b [כי לבני] 12 הכוהנ[ים] ראו להזהיר בדבר הזה בשל שלוא י[היו] 13a מסיאים את העם עוון
(15) <u>*No one shall profane the sacred donations of the people of Israel, which they offer to the Lord*</u>, (16) <u>*causing them to bear guilt requiring a guilt-offering, by eating their sacred donations*</u>: for I am the Lord; I sanctify them.	(11b) [For the sons of] (12) <u>*the priest[s] are responsible to take [c]are of this matter [so as not to]*</u> (13a) <u>*bring guilt upon the people.*</u> *(Cause the people to bear punishment)*

Bernstein describes the priests' responsibility to instruct the people how not to be guilty as follows: "Leviticus 22:16 is not cited with כאשר כתוב ('as it is written') or כאשר אמר ('as it says') as the basis of the law, but there is no doubt from MMT's formulation that it is the biblical source for this sentence, warning the priests not to cause laypersons to incur guilt."[48] B11a–

45. Schiffman, *Courtyards*, 124.

46. Qimron and Strugnell, *DJD* X, 151. Based upon Qimron, "The sect interpreted the law as referring to the cereal offering that should be eaten before sunset so that nothing would be left over for the next morning."

47. Qimron and Strugnell, *DJD* X, 152.

48. Bernstein, *Reading and Re-Reading Scripture*, 460. Bernstein comments that the author of MMT applied the passage from Leviticus to the law in terms of the proper

13b summarizes Leviticus regarding the priests' responsibility, including Aaron and his sons, to remember God's command not to profane the holy things of the people of Israel.

The ideology regarding the unclean period until the sun goes down in Lev 22:27 is echoed in B 15–16a.[49] People who have diseases, such as leprosy, or who have contact with the dead are considered unclean until evening (Lev 22:24–25).

Lev 22:7	B 15–16a
וּבָא הַשֶּׁמֶשׁ וְטָהֵר וְאַחַר יֹאכַל מִן־הַקֳּדָשִׁים כִּי לַחְמוֹ הוּא	15 לכול אלה להערי[בו]ת השמש להיות טהור[י]ם 16a בשל שא יהיה הטהר מזה על הטמה
<u>*When the sun sets he shall be clean*</u>; and afterwards he may eat of the sacred donations, for they are his food.	(15) <u>*it is at sun[se]t that all become pure*</u> (16) so that the pure may sprinkle upon the impure one.

B 15 says, "the sun must set" (הערִיבות השמש) while Lev 22:7 says, "when the sun sets (וּבָא הַשֶּׁמֶשׁ)," but since only Lev 22:7 possesses this detailed explanation, its influence is clear.

The First-Fruits of the Fourth Year

B 62–63 discusses the fruits of the fourth year considered to be holy so that they can be sacrificed to the priest (cf. 11QT[a] 60:2–14). It is apparent that B 62–63 adapted the words from Lev 19:23–25, when we compare the words from both texts.[50] The following example contains verbal overlaps and compatible ideas.

---

time for the consumption of offering. Even though it was not a direct citation, it is very clear that 4QMMT is influenced by Levitical consumption rules for offerings.

49. Deuteronomy 23:11 states, "bathe himself in water, and as the sun sets, he may come inside the camp"; however, this passage is not dealing with sacred food but with impurity of "a nocturnal emission."

50. MMT depends upon Levitical expressions: הארץ in Leviticus and ארץ ישראל in MMT; וּנְטַעְתֶּם in Leviticus and מטעת in MMT; עֵץ מַאֲכָל in Leviticus and עצי המאכל in MMT; הכה in Leviticus and כוהנים in MMT. Leviticus 19:24 commands that the first fruits should be offered to the Lord (הִלּוּלִים לַיהוָה) and Lev 23:10 commands that the first fruits of the harvest be offered to the priest. Qimron and Strugnell observe that B 62–63 and Lev 19:23–25 have similar words but the receiver (subject) of the first fruit is different. MMT combine Lev 19:23–25 and 23:10 to make this law. See Qimron and Strugnell, *DJD* X, 164; Yadin, "4QMMT," 130–49.

Lev 19:24–25

24 וּבַשָּׁנָה הָרְבִיעִת יִהְיֶה כָּל־פִּרְיוֹ קֹדֶשׁ הִלּוּלִים לַיהוָה

25 וּבַשָּׁנָה הַחֲמִישִׁת תֹּאכְלוּ אֶת־פִּרְיוֹ לְהוֹסִיף לָכֶם תְּבוּאָתוֹ אֲנִי יְהוָה אֱלֹהֵיכֶם

(24) *In the fourth year all their fruit shall be set apart for rejoicing in the Lord.* (25) But in the fifth year you may eat of their fruit, that their yield may be increased for you: I am the Lord your God.

Lev 23:10

דַּבֵּר אֶל־בְּנֵי יִשְׂרָאֵל וְאָמַרְתָּ אֲלֵהֶם כִּי־תָבֹאוּ אֶל־הָאָרֶץ אֲשֶׁר אֲנִי נֹתֵן לָכֶם וּקְצַרְתֶּם אֶת־קְצִירָהּ וַהֲבֵאתֶם אֶת־עֹמֶר רֵאשִׁית קְצִירְכֶם אֶל־הַכֹּהֵן

Speak to the people of Israel and say to them: When you enter the land that I am giving you and you reap its harvest, *you shall bring the sheaf of the* **first fruits** *of your harvest* **to the priest**.

B 62b–63[51]

62b ו֯א֯ף ע[ל מ]טע֯ת עצ[י]המאכל הנטע
63 בארץ ישראל כ֯ר֯א֯ש֯י֯ת֯ הוא לכוהנים

(62b) *And co[ncerning the plan]tation of fruits tree[s] planted* (63) in the Land of Israel: *they are to be dealt with* **like first fruits** *belonging* **to the priests**

Leviticus 19:24–25 and 23:10 concern the first fruits from a tree planted for the first time. MMT echoes the words and contents from Lev 19:23–25[52] by stating that the fruit of the first three years are not edible, according to biblical law, because the fruit was considered as uncircumcised (ערלה) and not holy. The fruits of the fourth year were considered holy (קֹדֶשׁ)[53] and all of these fruits belong to the Lord and should be offered to the Lord with praise (הִלּוּלִים לַיהוָה). Since the land belongs to the Lord, all of the first fruits should be offered to the Lord.

Qimron and Strugnell suggest that "the halakha in MMT seems to say that the fruits of the tree or the vineyard in its fourth year belong to the

51. In the sectarian group, they "often equate the Torah's 'holy' with perquisites of the priests." And the priests should eat these foods. The theme of holiness of the fruits of the fourth year (Lev 19:23–25), the tenth of the cattle and flock (Lev 27:32) seems to influence the composition of MMT. See Harrington, "Holiness in the Laws of MMT," 124.

52. Ezekiel 44:30 references first fruits to the priest; however, it does not include the years, as Leviticus does.

53. The fruits of the fourth year ("holy for giving praise") also appear among the priestly gifts itemized in the Temple Scroll at the beginning of col. 60. Qimron and Strugnell, *DJD* X, 165; Schiffman, *Courtyards*, 140–43.

priests, just as the first fruits belong to the priests."[54] This concept is from the biblical law found in several passages from Leviticus dealing with fruit tithe to the priest.[55] B 62–63 uses Lev 19:23–25 and 23:10, two separated laws, in one place: "the fruit produced by such trees in their fourth year is to be dealt with like first fruit belonging to the Priest" (B 62–63).

d. Impurity of Lepers

B 64b–67a concerns impurity of lepers and is dependent upon Lev 14:8. The laws of impurity of lepers in halakha in early rabbinic sources are very detailed because the purity process was very complicated. The main difficulty lay in identifying the various types of leprosy and in defining the degrees of purity and impurity proper to each type. Most of the halakha about lepers contain the detailed symptoms, but MMT is not concerned with such details.[56] Since MMT is more concerned with preserving the holiness of the temple, it deals with how priests keep lepers away from the temple and from objects that are ritually pure. The degree of lepers' impurity during the various stages of their purification is adapted by MMT from the biblical laws.[57] The following contains verbal overlaps and similar uses of phrasing and ideas.

54. Qimron and Strugnell, *DJD* X, 164. According to Lev 27:9–34, the offering was to be presented to the priest.

55. Leviticus 27:30 states that such a tithe is to be given to the priests (cf. Lev 27:30–32 and MMT B 62–64 the law about the fruits of the tree). See Qimron and Strugnell, *DJD* X, 164.

56. Qimron and Strugnell, *DJD* X, 166.

57. On general purity rules such as trees, lepers, and sacred food, Leviticus highly influences the structure and contents of B 62–72 and B 68 B and begins with priestly "opinion and explanations" by using a introductory phrase "and you know." See Maier, "Purity at Qumran," 91–124, esp. 97–105; Miller, *Performances of Ancient Jewish Letters*, 236.

Lev 14:8	B 64b–67a
וְכִבֶּס֩ הַמִּטַּהֵ֨ר אֶת־בְּגָדָ֜יו וְגִלַּ֣ח אֶת־כָּל־שְׂעָר֗וֹ וְרָחַ֤ץ בַּמַּ֙יִם֙ וְטָהֵ֔ר וְאַחַ֖ר יָב֣וֹא אֶל־הַֽמַּחֲנֶ֑ה וְיָשַׁ֛ב מִח֥וּץ לְאָהֳל֖וֹ שִׁבְעַ֥ת יָמִֽים	64b ואף על הצרׄועים אׄנחנו 65 א[ומרים שלוא י]בואו עם טהרת הקוד[ש] כי בדד 66 [יהיו מחוץ לבית ו]אף כתוב שמעת שיגלחׄ וכבס [י]שב מחוץ 67a [לאוהלו שבעת י]מים
The one who is to be cleansed shall *wash his clothes, and shave off all his hair, and bathe himself in water*, and he shall be clean. After that he shall come into the camp, but shall **live outside his tent for seven days**.	(64b) And also concerning lepers we (65) s[ay that they should not] enter (a place) with hol[y] purity, but in isolation (66) [they shall **stay outside a house**. And] also it is written that */from/ the moment he shaves and washes* [he should] **stay outside** (67a) [**his tent (or: his house) for seven d**]**ays.**

Leviticus distinguishes between stages in the purification of a healed leper with directives for treating each stage, and MMT follows this ordering of purification stages.

The first stage to become pure, according to Lev 14:8, is to wash (וְכִבֶּס) and shave (וְגִלַּח),[58] applied in B 66 as "he shaves and washes" (שיגלח וכבס). The word אהל in the laws of Torah is interpreted in the DSS as a "house" or "any dwelling place"; MMT takes the word אהל in the verse "but live outside his tent" (וְיָשַׁב מִחוּץ לְאָהֳלוֹ) in Lev 14:8 to be בית "house."[59] In this first stage of purification, lepers are to be isolated inside cities since they defile houses if they enter. MMT also does not permit lepers (including healed ones) to enter the house because sacred food can be found there.

The second stage of purification is to live outside the tent for seven days (Lev 14:8), an idea found in B 66–67a, and to wait until sunset to eat or touch sacred food.[60] With the process of Levitical purification in mind, MMT composes new instructions for the Israelites by following the order of Lev 14 in its stages of purification in B 68–70 and Lev 14:19–20 for the priestly role in purifying lepers.

58. The process of becoming clean by washing his clothes and shaving off all his hair is found mainly in Leviticus and somewhat in Numbers (6:9); however, they are not related to purity with lepers. B 64b–67a is closer to Lev 14:18 and depends upon this passage (cf. Lev 15:13; 16:28). See Qimron and Strugnell, *DJD* X, 153. Werrett, *Ritual Purity and the Dead Sea Scrolls*, 186; Bernstein, "Employment and Interpretation," 42; Feder, "The Polemic Regarding Skin Disease in 4QMMT," 55–70.

59. Qimron and Strugnell, *DJD* X, 134.

60. Werrett, *Ritual Purity*, 187. Leviticus 22:7: "When the sun goes down he shall be clean, and afterward he may eat of the holy things, because they are his food."

Lev 14:19–20

19 וְעָשָׂה הַכֹּהֵן אֶת־הַחַטָּאת וְכִפֶּר עַל־הַמִּטַּהֵר מִטֻּמְאָתוֹ וְאַחַר יִשְׁחַט אֶת־הָעֹלָה
20 וְהֶעֱלָה הַכֹּהֵן אֶת־הָעֹלָה וְאֶת־הַמִּנְחָה הַמִּזְבֵּחָה וְכִפֶּר עָלָיו הַכֹּהֵן וְטָהֵר

(19) *the priest shall offer the sin-offering, to make atonement for the one to be cleansed from his uncleanness.* Afterwards he shall slaughter the burnt-offering (20) *and the priest shall offer the burnt-offering and the grain-offering on the altar. Thus the priest shall make atonement on his behalf and he shall be clean.*

B 68b–70

68b [ואתם יודעים
69 שעל השוגג שלוא] [יעשה את המצוה ונעל]הׄ ממנו [להביא
70 חׄטאת ועׄ[ל העושה ביד רמה כתוב שהו]אׄהׄ בׄ[וזה ו]מׄגדׄ[ף]

(68b) [And you know (69) *that the one who unknowingly breaks a commandment] [and the matter escape]s his notice, [he must bring a]* (70) *sin offering. But as [for the one who intentionally sins, it is written that h]e is a d[espiser and] a blasphe[me]*

B 68–70 concerns sacrifice (ונעל]הׄ) and sin offering (חטאת) for those who unknowingly break a commandment. In Lev 14:20, the priest offers burnt offerings (עֹלָה) and grain offerings (מִנְחָה) to make lepers clean, but B 69–70 includes an offering without including the priest's role, though with a strong emphasis (להביא) on the purification of offerings as in Lev 14.[61] In summation, B 64b–70 depends heavily on the Levitical way of purifying the lepers through a specific process.

Purification Process

B 71–72 concerns the last stage of purification, based on Lev 14 and 22:7. This passage maintains the view that if a leper has made his purification offering, he might be allowed to eat the sacred food (להאכילׄםׄ מהקודשים) without waiting until sunset on the eighth day. The ruling in MMT is in accordance with the more stringent approach characteristic of the sect in matters of ritual purity.[62]

61. Leviticus 14:31 provides one for a sin offering and the other for a burnt offering, along with a grain offering. And the priest shall make atonement before the Lord for him who is being cleansed.

62. Qimron and Strugnell, *DJD* X, 169. The Hebrew Bible in Lev 14 does not mention sunset but MMT requires it and it is possible that they found this support from Lev 14:21–23. The word בַּיּוֹם הַשְּׁמִינִי on the eighth day in Lev 14:23 occurs at the end of B 72.

Lev 22:7	B 71–72b
וּבָא הַשֶּׁמֶשׁ וְטָהֵר וְאַחַר יֹאכַל מִן־הַקֳּדָשִׁים כִּי לַחְמוֹ הוּא	71 [ואף בהיות להמה טמאות נגע] אין להאכילם [מהקוד]שים 72b עד בוא השמש ביום ה]שמיני
When the sun sets he shall be clean; and afterwards he may eat of the sacred donations, for they are his food.	(71) [*Moreover, while they (still) have the impurity*] *of leprosy, one should not let them eat of the sacred food* (72) *until sunset* on the eight day.

The mention of sunset (עד בוא השמש) in B 72b has been influenced by Lev 22:7 "when the sun goes down" (וּבָא הַשֶּׁמֶשׁ)."[63] The process of the purification stage is stricter in MMT, since the sect apparently demanded a purification period of seven (full) days before eating sacred food, waiting until sunset on the eighth day to ensure the completed time for purification.

The rulings in Leviticus for the stages of purification control not only the content but also the structure of B 64–72. The three stages in the purification of a healed leper from Lev 14 are followed closely in MMT: he should wash with water (B 66; Lev 14:9), shave and immerse on the seventh day (Lev 14:20), and bring his offering on the eighth day (B 71–72b). Leviticus 14 governs MMT in its requirement that the sacred food be clean and holy, separated from lepers.

Illegal Mixtures and Marriages

The theme of holiness in Leviticus becomes very significant in MMT in attributing the holiness of God to the entire people of Israel. B 75–82 does not allow priests to marry ordinary Israelites; this seems to be against Lev 21:7–15, which allows a priest to marry any Israelite; however, the restated law in B 75–82 is ambiguous. Qimron and Strugnell say, "there is evidence that in the Second Temple period priests would marry only women from priestly families."[64] Intermarrying is significant for a priest's holiness, but B 75–82 also deals with fornication, clean animals, and sowing plants. The next example contains an explicit quotation.

63. The Hebrew Bible mentions both the purification of the leper and eating of hallowed things after purification and sunset. The reference in Lev 22:7 is to the eating of a hallowed thing by anyone who touches an impure person, not by a leper. See Jacob Milgrom, "The Scriptural Foundation," 94. Qimron points out "the leper must wait until sunset on the eight day of his purification before he may eat of the sacred food," which eventually seemed to make Levitical law become stricter. See Qimron and Strugnell, *DJD X*, 153; Grabbe, "4QMMT and Second Temple Jewish Society," 89–108.

64. Qimron and Strugnell, *DJD* X, 174; Werrett, *Ritual Purity*, 201–2.

Lev 19:19	B 76b–79
אֶת־חֻקֹּתַי֮ תִּשְׁמֹרוּ֒ בְּהֶמְתְּךָ֙ לֹא־תַרְבִּ֣יעַ כִּלְאַ֔יִם שָׂדְךָ֖ לֹא־תִזְרַ֣ע כִּלְאָ֑יִם וּבֶ֤גֶד כִּלְאַ֨יִם֙ שַֽׁעַטְנֵ֔ז לֹ֥א יַעֲלֶ֖ה עָלֶֽיךָ	76b ועל בה[מתו הטהורה] 77 כתוב שלוא לרבעה כלאים ועל לבוש[ו כתוב שלוא] 78 יהיה שעטנז ושלוא לזרוע שדו וכ[רמו כלאים] 79 [בֿ]גלל שהֿמה ובני אהרון ק[דושי קדושים]
You shall keep my statutes. **You shall not let your animals breed with a different kind; you shall not sow your field with two kinds of seed; nor shall you put on a garment made of two different materials.**	(76) Concerning the [pure] an[imal] (77) **it is written that one must not let it mate with another species; and concerning his clothes [it is written that they should not]** (78) **be of mixed stuff; and he must not sow his field and vi[neyard with mixed species].** (79) [Be]cause they (Israel) are holy, and the sons of Aaron are ho[liest of holy]

B 77–79 uses similar expressions and ideology as Lev 19:19, concerning not mixing different kinds of seed. While B 77–79 includes species, clothes, mixed seed, and vineyard with mixed species (כלאים), MMT might have harmonized Lev 19:19 and Deut 22:9, which enjoins one to "not sow a vineyard with two kinds of seed," though Lev 19:19 controls the contents and ideology of B 77–79. The word כלאים (improper mixture or mingled) in Leviticus sets the boundary that makes the people and nation holy before the Lord,[65] and MMT adapts this use of כלאים.

The subject of fornication and illegal marriage in B 75–76a, 80–82a is based on Lev 21:7, 13–15. The marriage of the priest in Lev 21:13–14 influences B 80–82 to prohibit a priest from marrying anyone from the laity. Qimron suggests this is based on Lev 21, where זֹנָה refers to a woman who is not suitable because she is not from a priestly family.[66] MMT designates "Israel as holy and the priests as most holy."[67] The following example is based upon my own use of electronic search instruments and seems to confirm that the use of Leviticus is more widespread than most scholars have previously thought.

65. MMT seems to be concerned with the purity of the sanctuary and congregation and holiness, and its guidelines from Leviticus might have influenced the author of MMT. See Sharp, "Phinehan Zeal," 208–22.

66. Qimron, *DJD* X, 172–73; Frevel, "Separate Yourself," 220–50; Harrington, "Intermarriage in Qumran Texts," 251–73, esp. 257–59.

67. Himmelfarb, *Between Temple and Torah*, 35.

Lev 21:7, 13–15

7 אִשָּׁה זֹנָה וַחֲלָלָה לֹא יִקָּחוּ וְאִשָּׁה גְּרוּשָׁה
מֵאִישָׁהּ לֹא יִקָּחוּ כִּי־קָדֹשׁ הוּא לֵאלֹהָיו
13 וְהוּא אִשָּׁה בִבְתוּלֶיהָ יִקָּח
14 אַלְמָנָה וּגְרוּשָׁה וַחֲלָלָה זֹנָה אֶת־אֵלֶּה לֹא יִקָּח
כִּי אִם־בְּתוּלָה מֵעַמָּיו יִקַּח אִשָּׁה
15 וְלֹא־יְחַלֵּל זַרְעוֹ בְּעַמָּיו כִּי אֲנִי יְהוָה מְקַדְּשׁוֹ

(7) *They shall not marry a prostitute or a woman who has been defiled; neither shall they marry a woman divorced from her husband. For they are holy to their God* (13) *He shall marry only a woman who is a virgin.* (14) *A widow, or a divorced woman, or a woman who has been defiled, a prostitute, these he shall not marry. He shall marry a virgin of his own kin,* (15) that he may not profane his offspring among his kin; for I am the Lord; I sanctify him.

B 75–76a

75 ועל הזנות הנْעْ[ס]ה בתוכ הע[ם והמה
בני זרע]
76a קדש כ֯שכתוב קודש ישראל

(75) *Concerning the fornication which is pr[act]iced among the pe[ople, although they are children of the holy seed]* (76) (of) holiness, as it is written, Israel is holy.

B 80–82a

80 [וא]תמ יודْעים שמקצת הכוהנים וה[עם
מתערבים]
81 [והם] ומטמאי[ם]את זרע[הקודש ואף]
82a את [זרע]ם ע֯ם הזונות

(80) [*But y]ou know that a part of priests and of the [people mingle]* (81) *[And they] unite with each other and pollute the [holy] seed [as well as]* (82a) *their (own) [seed] with fornications.*

The priest must take as his wife a virgin from his own family (מֵעַמָּיו), not a widow, divorcee, profaned woman, or harlot.[68] Since the limitations for marriage for the priest are very stringent, Lev 21:13–14 lists the illegitimate unions in stages. The priest should marry from his own people or Israelites to preserve a pure pedigree throughout the priesthood. This prohibition is due to a ban against the mixing of kinds, but it also expresses the need to protect the holiness of both priest and people in 81–82a: "And they unite with each other and pollute the holy seed as well as their own seed" (והם מתוכבים ומטמאים את זרע הקודש ואף את זרעם). Leviticus 21:15 states, "that he may not profane his offspring among his kin" (וְלֹא־יְחַלֵּל זַרְעוֹ בְּעַמָּיו). B 80–82a uses the words people (העם), seed (זרע), and defile (טמא) from Lev 21:13–15. MMT B 80–82a extends this law from the high priest to other priests. MMT applies the biblical law in a stricter way concerning the priests, as well as the people, in order to become holy (cf. Lev 21:7, 13–15). In Lev 21:7 marriage with an outsider (זֹנָה) defiles the holy seed of lay Israelites as much as priestly marriages with outsiders defile their seed.[69]

68. Its literal meaning is "from his own people," which has been understood as a reference to taking a wife from the people of Israel (Ezek 44:22).

69. According to Himmelfarb, the holy seed in B 81 must "refer to priests, since it is (male) priests who are forbidden to marry the אִשָּׁה זֹנָה in Lev 21:7." See Himmelfarb, *Between Temple*, 35; Wright, "Justification and Eschatology," 104–32.

Israelites and priests alike are subject to the rule of Lev 21:7,[70] hence the stricter provision in B 75–82.

USE OF LEVITICUS IN MMT SECTION C

Section C of MMT is dominated by Deuteronomy.[71] However, the command to be holy and the regulations on cursing and blessing from Leviticus influence MMT explicitly and implicitly. In this section, I will briefly attempt to show that Leviticus influenced section C with respect to separation from the majority and through blessing and cursing. In Lev 26, God separated his people from uncleanness with warnings and blessings (Lev 26:3–14) and with cursing (Lev 26:14–39). These two subjects are placed at the end of each section in Leviticus to enjoin the Israelites to remember. MMT not only depends upon Leviticus, but also adds a detailed explanation of the reason for remembering in C 31–32, "for your own welfare and for the welfare of Israel."

Separate from the Majority

In the epilogue (the hortatory conclusion), the author of MMT echoes that the people should be separated from their uncleanness, which clearly is found in Leviticus.[72] The following example contains similar use of phrasing and ideas, based on my own use of electronic search instruments and offers new insights to the discussion of the use of Leviticus in MMT.

70. Milgrom, *Leviticus 17–22*, 186.

71. Bernstein, "Employment and Interpretation," 29–51; Brooke, "Explicit Presentation," 67–88.

72. The theme of holiness heavily influences MMT, Temple Scroll, and D. In MMT, some former separation already had taken place (C 7), which echoes Leviticus' theme on separation to be holy. See Davies, "Judaism(s) of the Damascus Document," 27–43; Schiffman, *Qumran and Jersalem*, 112–17.

Lev 15:31a; 20:24, 26	C 7b
15:31a וְהִזַּרְתֶּ֥ם אֶת־בְּנֵֽי־יִשְׂרָאֵ֖ל מִטֻּמְאָתָ֑ם 20:24b אֲנִ֞י יְהוָ֣ה אֱלֹהֵיכֶ֔ם אֲשֶׁר־הִבְדַּ֥לְתִּי אֶתְכֶ֖ם מִן־הָֽעַמִּֽים 20:26 וִהְיִ֤יתֶם לִי֙ קְדֹשִׁ֔ים כִּ֥י קָד֖וֹשׁ אֲנִ֣י יְהוָ֑ה וָאַבְדִּ֥ל אֶתְכֶ֛ם מִן־הָֽעַמִּ֖ים לִהְי֥וֹת לִֽי	[ואתם יודעים ש]פ֯רשנו מרוב הע֯[ם ומכול טמאתם] C 8 [ו]מ֯התערב בדברים האלה ומ֯לבוא ע֯[מהם] לג֯ב אלה
(15:31) Thus you shall keep *the people of Israel separate from their uncleanness*, (20:24) . . . I am the Lord your God; *I have* separated *you from the peoples.* (20:26) You shall be holy to me; for I the Lord am holy, and *I have separated you from the other peoples* to be mine.	(C 7) [But you know that] *we have separated from the majority of the peo[ple and from all their uncleanness]* (C8) [and] from being party to these matters or going along w[ith them] in these things.

The theme of purity and holiness is significant in Leviticus (16–26), a theme that demands separation from the majority of the people and objects in order to keep holiness within the community.[73] Grossman states,

> Which [4QMMT C7] gives the reader reason to understand the communal separation as a response to the inappropriate behaviour of the rest of the populace, rather than as a poor reflection on the community or on the reader personally . . . in place of historic implications, this covenantal reader might focus on the ongoing and personalized significance of the text, which reflects the covenanter's own importance as an interpreter of Torah and his own place as an obedient follower of God's commandments.[74]

There are no explicit texts linking Leviticus and MMT in this case, but the priestly opinions in C seem to be influenced by Leviticus' theme of holiness and encouragement of the Israelites to be obedient to the commandments, which also reflects the covenant that God established.

Blessings and Curses

The blessings and curses in section C are based on various scriptures.[75] Section C 20–21 (4Q398 11–13 3–4) mentions the blessings and curses in the book of Moses.

73. Bar-Asher Siegal, "Who Separated from Whom and Why?," 229–56.

74. Grossman, *Reading for History*, 83.

75. Section C 15–6 "[that you call them to] your [mind] and return [to him with al]l your heart and with [al]l [your] soul" is based on Deut 4:30 and 30:1–2. Section C commands Israel to return to God and his commandments, especially "at the end of days."

C 20–21 ו֯אנחנו מכירים שבאוו מקצת הברכות והקללו֯ת֯ שכתוב בס֯[פר מו]שה

And so we see that some of the blessings and curses have already come that are written in the b[ook of Mo]ses.

C 20–21 describes a biblical theme[76] and "MMT's perspective on the curses and blessings of the Mosaic covenant of the Torah is one of progressive fulfillment in the course of a theological perspective of salvation history."[77] The command for the Israelites to return to the Lord in C 21–22 echoes not only Deut 30:1–4 but also Lev 26 that the warning and judgement of the Lord[78] would not be applied if the Israelites return to the Lord in repentance.

MMT uses the imperative form in the C section to call on the people to "remember" (4Q398 11–13, 6 and 4Q399 1 i, 9), which reminds the reader of Lev 26. It is the Lord's re-established covenant (Lev 26:42 and 45) that requires the Israelites to remember. In these texts, three imperatives are found: זכור, והתבנן, זכור. MMT emphasizes the significance of remembering and following the written commands from the Torah.[79]

4Q398 frgs. 11–13, 6 וה○[– –]ז֯כ֯ו֯ר֯ את מלכי ישרא[ל] והתבנן במעשיהמ֯ה֯
And the [. . .] [Now] remember the kings of Israe[l] and consider their works carefully.

4Q398 frgs. 14–17 ii, 1 זכור [את] דויד שהיא איש חסדים
Remember David, he was a pious man

MMT encourages the reader to "remove your evil thoughts and the counsel of Belial" (C 29), a statement that could be related to terms of warning, judgement, and blessing from Lev 26. This section from MMT points out that their effort to stay away from evil and turn back to the Lord had not been successful. The final hope that the audience might "rejoice at the end

Also this list of blessings and curses form the concluding section of biblical sources: the Book of the Covenant (Exod 23:20–31), the Deuteronomic Code (Deut 28:1–68), and the Holiness Code (Lev 26:3–45). See Wilson and Wills, "Literary Sources," 275–88; Fraade, "Rhetoric and Hermeneutics," 150–61.

76. Fraade, *Legal Fictions*, 95.

77. Hogeterp, "4QMMT and Paradigms," 359–79, esp. 375.

78. MMT collected laws from the Levitical version of the blessings and curses (Lev 26:3–46, esp. 40–45). In the Temple Scroll, the blessings and curses from Deut 28 and Lev 26 influence cols. 56:12–21. See Fraade, *Legal Fictions*, 95–97; Kessler, "Patterns of Descriptive Curse Formulae," 943–84, esp. 950–51; von Weissenberg, *4QMMT*, 127; Anderson, "Curses and Blessings," 47–60.

79. "Remember" and "consider" in C 23, "remember" in C 25, and "consider" and "ask" in C 28.

of time, finding that some of our statements are correct" (C 30) is related to warnings and covenants for the future in Lev 26.

CONSIDERING LEVITICUS IN MMT OVERALL

The discussion in section B shows that purity laws with regard to slaughtering, sacrifice, and illegal marriages in B are closely related to Leviticus explicitly and implicitly. Both Qimron and Werrett agree that 4QMMT's halakhic laws are systematic, stringent, and consistent.[80] In addition, von Weissenberg supports the view that the author(s) of MMT had a biblical model in mind, especially Deuteronomy.[81] However, as I have attempted to show in this chapter, the author(s) of MMT relied on Leviticus more heavily than previous scholars have recognised. As an example, most of the purity rulings in MMT B follow the order of purity laws in Leviticus. Many parts of the laws in MMT depend upon the order of the laws in Leviticus, with minor exceptions. Though B 64–72 does not follow the order of Leviticus, they implicitly follow borrowed ideology from Leviticus.

MMT composes laws in B with slight changes, but the overall structure of MMT mostly follows the order in Leviticus. The evidence from most of the examples in this chapter is as follows:

B 5–8	Lev 6:19–21		
B 9–16	Lev 22:7	B 64–72	Lev 4:13–14, 27–28; 13:46; 22:7
B 15–17	Lev 7:15; 19:6	B 71–72	Lev 22:7
B 21–24	Lev 11:4–5, 27–28, 39–40	B 75–82	Lev 21:7, 13–15
B 27–33	Lev 17:3	C 7–8	Lev 16–26
B 62–63	Lev 19:23–25	C 20–22	Lev 26:15, 31–32

80. Qimron and Strugnell, *DJD* X, 190.

81. Weissenberg, "Centrality of the Temple," 231. Weissenberg suggests the author(s) of MMT may have been influenced by the earlier halakhic issues such as CD/D or 11QT, which could have explained the different genre. See 230–31, however; according to my research in this chapter, the author(s) of MMT have been influenced by Leviticus significantly in terms of its contents and structure in the similarities between the two texts.

This structure depends, with minor exceptions, on Levitical order and structure.[82] Based upon these data, it is fair to say that Leviticus influences the structure of MMT, and the compiler of MMT likely has the structure of Leviticus in mind in its composition and uses it as a primary source. In light of the fact that MMT was originally addressed to outsiders, clearly Leviticus and its interpretation would have been a widespread issue of contention. The multiple copies of MMT imply that the text was reproduced, probably for internal purposes in the community as a teaching tool. This suggests that Leviticus and its interpretation were a significant part of the curriculum.

CONCLUSION

In this chapter, I have shown that Leviticus influences the genre, content, structure, and purpose of MMT. Various sections of MMT are closely influenced by Leviticus' ideology, especially in the B section; the blessing and cursing in Lev 26 shape a key aspect of the ideology of the C section. From this research, we can see clearly that issues such as slaughtering, sacrifice, marriage, judgement, and blessing, all of which are important topics in Leviticus, indicate the close dependence of MMT on Leviticus.

When MMT commands the Israelites to be pure and holy, it is influenced by the theme of holiness in Leviticus. In constructing this so-called letter, the compiler of MMT reflects on a wide range of cultic practices from Leviticus, with extensions and greater strictness, using Leviticus' texts to persuade his audience to follow the laws correctly in order that the holiness of the community might be preserved.

In section B, the author's emphasis on maintaining purity uses Leviticus to explain the process of slaughtering and sacrifice and the prohibition of illegal mixed marriages. MMT uses Levitical texts to explain the place of slaughter,[83] purity of hides and bones,[84] and the slaughter of pregnant animals.[85] Significantly, the author of B combines contradictory laws from Leviticus to produce a clearer law to help the audience understand the text.[86]

82. In Lev 22:7 the idea that after the sun goes down he shall be clean influences both B 15–16 and 71–72, since these two texts deal with similar leprous issues and its cleanness. B 71–72 may have been added later; however, the selected texts in MMT in this chapter mostly follow the order in Leviticus. Cf. Qimron and Strugnell, *DJD* X, 136.

83. B 27–33 / Lev 17:3.

84. B 21–24 / Lev 11:24–25, 27–28, 39–40.

85. B 36–38 / Lev 22:28.

86. B 10–11 / Lev 6:19–21; 7:15; 19:6.

In B 64–72, MMT not only borrows the ideology of Leviticus but also follows the detailed process of purification provided by Leviticus.

Prohibitions regarding illegal mixture and marriage from Lev 21 are also a base text for B 75–82, with the purpose of protecting the priests and ensuring that the people are holy. Based upon all of this evidence, we can conclude that without Leviticus, it would have been difficult for the author of MMT to compose section B.

In Section C, though the author of MMT does not duplicate passages from Leviticus explicitly, the motif of blessing and cursing from Lev 26 is applied in C implicitly; the priestly encouragement to the Israelites to be separated from the majority to become clean is obviously influenced by Levitical texts. Overall, the author of MMT uses Leviticus texts and legal passages to persuade and convince the audience to accept the new reconstructed law to maintain purity in order to keep the covenant with the Lord.

As the survey in this chapter shows, parallels between MMT and Leviticus indicate that the book of Leviticus as a whole prompted, in large part, the order of the construction of MMT as it is now found. The influence of Leviticus on the process of the composition of MMT is clear. Leviticus provided the author with the authoritative tool for outlining and prescribing the sacred space, which was so fundamental to priestly identity.

VII

Leviticus in Other Texts

INTRODUCTION

In this chapter I will summarize the use of Leviticus in several other texts from the Qumran Caves that I did not discuss in previous chapters. The aim of this chapter is to show the breadth of the influence of Leviticus throughout the scrolls' corpus, both in early or pre-sectarian compositions (such as Jubilees and the Temple Scroll), and also in traditions contemporary with sectarian compositions (such as D and MMT). Early or pre-sectarian compositions are identified as such through the absence of technical sectarian terminology and scholarly consensus concerning the likely date of the composition. The traditions contemporary with sectarian compositions or in sectarian compositions themselves are to be found in works whose final form seems to belong to the first century BCE, not least because the manuscript evidence implies such a date.

Chapter II showed that Leviticus scrolls are extant in various sizes and languages. Not only does this indicate the widespread use of Leviticus, but also it very probably indicates that Leviticus was used in various settings for a range of purposes. Chapters III—VI provide evidence that Leviticus has been used in certain compositions to control literary structure, textual content, and thematic ideology.[1] In summary, Leviticus was a significant

1. Previous chapters highlight the significant use of Leviticus in matters such as chronology (III), cult (IV, V and VI), structure (III, V and VII), Sabbath, and covenant

influence in Jewish literature as is attested in the Dead Sea Scrolls from the Qumran Caves. This chapter will describe and analyse the use of Leviticus in several other compositions.

Since we have very limited, incomplete documents, this chapter will discuss the use of Leviticus pragmatically. It is not possible to look at every composition for hints of Leviticus, since many manuscripts are fragmentary and what could be said about them would be of limited value to my overall argument. Thus, I will consider the most likely identifications of Leviticus in various scrolls, giving examples that directly or indirectly show the influence of Leviticus in relation to several matters that have already been identified as significant in earlier chapters. Thus this chapter will largely confirm the picture that I have portrayed in the detailed presentation of the four compositions in chapters III–VI.

As outlined in chapter I, in order to have a general idea of the use of Leviticus in other compositions, I have depended upon Johann Maier's index[2] and *Biblical Quotations and Allusions in Second Temple Jewish Literature*[3] as basic resources for identifying verbal overlaps and other allusions. Those two indexes are very helpful for understanding the way Leviticus has been used in other compositions. However, my research uncovered even wider use of Leviticus than those resources suggested. Through the use of selective searches with Accordance Bible software, I was able to determine that those two indexes missed some possible allusions. As a result, this chapter includes more examples than were proposed in the two indexes.

I have arranged the discussion of these other texts in relation to two eras: early or pre-sectarian traditions (third to second centuries BCE), and traditions in compositions whose final form seems to belong to the first century BCE. The purpose of this chapter is not only to establish the influence of Leviticus on other compositions, but also to highlight the use of Leviticus from earlier to later traditions to show the wide range and continuous use of Leviticus in these scrolls from the Qumran Caves.

(III, IV, V, and VI). Special attention has been paid to the role of Lev 26 (III, IV, V, and VI).

2. Maier, *Die Qumran-Essener*, 161–82.

3. Lange and Weigold, *Biblical Quotations*, 81–88.

DEPENDENCE ON LEVITICUS IN OTHER COMPOSITIONS

Early or Pre-sectarian Traditions (Third to Second Centuries BCE)

The most extensive examples of the use of Leviticus in early or pre-sectarian traditions are the Aramaic Levi Document and the Genesis Apocryphon. These early pre-sectarian (or non-sectarian) works have been described as socially disembodied, since they have no direct reference to any movement or following with which they were explicitly associated.[4] The Aramaic Levi Document as a composition can be dated "to the third century or very early second century BCE."[5] The Genesis Apocryphon as a composition is variously dated between the late third century and the early first century BCE.[6] The Apocryphon of Jeremiah is dated to the second century BCE because of its historical scheme and textual affinities.[7] The use of Leviticus in these early or pre-sectarian traditions indicates the ongoing and pervasive significance of the book in the late Second Temple period.

Aramaic Levi Document (ALD)

The fragments of ALD indicate that the work was known at Qumran. In these fragmentary Aramaic texts, certain themes, such as priesthood and sacrificial processes, are dependent upon Leviticus. As mentioned the ALD was composed in the third or early second century BCE.[8] It concerns Levi's consecration to the priesthood and his teaching to his children.[9] The

4. Fraade, "Interpretative Authority," 46–69.

5. Greenfield et al., *The Aramaic Levi Document*, 19. The editors give the following reasons for that dating: the date of the manuscripts, the quotation of ALD in other compositions (D), and the influence of ALD on works such as Jubilees.

6. See the lengthy discussions in Machiela, *The Dead Sea Genesis Apocryphon*, 7–17. Machiela himself prefers "a date near the early end of this spectrum (preceding Jubilees and perhaps even I En 106–107)" (17).

7. See the extensive discussion concerning dating in Dimant, *DJD* XXX, 110–16.

8. Bonani et al., "Radiocarbon Dating," 843–49; Greenfield et al., *The Aramaic Levi Document*, 3–5, 20; Stone and Greenfield, "Aramaic Levi Document," 1–72, esp. 3–4; Schattner-Rieser, "Levi in the Third Sky," 800–819.

9. These Aramaic texts are a relatively early date, clearly before the time of the Qumran community, in the early second, or even in the third century BCE. The selected biblical passages deal with the priesthood and priests who are instructed by their ideal forefathers. See Collins, *Oxford Handbook of Apocalyptic Literature*, 227; Baumgarten, "Some 'Qumranic' Observations," 393–401; Stuckenbruck, "Pseudepigraphy and First Person Discourse," 295–326.

surviving manuscript has no beginning or end. The texts are fragmentary, which makes it difficult to determine its literary genre. What follows is one significant example from ALD 8:1–6[10] that is dependent upon Lev 1:5, 8–9 and 2:13.

The first part of the example involves Lev 1:5 and 8 concerning the process of sacrifice and is found in ALD 8:1. The following example contains similar use of phrasing and ideas; I have added Lev 1:8 to this example from my own use of electronic search instruments.

Lev 1:8	ALD 8:1
וְעָרְכוּ בְּנֵי אַהֲרֹן הַכֹּהֲנִים אֵת הַנְּתָחִים אֶת־הָרֹאשׁ וְאֶת־הַפָּדֶר עַל־הָעֵצִים אֲשֶׁר עַל־הָאֵשׁ אֲשֶׁר עַל־הַמִּזְבֵּחַ	וכדי הנסקת מן אעי אלין על מדבחא ונורא ישרא להדלקא כהון והא באדין תשרא למזרק לע דמא כותלי מדבחה
Aaron's sons the priests shall arrange the parts, with the head and the suet, <u>*on the wood that is on the fire on the altar*</u>	And when you have offered up any of these woods upon the altar and <u>*the fire begins to burn them, you should then begin to sprinkle the blood on the sides of the altar*</u>.
Lev 1:5b	
וְהִקְרִיבוּ בְּנֵי אַהֲרֹן הַכֹּהֲנִים אֶת־הַדָּם וְזָרְקוּ אֶת־הַדָּם עַל־הַמִּזְבֵּחַ סָבִיב אֲשֶׁר־פֶּתַח אֹהֶל מוֹעֵד	
Aaron's sons the priests shall offer <u>*the blood, dashing the blood against all sides of the altar*</u> that is at the entrance of the tent of meeting.	

Aramaic Levi Document 8:1 depends upon Lev 1:5 and 8: preparing the offerings, burning them, and sprinkling the blood on the sides of altar. The process of sacrifice in Lev 1 is not exactly applied in ALD 8:1, though the prescriptions for sacrificial procedures found in ALD 8:1 are likely to be from Leviticus, since ALD 8:4–6 continually echoes the Levitical processes of sacrificial offerings.

The second part of this example concerns a parallel which shows the detailed order in Lev 1:8–9 and 2:13[11] as an influence in ALD 8:4–6. The fol-

10. The numbering follows the Aramaic text based on Bodleian manuscripts c and d, which contain better preserved text that contains multiple overlaps with 1QLevi 45, 4QLevi[f] 2–6, and 4QLevi[d] 2. The Qumran manuscripts are very fragmentary so for ease of reference the better preserved medieval manuscripts are used as the point of reference. The edition used for ALD is that of Greenfield et al., *The Aramaic Levi Document*.

11. Lev 1:5 ("throw the blood against the sides of the altar") influenced ALD 8:1 ("you should then begin to sprinkle the blood on the sides of altar"). Since both ALD

lowing example contains similar use of phrasing and ideas; I have added Lev 2:13 from my use of electronic search instruments that seems to confirm the use of Leviticus is more widespread than most scholars have previously thought.

Lev 1:9 וְקִרְבּ֥וֹ וּכְרָעָ֖יו יִרְחַ֣ץ בַּמָּ֑יִם	ALD 8:4b ובתר ידכאהא רגלין רחיען עם קרביא
but <u>*its entrails and its legs shall be washed with water*</u> (cf. Lev 1:12–13).	And after <u>*the haunches the hindquarters are washed, with the entrails*</u>
Lev 2:13 וְכָל־קָרְבַּ֣ן מִנְחָתְךָ֮ בַּמֶּ֣לַח תִּמְלָח֒ וְלֹ֣א תַשְׁבִּ֗ית מֶ֚לַח בְּרִ֣ית אֱלֹהֶ֔יךָ מֵעַ֖ל מִנְחָתֶ֑ךָ עַ֥ל כָּל־קָרְבָּנְךָ֖ תַּקְרִ֥יב מֶֽלַח	ALD 8:5 וכולהון מליחין במלח כדי חזה להון כמסתהון
<u>*You shall not omit from your grain-offerings the salt of the covenant with your God; with all your offerings you shall offer salt.*</u>	<u>*All of them salted with salt as is fitting for them in their proper amount*</u>
Lev 1:9 עֹלָ֥ה אִשֵּׁ֛ה רֵֽיחַ־נִיח֖וֹחַ לַיהוָֽה	ALD 8:6 לריח ניחח קודם אל עליון
<u>*an offering by fire of pleasing odour to the Lord.*</u>	As a <u>*pleasing odour before the Most High God*</u>

The process of sacrifice in ALD—washing (8:4), salting (8:5), and pleasing odor (8:6)—is heavily dependent upon Lev 1:9 and 2:13.[12] Schiffman notes, "Aramaic Levi specifies the order in which the various parts of the animal, all slated, are to be offered," based upon passages from Leviticus[13]; specific instructions to sprinkle blood on the sides of the altar also occur frequently in Leviticus.[14] It is interesting that ALD used sacrificial laws from Lev 1. At the very least, this parallel shows that the author of ALD used Leviticus from the beginning.

Aramaic Levi Document 8:5 echoes Lev 2:13, which concerns seasoning a grain offering with salt. Notably, seasoning a grain offering with salt is not found in other texts in the Torah, except in Lev 2:13. Exodus 30:35

8:1 and Lev 1:6 used the word "sprinkle" (זרק), the idea of sprinkling or throwing the blood on the side of altar is probably influenced by Lev 1:5.

12. Greenfield et al., *Aramaic Levi Document*, 174; Stone and Eshel, "Aramaic Levi Document," 1498–510.

13. Schiffman, "Sacrifical Halakhah," 177–202, esp. 188.

14. Leviticus 1:5, 11; 3:2, 8, 13; 4:18; 5:9, etc.

contains the expression "seasoned with salt," but this refers to incense, not to a grain offering. The cultic practice described in Leviticus is used in this early pre-sectarian tradition, which clearly recognises the authority of the prescriptions of Leviticus. Since ALD emphasizes cultic practices, it is plausible that this document had a comprehensive view of atonement as their cultic practices are portrayed.[15] The process of the sacrifice offering in ALD 8:4–6 depend on both Lev 1:9 and 2:13.

These examples indicate that the ideology and sacrificial description from Leviticus significantly influence certain parts of the early ALD. The presence of such details from Leviticus in Aramaic traditions is suggestive of the influence of Leviticus in priestly circles where the traditions of ALD were used.

Genesis Apocryphon

The Genesis Apocryphon is one of the first Dead Sea Scrolls from Qumran Cave 1 to be discovered. Like ALD it is an Aramaic composition that is dependent upon earlier Hebrew scripture.[16] This scroll can be divided into at least three sections: Lamech (0–5:25), Noah (5:26–18:24), and Abram (18:25–22:34). The sacrificial law from Leviticus in Noah's description of his offering in col. 10:15–17 is influenced by Levitical traditions, such as those found in the book of Jubilees, that retell the stories of the patriarchs from Genesis in a "somewhat stylized fashion."[17] The parallels included in this section show the use of expressions and ideology from Leviticus in the Genesis Apocryphon and indicate how the rewriting of Genesis makes explicit the priestly concerns of some parts of Genesis itself.

In the first example, 1Q20 10:15 alludes strongly to Leviticus in use of the expression "he shall pour out at the base of the altar" (Lev 4:18) and follows the procedure of performing sacrifice prescribed in Leviticus. The following example contains verbal overlaps and similar use of phrasing and ideas. Also Lev 4:18 and 19 are added from my own use of electronic search instruments.

15. Stone, "Enoch, Aramaic Levi," 159–70, esp. 168–69. A second important feature of the Aramaic Levi Document is the subsuming of all the messianic functions, both priestly and royal, under the priestly figure. This is clearly a very particular and distinctive point of view.

16. Bernstein, "The Genesis Apocryphon," 157–75, esp. 157–18; Crawford, *Rewriting Scripture*, 107; Qimron, "Toward a New Edition," 11–18.

17. Fitzmyer, *The Genesis Apocryphon*, 16.

Lev 4:18b

וְאֵת כָּל־הַדָּם יִשְׁפֹּךְ אֶל־יְסוֹד מִזְבַּח

and the rest of the blood he shall **pour out at the base of the altar** (cf. Lev 4:7).

1Q20 10:15

. . . דמהון לאיסוד מדבחא אשד[ת ו]כול בשרהון
על מדבחא אקטרת ותליתי לבני שפנינא

. . . [I] **poured out their blood at the base of the altar,** [and] *I burned all their flesh on the altar*, and thirdly the turtledoves.

Lev 4:19

וְאֵת כָּל־חֶלְבּוֹ יָרִים מִמֶּנּוּ וְהִקְטִיר הַמִּזְבֵּחָה

He shall remove all its fat and turn it into smoke on the altar.

Lev 2:13

וְכָל־קָרְבַּן מִנְחָתְךָ בַּמֶּלַח תִּמְלָח וְלֹא תַשְׁבִּית מֶלַח
בְּרִית אֱלֹהֶיךָ מֵעַל מִנְחָתֶךָ עַל כָּל־קָרְבָּנְךָ תַּקְרִיב
מֶלַח

You shall not omit from your **grain-offerings** *the salt of the covenant with your God; with all your offerings you shall offer salt.*

1Q20 10:16

[ ]ן על מדבחא קרבנא ○○○○○○○הון עליה יהבת
סולת נשיפא פילא במשח עם לבונא למנחא

[. . .] on the altar as an offering [. . .] upon it I placed fine flour soaked with oil together with frankincense as a **grain offering**.

1Q20 10:17

ן מ○○○○○○○○○○○ם בכלהון מלחא הוית יהב[ ]

[. . .] Upon all of them I was sprinkling salt.

1Q20 10:15 echoes especially Lev 4:18b in that "pour out the blood at the base of the altar" is mainly found in Leviticus (but only once in Exod 29:12).[18] The language in 10:15 "at the base of the altar" reflects Lev 4:7 and 18b.[19] In col. 10:15–17 the detailed process of sacrificial offering is based upon Lev 2:13 and Lev 4:18b–19, though the order has been changed. The particular expression and ideology of Leviticus clearly influence the description of the sacrifice in col. 10.[20]

However, the description in col. 10:15–17 is more deliberate about the order of the procedure, suggesting that the Genesis Apocryphon is careful

18. Bernstein, "Genesis Apocryphon," 157–75, esp. 169; Machiela, *The Dead Sea Genesis Apocryphon*, 52–53; Falk, *The Parabiblical Texts*, 69–70. Based upon Falk's description, Lev 4:13–21 specifies a bull for a sin offering and the separate burning of fat and pouring out of blood; whereas, Num 15:22–26 specifies a bull for a burnt offering along with grain and drink offering, and a male goat for a sin offering. The rabbis harmonized the two regarding Lev 4 as the general case and Num 15 as a specifiable case.

19. Bernstein, "The Genesis Apocryphon," 651–71, esp. 663. Bernsten also comments on the use of Leviticus 3:17 in 1Q20 11:16–17, which retells Gen 9:3–4 with some phraseology from Lev 3:17.

20. Bernstein, *Reading and Re-Reading Scripture*, 166–68.

to reflect on the scriptural precedents by mentioning the pouring out of blood and seasoning of all the elements, not just the sacrifice itself.[21]

The second example is the story of Noah's planting a vineyard in 1Q20 12:13–15, which is dependent upon Lev 19:23–25. The following example contains similar use of phrasing and ideas and verbal overlaps.

Lev 19:23	1Q20 12:13
וְכִֽי־תָבֹ֣אוּ אֶל־הָאָ֗רֶץ וּנְטַעְתֶּם֙ כָּל־עֵ֣ץ מַאֲכָ֔ל וַעֲרַלְתֶּ֥ם עָרְלָת֖וֹ אֶת־פִּרְי֑וֹ שָׁלֹ֣שׁ שָׁנִ֗ים יִהְיֶ֥ה לָכֶ֛ם עֲרֵלִ֖ים לֹ֥א יֵאָכֵֽל	[ו]שׁרית אנה ובני כולהון למפלח בארעא ונצבת כרם רב בלובר טורא ולשנין ארבע עבד לי חמר
When you come into the land and plant all kinds of trees for food, then you shall regard their fruit as forbidden; *for three years it shall be forbidden to you; it must not be eaten.*	Then I began to cultivate the earth together with all my sons. I planted a large vineyard on Mount Lubar; *when* **four years** *had passed, it produced wine for me*
Lev 19:24	1Q20 12:14
וּבַשָּׁנָה֙ הָרְבִיעִ֔ת יִהְיֶ֖ה כָּל־פִּרְי֑וֹ קֹ֥דֶשׁ הִלּוּלִ֖ים לַיהוָֽה	. . . כׄול . . . וׄכדי . . . רגלא קדמיא ביום חד לרגלא קדמיא די בׄחודשא
In the fourth year *all their fruit shall be set apart for rejoicing in the Lord*.	. . . all . . . And when the first festival . . ., on the first day of the first feast of the month
Lev 19:25	1Q20 12:15
וּבַשָּׁנָ֣ה הַחֲמִישִׁ֗ת תֹּֽאכְלוּ֙ אֶת־פִּרְי֔וֹ לְהוֹסִ֥יף לָכֶ֖ם תְּבוּאָת֑וֹ אֲנִ֖י יְהוָ֥ה אֱלֹהֵיכֶֽם	[—]°°° די כרמי כומרא דן פתחת ושרית למשתיה ביום חד לשתא חמישׁיׄתׄא
But **in the fifth year** *you may eat of their fruit*, that their yield may be increased for you: I am the Lord your God.	[. . .] that belonged to my vineyard. I opened this vessel and *began to drink it on the first day of* **the fifth year** *since planting*.

The ideology and expression of 1Q20 12:13–15 in terms of drinking wine on the first day of the fifth year is based upon Lev 19:23–25. The Apocryphon (12:19; 15:21) alters the account of Noah's drunkenness in light of the prescriptions of Leviticus about viniculture. In addition, the time period after which it is permitted to eat the fruit in the fifth year in Lev 19:25 is not found anywhere else in the Torah. Therefore, 1Q20 12:15 depends upon Lev 19:25, indicating that Leviticus strongly influences the Genesis Apocryphon in this section. Leviticus influences the Genesis Apocryphon to show in particular how the righteous Noah kept the law and how his deeds can be

21. Falk, *Parabiblical Texts,* 70 (cf. Lev 7:26/1Q20 11:17).

understood as appropriate actions to be copied by those who read or hear these stories about him.[22]

Apocryphon of Jeremiah

In this section I will briefly mention two reflections of Leviticus, one in 4Q385a (apocrJer C[a]) and one in 4Q390 (apocrJer E). The Apocryphon of Jeremiah (4QapocrJer) is a prophetic style text written in Hebrew from the viewpoint of Moses and full of the language of Jeremiah. As mentioned it is most likely to be a non-sectarian composition from the second century BCE. 4Q385a and 4Q390 also contain rules and commands from the Torah and point the judgement of God to the disobedient, all of which are matters found in Leviticus as well as other scriptural passages. At least two examples from Lev 26, on disobedience and judgement, seem to be reflected in the Apocryphon of Jeremiah, although the language of Jeremiah is also present.[23]

First, many of the motifs linked with disobedience by not keeping God's covenant in 4Q385a 18ia_b:8–9 seem to have ideas which are compatible with Lev 26, as is its warning using the conditional clause as follows:

Lev 26:14	4Q385a 18ia_b:8
וְאִם־לֹ֖א תִשְׁמְע֣וּ לִ֑י וְלֹ֣א תַעֲשׂ֔וּ אֵ֥ת כָּל־הַמִּצְוֺ֖ת הָאֵֽלֶּה	[וישמעו] בקול ירמיה לדברים אשר צוהו אלהים
But *if you will not obey me, and do not observe all these commandments*	*[that they should listen] to the voice of Jeremiah concerning the things which God had commanded him*
Lev 26:21	4Q385a 18ia_b:9
וְאִם־תֵּלְכ֤וּ עִמִּי֙ קֶ֔רִי וְלֹ֥א תֹאב֖וּ לִשְׁמֹ֣עַ לִ֑י וְיָסַפְתִּ֤י עֲלֵיכֶם֙ מַכָּ֔ה שֶׁ֖בַע כְּחַטֹּאתֵיכֶֽם	[לעשות]ושמרו את ברית אלהי אבותיהם בארץ֯
If you continue hostile to me, and will not obey me, I will continue to plague you sevenfold for your sins	*[to do,] that they should keep the covenant of the God of their fathers in the land*

22. The Genesis Apocryphon often uses the expression, "The Great Holy One," to show the nature of God's holiness (1Q20 2:14, 20, 23; 6:2, 13, 15; 12:17). See Kugel, *A Walk through Jubilees*, 310–11.

23. Davis, *The Cave 4 Apocryphon of Jeremiah*, 192–93.

4Q385a 3a c:6

[ותשכחו את]מׄועדי
בריתי ותחׄ[ללו את שמי ואת קדשי]

[you forgot] the festivals of My covenant, and you pro[faned My name and My holy things,]

4Q385a 3a c:7

[ותטמאו את] מקדשי ותזבחו[את זבחיכם
ל]שעירים ו[. . .]

[you defiled] My Temple, and you offered [your sacrifices to the] goat-demons and [. . .]

The warning of God to the Israelites about judgement in Lev 26:14, 18, 21, 27 is reflected, albeit not in a strong way, in 4Q385a 18ia_b:8–9. The Apocryphon of Jeremiah uses the past tense to remind the Israelites of their disobedience to God's covenant and commands.

Second, the Lord's judgement with the sword and concern with the remnant from Lev 26:25 and 36 is reflected in the ideology and expressions in 4Q390 1:9–10.

Lev 26:25	4Q390 1:9
וְהֵבֵאתִי עֲלֵיכֶם חֶרֶב נֹקֶמֶת נְקַם־בְּרִית וְנֶאֱסַפְתֶּם אֶל־עָרֵיכֶם וְשִׁלַּחְתִּי דֶבֶר בְּתוֹכְכֶם וְנִתַּתֶּם בְּיַד־אוֹיֵב	והסתרתי פני מהמה ונתתים ביד איביהם והסגרתׄ[ים]
I will bring the sword against you, executing vengeance for the covenant; and if you withdraw within your cities, I will send pestilence among you, *and you shall be delivered into enemy hands*.	So I shall hide my face from them, *give them into the hand of their enemies, and hand [them] over*
Lev 26:36	4Q390 1:10
וְהַנִּשְׁאָרִים בָּכֶם וְהֵבֵאתִי מֹרֶךְ בִּלְבָבָם בְּאַרְצֹת אֹיְבֵיהֶם	לחרב והשארתי מהם פׄליטים למע[ן] אשר לא יׄ[כ]ל[ו]בחמתי
And as for those of you who survive, I will send faintness into their hearts in the lands of their enemies	*to the sword.* But *I shall cause a remnant from them* to escape in order that [t]he[y might] not [be complet]ely des[troyed] in my wrath.

In the parallel above, 4Q390 1:9–10 seems to echo Lev 26:25 and 36, regarding God's judgement with the sword. The idea of the remnant in Lev 26:36 and of God's faithfulness to the covenant with the forefathers in

Lev 26:42 seem to be echoed in 4Q390 1:9–10, both in terms of words and ideology.

Works Whose Final Form Belongs to the First Century BCE

4QTohorot A (4Q274)

4QTohorot A is a legal text concerned with purification laws. Although some of the topics discussed in the composition could reflect debates from earlier periods, it is likely that the final form of the work belongs in the first century BCE. The one manuscript copy that survives is written in a script from the early Herodian period, which is estimated to be the first century BCE.[24] The meaning of Tohorot (טהרות) is "cleanliness" or "purity," as in the last six orders of the Mishnah, which concern themes of impurity, ritual impurity, uncleanness from leprosy, unclean foods, ritual immersion, and uncleanness of unwashed hands.[25] Here I will discuss just one example of a purity law from Leviticus that has influenced the language of 4QTohorot A.

The ideology and expressions of this purity law from Leviticus are reflected heavily in 4Q274. In Lev 15:1–33 the emphasis throughout is on four matters: 1) the character of the discharge that signifies flux-uncleanness, 2) the effects of the status of uncleanness; objects that are subject to uncleanness, 3) how the uncleanness is transmitted, and 4) the mode of purification and attendant cultic rite signifying the regaining of the normal status of cleanness. The purity laws in 4QTohorot A are presented in several ways as dependent upon Leviticus. For example, the texts in 4Q274 1i:3–5 echo Levitical language and ideology with respect to menstrual impurity in women. The following example contains verbal overlaps and similar use of phrasing and ideas.

Lev 13:45b–46a	4Q274 1i:3b–4a
45b וְטָמֵ֥א טָמֵ֖א יִקְרָֽא 46a כָּל־יְמֵ֞י אֲשֶׁ֨ר הַנֶּ֥גַע בּ֛וֹ יִטְמָ֖א	3b כי הוא אשר אמר טמא טמא 4a יקרא כול ימי היותׄ [בו הנ]גׄע
(45b) and cry out, '**<u>Unclean, unclean</u>**.' (46a) He shall remain unclean as long as he has the disease	(3b) For as it says, "'**<u>Unclean, unclean</u>**,' (4a) he shall cry all the days which [he] has [the afflic]tion"

24. Baumgarten, "Tohorot," in *DJD* XXXV, 79–122, esp. 99.

25. Avemarie, "'Tohorat Ha-Rabbim' and 'Mashqeh Ha-Rabbim,'" 215–29.

Lev 15:5

וְאִ֗ישׁ אֲשֶׁ֥ר יִגַּ֖ע בְּמִשְׁכָּב֑וֹ יְכַבֵּ֧ס בְּגָדָ֛יו וְרָחַ֥ץ בַּמַּ֖יִם וְטָמֵ֥א עַד־הָעָֽרֶב

Anyone who touches his bed shall wash his clothes, and bathe in water, and be unclean until the evening.

4Q274 1i:5a

ואֹם נגעה תכבס בגדיה ורחצה ואחר תוכל

And **if she has touched anything, she shall wash her clothes and bathe** and then she may eat

Lev 15:19

וְאִשָּׁה֙ כִּֽי־תִהְיֶ֣ה זָבָ֔ה דָּ֛ם יִהְיֶ֥ה זֹבָ֖הּ בִּבְשָׂרָ֑הּ שִׁבְעַ֤ת יָמִים֙ תִּהְיֶ֣ה בְנִדָּתָ֔הּ וְכָל־הַנֹּגֵ֥עַ בָּ֖הּ יִטְמָ֥א עַד־הָעָֽרֶב

When a woman has a discharge of blood that is her regular discharge from her body, *she shall be in her impurity for* **seven days**, *and whoever touches her shall be unclean until the evening.*

4Q274 1i:4b–5a

4b והזבהׄ דם לשבעת הימים אל תגע בזב ובכול
כלי [א]שר יגע בו הזב ושׁ[כב]
5a עליו או אשר ישב עליו

(4b) And *she who has a flow of blood, for* **seven days** *let her not touch the man who has a discharge or any vessel [t]hat he touches or* (5a) *that he has lain upon or sat upon*

The expression, "Unclean, unclean," in 4Q274 1i:3b is a verbal overlap found only in Lev 13:45. The process to become clean in 4Q274 is almost the same as the description of purification in Lev 15.[26] The requirement to be clean before eating food in 4Q274 1i, 5a is found in Lev 15:5 and 22:4: "none . . . may eat of the holy things until he is clean." The expression "may eat" in relation to eating holy or clean food is found in Leviticus repeatedly.[27]

The term "seven days" in relation to the period for becoming clean in 4Q274 1i:4b–5a related to a woman's menstrual impurity, is found mainly in Leviticus. For example, the woman with a discharge of blood in her body who should not be touched for seven days mentioned in Lev 15:19 is reflected in 4Q274 1i:4b–5a. The expression and ideology of the purity law in Lev 15 is clearly the base text for 4Q274.[28] The use of Leviticus in 4QTohorot A seems to reflect an aspiration that the laws of Leviticus should be strictly observed in daily life and not just understood as the expression of an ideal.

26. Baumgarten, *DJD* XXXV, 102–5; Keady, *Vulnerability and Valour*, 130–33.

27. Leviticus 11:2, 3, 9, 21–22, 39; 19:25; 25:12, etc.

28. Most of Lev 15 is related to the texts from Tohorot A. Leviticus 15 describes the boundary of the unclean regarding discharge of a woman, as follows: 1) whoever touches her shall be unclean until evening; 2) anything that she lies or sits on during her impurity shall be unclean; 3) anyone who touches her bedding, and anyone who touches any object on which she has sat, shall be unclean; 4) and if a man lies with her, her impurity is communicated to him. These details seem to be applied to Tohorot.

War Scroll

In this brief section I will not consider all the manuscripts of the War Scroll but focus on two examples of the influence of Leviticus that are clear in the principal copy of the Rule, 1QM (1Q33). The purpose of this section is to show that Leviticus is not only of interest to those concerned with composing legal texts, but is also in the minds of those who wrote other compositions.

The War Scroll is an eschatological ritual work with apocalyptic motifs that was probably compiled over several generations. The version present in 1QM was written in the early Herodian period (30–1 BCE). Many texts from Qumran have an eschatological orientation, such as 1QSa and 11QMelch; however, one of the most elaborate and distinctive eschatological compositions is the War Scroll.

In 1Q33 17:2–3, the judgement of God against Nadab and Abihu and God's eternal covenant is dependent upon Lev 10:1–3 and Lev 24:8; 26:36, 42. 1Q33 17:2–3 is based upon the ideology of Leviticus: though God's judgement happened, God's faithfulness to the covenant remains.

First, the compiler of the War Scroll preferred Levitical texts rather than other texts from the Torah; in this case, it appears that 1Q33 17:2 is based upon Lev 10:1–3.

Lev 10:1

וַיִּקְחוּ בְנֵי־אַהֲרֹן נָדָב וַאֲבִיהוּא אִישׁ מַחְתָּתוֹ וַיִּתְּנוּ בָהֵן אֵשׁ וַיָּשִׂימוּ עָלֶיהָ קְטֹרֶת וַיַּקְרִבוּ לִפְנֵי יְהוָה אֵשׁ זָרָה אֲשֶׁר לֹא צִוָּה אֹתָם

Now **<u>Aaron</u>**<u>'</u>**<u>s sons, Nadab and Abihu</u>**, each took his censer, put fire in it, and laid incense on it; and they offered unholy fire before the Lord, such as he had not commanded them.

Lev 10:2

וַתֵּצֵא אֵשׁ מִלִּפְנֵי יְהוָה וַתֹּאכַל אוֹתָם וַיָּמֻתוּ לִפְנֵי יְהוָה

<u>*And fire came out from the presence of the Lord and consumed them, and they died before the Lord.*</u>

Num 3:4

וַיָּמָת נָדָב וַאֲבִיהוּא לִפְנֵי יְהוָה בְּהַקְרִבָם אֵשׁ זָרָה

But Nadab and Abihu died before the Lord when they offered unauthorized fire (cf. 26:61)

1Q33 17:2

ואתמה זכורו משפט̊[נדב ואבי]הוא בני אהרון אשר התקדש אל במשפטם לעיני [כול העם

But, as for you, remember the judgment [of **<u>Nadab and Abi]hu, the sons of Aaron,</u>** by <u>*whose judgment God showed Himself holy before [all the people*</u>.

Both Lev 10:1–2 and Num 3:4; 26:61 mention the judgement of God upon Nadab and Abihu found in 1Q33 17:2, but 1Q33 17:2 adds a further comment on the nature of God's holiness which reflects the phrasing of Leviticus. As a result it seems that the author of 1Q33 17 has Leviticus in mind rather than the passages from Numbers. As Brooke notes, "it is not simply a spiritualisation of war, the depiction of the combat between good and evil as an internal spiritual struggle; it is a ritual campaign manual for those who have to fight an external enemy."[29] These struggles and wars also seem to be echoed in Lev 26, which concerns judgement on those who do not listen to God's commands.

The phrase "remember the judgement [of Nadab and Abi]hu" (ואתמה זכורו משפט֯ [נדב ואבי]הוא) seems to be related to the future judgement found in Lev 26.[30] Warning about future judgement and the remnant in Lev 26:36 and 42 is possibly reflected in 1Q33 17:3 and 1Q33 13:7 with compatible ideas and some similar phrasing as follows. The following example contains similar use of phrasing and compatible ideas, based upon my own use of electronic search instruments, showing that the use of Leviticus is more widespread than noted from previous investigations by scholars.

Lev 26:36a	1Q33 17:2b–3
וְהַנִּשְׁאָרִים בָּכֶם וְהֵבֵאתִי מֹרֶךְ בִּלְבָבָם בְּאַרְצֹת אֹיְבֵיהֶם	2b [ואלעזר 3 ואיתמר החזיק לו לברית [כהונת] עֹולמים
And *as for those of you who survive*, I will send faintness into their hearts in the lands of their enemies	(2b) But *Eleazar]* (3) *and Ithamar He preserved for Himself for an eternal covenant [of priesthood.*]
Lev 26:42	1Q33 13:7b
וְזָכַרְתִּי אֶת־בְּרִיתִי יַעֲקוֹב וְאַף אֶת־בְּרִיתִי יִצְחָק וְאַף אֶת־בְּרִיתִי אַבְרָהָם אֶזְכֹּר וְהָאָרֶץ אֶזְכֹּר	וברית [כ]רתה לאבותינו ותקימה לזרעם
Then will I remember my covenant with Jacob; *I will remember also my covenant with Isaac and also my covenant with Abraham*, and I will remember the land.	*You made a covenant with our fathers*, and established it *for their seed*

The judgment of God, remnant, and covenant in Lev 26 is reflected in 1Q33 17:2b–3 and 13:7b, probably borrowing the ideology and motif of God's judgment from Leviticus[31] and applying it in the composition of

29. Brooke, "Text, Timing, and Terror," 49–66, esp. 56.

30. Strugnell et al., *DJD* XXXIV, 520.

31. Peters and Eshel, "Cutting Off and Cutting Down Shechem," 237–59; Duhaime, "War Scroll," 3116–51, esp. 3145.

1Q33. These passages seem to share certain ideas with key sections of the Damascus Document as described in chapter V.

4QHalakah A (4Q251)

4Q251 (4QHalakha A) dealing with halakhic issues is one of three Halakha texts (4Q251, 4Q264a and 4Q472). 4Q251 consists of twenty-six fragments. Its script is formal Hebrew handwriting, dating to the early Herodian period.[32] The date of composition is probably earlier, but like 4Q274 its final form probably belongs in the first century BCE. Some of the halakhic issues in 4Q251 are dependent upon Leviticus.[33] This section provides one example of laws concerning sexual prohibitions in the family in Lev 18 and 20 that are reflected in 4Q251 17, 1–6. The following example contains similar use of phrasing and ideas.

Lev 18:8	4Q251 17:1
עֶרְוַ֥ת אֵֽשֶׁת־אָבִ֖יךָ לֹ֣א תְגַלֵּ֑ה עֶרְוַ֥ת אָבִ֖יךָ הִֽוא	על העריות[. . .]
You shall not uncover the nakedness of your father's wife; it is the nakedness of your father.	Concerning prohibited relationships: [. . .]
Lev 18:12	4Q251 17:2
עֶרְוַ֥ת אֲחוֹת־אָבִ֖יךָ לֹ֣א תְגַלֵּ֑ה שְׁאֵ֥ר אָבִ֖יךָ הִֽוא	אל יקח איש את א[שת אביו ולא יגלה את כנף אביו לא יקח איש]
You shall not uncover the nakedness of your father's sister; she is your father's flesh.	*Let no man take the w[ife of his father, let him not uncover the skirt of his father. Let no one take]*
Lev 18:13	4Q251 17:3
עֶרְוַ֥ת אֲחוֹת־אִמְּךָ֖ לֹ֣א תְגַלֵּ֑ה כִּֽי־שְׁאֵ֥ר אִמְּךָ֖ הִֽוא	את בת אחיו ואת בת א[חותו . . . -אל יגלה]
You shall not uncover the nakedness of your mother's sister, for she is your mother's flesh.	*his brother's daughter or the daughter of [his] si[ster* . . . *Let no] man [uncover]*

32. Charlesworth, ed., *The Dead Sea Scrolls*, 271.

33. The sacrificial law from Lev 7:13 appears in 4Q251 9:4, sexual law from Lev 18:13 appears in (4Q251) 11:12, the harvest rules from Lev 19:23–25 appear in 4Q251 10:8–9, the law about a pregnant animal from Lev 22:27–28 appears in 4Q251 12:1–2, the rule about firstfruits from Lev 23:17 appears in (4Q251) 9:4, and Jubilee from Lev 27:21 appears in 4Q251 14:2. The author of 4Q251 adopts various laws, rules, and commands from Leviticus to reconstruct its texts. See Metso, "Shifts in Convenantal Discourse," 497–512, esp. 499–500.

Lev 20:19	4Q251 17:4
וְעֶרְוַת אֲחוֹת אִמְּךָ וַאֲחוֹת אָבִיךָ לֹא תְגַלֵּה כִּי אֶת־ שְׁאֵרוֹ הֶעֱרָה עֲוֺנָם יִשָּׂאוּ׃	איש את ערות אׄחות אׄ[מו או אביו זמה היא ואשה לא תהיה לאחי]
You shall not uncover the nakedness of your mother's sister or of your father's sister, for that is to lay bare one's own flesh; they shall be subject to punishment.	*the nakedness of the sister of [his] mo[ther or his father*, it is wickedness. And no woman shall be the wife of the brother of]

Leviticus 18:6–18 deals with prohibited relationships that may have influenced 4Q251 17 since this text includes most of the prohibited relationships from Lev 18; however, 4Q251 17:3 extends this prohibited relationship to include a brother's or sister's daughter. Though Leviticus 18 and 20 also deal with relationships with animals, 4Q251 deals only with human relationships.[34]

4Q251 17:1–2, which begins with the prohibited relationship with a wife of a son's father (Lev 18:7), is reconstructed in 4Q251 17:3 to include a brother's or wife's daughter, which is missing in Lev 18:11–12.[35] 4Q251 does not contain all the detailed prohibited relationships from Lev 18, but 4Q251 at least follows the order of Lev 18 and adds more material based on Lev 18. Something of the same concern with Lev 18 and 20 is reflected in the harmonized version of the chapters in 11QpalaeoLev^{a}.

The Rule of the Community (1QS)

Although there are several versions of the Rule of the Community from Qumran Cave 4, in this section I will simply discuss some of the evidence for the use of Leviticus in the Cave 1 version of the Rule (1QS). 1QS is dated to the first half of the first century BCE. 1QS contains several sections concerned with ritual purity and the metaphorical use of temple language; it also describes communal meals.[36] This section provides three examples

34. CD A 5:7b–11a mentions the prohibition against uncle-niece marriages, which is parallel to Lev 18:12–13; the prohibition of marriage between an uncle and a niece is recorded also in 11QT^{a} LXVI:15–17 and 4QHalakha A f17:2. The subject matters in 4QHalakha A overlap with the Damascus Document, 11QT^{a}, and 4QMMT, documents, or segments of those documents. 4QHalakha A seems to belong in the same category of halakhic works of general, non-sectarian origin. See Dávid et al., eds., *The Hebrew Bible in Light of the Dead Sea Scrolls*, 442.

35. Cf. Lev 20:19.

36. Metso, "The Textual Traditions," 141–47; Metso, "Qumran Community Structure," 283–300. Metso also mentions the paraphrase of Lev 12:1–4 in 4Q265 and the use of Lev 19:17 in 4Q477; Metso, *The Serekh Texts*, 57–58.

of the reflection of Leviticus in 1QS: separation from uncleanness, sacrifice, and covenant.[37]

The theme of separating clean from unclean in Leviticus is reflected in 1QS in various places.[38]

Lev 15:31

וְהִזַּרְתֶּם אֶת־בְּנֵי־יִשְׂרָאֵל מִטֻּמְאָתָם וְלֹא יָמֻתוּ בְּטֻמְאָתָם בְּטַמְּאָם אֶת־מִשְׁכָּנִי אֲשֶׁר בְּתוֹכָם

Thus you shall keep the people of Israel *separate from their uncleanness*, so that they do not die in their uncleanness by defiling my tabernacle that is in their midst.

1QS 8:24

ואם בשגגה יעשה והובדל מן הטהרה

But if the sinner transgressed unintentionally, then he is *to be separated from the pure food*

Lev 20:25a

וְהִבְדַּלְתֶּם בֵּין־הַבְּהֵמָה הַטְּהֹרָה לַטְּמֵאָה וּבֵין־הָעוֹף הַטָּמֵא לַטָּהֹר

You shall therefore *make a distinction between the clean animal and the unclean, and between the unclean bird and the clean*.

1QS 9:9

לוא הזכו דרכם להבדל מעול וללכת בתמים דרך

Have failed to cleanse their path *by separating from perversity* and walking blamelessly.

1QS 9:20–21a

20 ולהשכילם כול הנמצא לעשות בעת הזואת
והבדל מכול איש ולוא הסר דרכו
21a מכול עול

(20) He shall instruct them in every legal finding that is to regulate their works in that time, and teach them *to separate from every man who fails to keep himself* (21a) *from perversity*

In Lev 15:31 and 20:25a two kinds of separation are commanded: separation between human beings and separation between animals. In 1QS, separation of human beings from perversity and from a pure meal echoes Lev 20: 25a in its concern to protect cleanness.[39]

37. Leviticus 19:18 seems to be the basis for communal behaviour as reflected in 1QS 7:8–9. See Metso, *Serekh Texts*, 46–7; Tzoref, "The Use of Scripture," 203–33, esp. 205.

38. 1QS 2:16; 5:1, 10, 18; 7:3, 5; 8:13, 24; 9:9, 20.

39. Gillihan, *Civic Ideology*, 313–16; Jassen, "Rule of the Community," 2923–74, esp. 2956.

More specifically, 1QS 8:10 deals with an acceptable sacrifice and proper atoning for the land. The author of 1QS introduces the concept of eternal statutes

(לחו {..} קות עולם), an expression found in Lev 16:31 that refers to Sabbath keeping.

Lev 16:31	1QS 8:10
שַׁבַּ֨ת שַׁבָּת֛וֹן הִיא֙ לָכֶ֔ם וְעִנִּיתֶ֖ם אֶת־נַפְשֹׁתֵיכֶ֑ם חֻקַּ֖ת עוֹלָֽם	להקם {. . . .} ברית לחו {..} קות עולם והיו לרצון לכפר בעד הארץ
It is a sabbath of complete rest to you, and you shall deny yourselves; *it is a statute forever*.	*Upholding* {. . . .} *the covenant of* {..} *eternal statutes*. They shall be an acceptable sacrifice, atoning for the land

The expression, "eternal statute," appears around twenty times in Exodus, Leviticus, and Numbers, but Leviticus contains more than ten references that include the prohibition of eating blood or drinking wine (Lev 3:17, 10:9), keeping the Sabbath (Lev 16:31), and celebrating feasts (Lev 23:4). In Leviticus the Sabbath is introduced as an eternal statute (Lev 16:31), which is connected with the desolation of the land in relation to not keeping the Sabbath. 1QS 8:10 does not refer to the Sabbath directly, but this text commands the community to uphold the eternal statutes that will be an acceptable sacrifice that atones for the land. Leviticus 16:31 links the eternal statute of the Sabbath with the land, which becomes a significant theme in the latter part of Leviticus. The request to be holy, a concept that sets the community apart (1QS 8:11),[40] sounds similar to the command to be holy in Leviticus. 1QS might have been used as authoritative for the communities at Qumran and elsewhere.[41]

The eternal covenant in 1QS 4:22 is influenced by Lev 26:42.

40. The expression (יבדלו קודש בתוך עצת אנשי היחד) "they shall be set apart as holy in the midst of the council of the men of the Yahad" in 1QS 8:11 implies that the entire sect is a segregated group (1Q8:10-11). See Regev, *Sectarian in Qumran*, 36.

41. Hempel, "Reflection on Literacy," 69–82, esp. 70–72.

Lev 24:8

בְּי֨וֹם הַשַּׁבָּ֜ת בְּי֣וֹם הַשַּׁבָּ֗ת יַעַרְכֶ֛נּוּ לִפְנֵ֥י יְהוָ֖ה תָּמִ֑יד
מֵאֵ֥ת בְּנֵֽי־יִשְׂרָאֵ֖ל בְּרִ֥ית עוֹלָֽם

Every sabbath day shall set them in order before the Lord regularly as a commitment of the people of Israel, *as a covenant forever*.

Lev 26:42

וְזָכַרְתִּ֖י אֶת־בְּרִיתִ֣י יַעֲק֑וֹב וְאַף֩ אֶת־בְּרִיתִ֨י יִצְחָ֜ק
וְאַף֩ אֶת־בְּרִיתִ֧י אַבְרָהָ֛ם אֶזְכֹּ֖ר וְהָאָ֥רֶץ אֶזְכֹּֽר

Then I will remember my covenant with Jacob, and *I will remember my covenant* with Isaac and my covenant with Abraham, and I will remember the land.

1QS 4:22b

. . . כיא בם בחר אל לברית עולמים

Indeed, *God has chosen them for an eternal covenant*

Thus, though 1QS does not use Leviticus texts explicitly, the ideology of the covenant of Lev 26 is present in 1QS 4:22b. Shani Tzoref states, "the characteristic is directly related to motive—the author of 1QS recasts biblical languages and concepts for his sectarian purposes, especially to present the Community as the righteous remnant of Israel, destined for salvation through proper observations of God's Torah."[42] The ideology in Lev 26 indicates that the covenant is forever, which confirms God's faithfulness.

These three examples of allusions to Leviticus in 1QS confirm the priestly outlook of the movement, some of whose members took up residence at Qumran.

CONCLUSION

I have attempted to show various uses of Leviticus in some other texts from the Qumran Caves. This chapter provides evidence that Leviticus significantly influenced other compositions in relation to sacrificial laws, purity laws, sexual laws, judgement, and covenant. The ideology and content of the Levitical passages are key factors in the composition of other texts from the Qumran Caves.

First, as in the other compositions considered in Chapters III–VI, Lev 26 is again a major source behind the composition of various texts. In the War Scroll, Apocryphon of Jeremiah, and 1QS, Lev 26 and its concern with judgement and covenant is clearly found with identical expressions

42. Tzoref, "Use of Scripture," 203–33.

and ideological motifs. Leviticus 26 is surely an important foundational chapter for several other texts from the Qumran Caves, not only early or pre-sectarian compositions, but also later traditions contemporary with sectarian documents.

Second, priestly laws, purity laws, and sexual laws from Leviticus are influential in both early or pre-sectarian times and also in later traditions from the Qumran Caves. Aramaic Levi Document uses the sacrificial process of Lev 1, and the Genesis Apocryphon is dependent on sacrificial law and eating the fruits in the fifth year as found in Leviticus. In addition, purity laws, sexual laws, and holiness from Lev 15, 18, 19, and 20 are found in the compositions discussed in this chapter. This research shows that the whole book of Leviticus influences a wide range of texts from the Qumran Caves, not just from a certain era, but in all periods of the three centuries before the fall of the temple in 70 CE.

Whoever collected all the manuscripts in the Qumran Caves was heir to a long tradition of the use and reuse of Leviticus. This chapter has not considered all the possible allusions to Leviticus in compositions other than Jubilees, the Temple Scroll, the Damascus Document, and MMT, but a varied sample of compositions, both non-sectarian and sectarian, confirms my thesis about the use of Leviticus in the late Second Temple period.

VIII

Conclusion

In this volume I have attempted to demonstrate how Leviticus has been read and used in the Second Temple period as is attested in the manuscripts from the Qumran Caves. The influence of Leviticus is widespread in sectarian and non-sectarian texts and in texts from earlier and later times. My research shows that some Second Temple texts are purposely concerned with the ideology and content of Leviticus, which is used in various ways to influence the structure, ideology, and content of certain compositions.

Chapter II briefly describes twenty-five Leviticus manuscripts; these manuscripts indicate that Leviticus was probably read and heard as much as any other scriptural book, with the possible exception of the Psalms. Many of the manuscripts of Leviticus can be classified as large or very large scrolls, which imply that they could have been used for public cultic purposes. This indicates that the use of Leviticus was not optional but primary for Jewish communities in the Second Temple period.

The twenty-five Leviticus scrolls seem to indicate that Leviticus was continuously influential from 250 BCE (4QExod–Lev^{f}) to the early first century CE (MasLev^{b}) and used for various purposes. The book of Leviticus was sometimes written with other texts, such as Numbers or Exodus, on a single skin, but most of the manuscripts of Leviticus that survive seem to contain just Leviticus by itself. The manuscripts generally support the view that the text of Leviticus was relatively stable, though a few of them contain minor variants.[1]

Several distinctive features of Leviticus scrolls from Qumran and elsewhere can be highlighted. Leviticus survives in three languages: Hebrew, Aramaic, and Greek. There are both square Hebrew and Palaeo-Hebrew manuscripts. Though no complete book of Leviticus survives, many of the Leviticus scrolls can be assumed to have contained the whole book. The manuscripts are in various sizes, which suggest that they had various functions in cultic, educational, and private settings.

In chapter III, I have shown the influence of Leviticus on Jubilees in two respects. The first of these concerns the structure of the final form of the book. Leviticus 26 in particular heavily influences Jubilees and controls its structure, which begins and ends with the theme of Sabbaths from Leviticus and narrates the texts in relation to the Sabbath theme. In addition, the term *jubilees* comes from Lev 25 and 27, and the heavy influence can be seen in that the entire book is based on a chronological system from Lev 25–27.

Second, Leviticus influences many of the themes of Jubilees. The author of Jubilees employs the themes of Leviticus—laws, chronology, covenant, and priestly ideology—in significant ways. The calendrical system in Jubilees is adapted from Leviticus to inform the appointed festival times, especially Sabbath observance. The understanding of Sabbath—that the Sabbath belonged to the Lord and that the Sabbath should be applied to the land as well as to the people of Israel—is also from Leviticus.

Leviticus 26:1–13, 14–46 includes God's promises of both blessing and judgement, according to whether or not Israel obeyed the commands. These two themes, blessing and judgement, in terms of God's covenant and God's plan of restoration for His chosen people, are prominent in the beginning of Jubilees, and Levitical laws and commands are apparently adapted by the author of Jubilees throughout.

Cumulatively, Leviticus influences Jubilees in terms of structure and content, chronology, and ideology, not just partially or in selected sections, but in the entire process of its composition. Whereas most modern readers can immediately recognize that Jubilees is a representation of Genesis and parts of Exodus, this volume has shown that the editorial frame of the book and much of its content is dependent upon Leviticus.

In chapter IV, I have shown that Leviticus extensively influences the structure, content, and ideology of the Temple Scroll. The use of first person

1. Tov suggests that there was only a single edition of Leviticus in circulation in the latter half of the Second Temple period. There are numerous minor variants between the manuscripts, but Leviticus is parallel to the several editions of Exodus and the two editions of Numbers that are attested. See Ulrich, "1Qpaleo-Lev–Num[a]," 341–47.

singular in Leviticus seems to affect the whole rewriting of the Temple Scroll, where the Lord is presented as speaking in the first person singular. "I am YHWH your God" is found frequently in Leviticus, whereas Exodus only uses this construction several times, suggesting that the compiler of the Temple Scroll had Leviticus in mind.

As with the book of Jubilees, Lev 26 plays a prominent role. The influence of Lev 26:42 is evident in 11QT[a] 29:2–10, the key editorial section of the Temple Scroll. This is made clear when the compiler of the Temple Scroll in col. 29:9–10 adapts the covenant with Jacob at Bethel from Lev 26:42, the only place where the covenant with Jacob is found. Though there are two different scholarly views about this covenant, both sides strongly agree that the Temple Scroll borrowed this key passage regarding the theology of the reestablishment of the covenant from Leviticus. Given this, the theology of the book of Leviticus may be assumed to control the ideology and structure of the Temple Scroll.

The Temple Scroll uses motifs from the book of Leviticus, such as cultic practices (11QT[a] 34:7–15; Lev 1:5–9), placement of lamp and lights (11QT[a] 9:12–14; Lev 24:2–4), and themes of land and sacrifice (11QT[a] 51:15, 19–21; Lev 20:24 and 26:1, 11QT[a] 2:5–8; Lev 3:2–11). These examples indicate that the author of the Temple Scroll borrows motifs from the book of Leviticus to compose a new text for ritual practices in a preeschatological period. For example, col. 34:7b–14 clearly follows the structure and order of Lev 1:5b–9b, with minor changes. 11QT[a] 9:12–14 ("lamps and light") borrows the concepts of arranging the lamps from Lev 24:2–4, and adds the statement that it should be a statute forever from Lev 24:2–4, again clearly showing the influence of the strict law from Lev 24:2–4.

Passages from Leviticus also serve as a base text for the Temple Scroll. One section of the purity laws in 11QT[a] 48:3–51:2, that is col. 48:3–5a, heavily depends on Lev 11:21–22, and other passages in col. 48:3–51:2 follow the structure, words, or expressions very closely. The purity laws from Leviticus and its emphasis on the theme of holiness (Lev 19:2) are especially evident in the Temple Scroll, even though the compiler had a choice of concepts from other Pentateuchal books. The many passages from Leviticus imply that the compiler of the Temple Scroll has the complete book of Leviticus in mind in its composition.

In chapter V, I have shown how the compiler of the Damascus Document used Leviticus with respect to its structure, content, and ideology. Once again Lev 26 is prominent. The warning in Lev 26 is consistently applied throughout D, as the structural outline shows. Several important themes from Leviticus are evident in D: the patriarchs and the covenant, Sabbath and land, Three Nets of Belial, and disobedience in general. Some of the references are clear verbal overlaps and some are more implicit; however, cumulatively Leviticus is very influential in the composition of D.

The theme of patriarchs and covenant with the forefathers, their obedience and God's faithfulness in Lev 26:42 and 45 is reflected in CD 1:4; 6:2; 20:17. The ideology of Sabbath and land in Leviticus is also found in CD 6:18 and 10:14, as the compiler of D relies upon themes found in Leviticus, namely that the land was devastated by the Lord because of disobedience (CD 5:21). Levitical purity laws in relation to fornication and defilement of the temple are found in the Three Nets of Belial in CD 4:15, 4:19–5:21, as it is used in Leviticus. The particular nature of fornication and of defiling the sanctuary, treated significantly in Leviticus, is reflected in D. Leviticus contains many cultic laws and commands the people were required to keep but were not observing. This disobedience is pointed out in CD 2:18, 21; 3:7b–8a, and 19:20.

Overall, Leviticus is a major resource not just for compiling the Damascus Document, but also for explaining the purposes and identity of the community behind the composition. The data and research in this chapter, especially concerning Lev 26 and the Holiness Code, show that Leviticus is a major foundational text for D.

In chapter VI, I have shown that Leviticus also influences the genre, content, structure, and purpose of MMT. Various sections of MMT are closely influenced by Leviticus' ideology, especially in the B section; the blessing and cursing in Lev 26 shape the ideology of the C section—Leviticus 26 appears yet again. From this research, we can see clearly that issues such as slaughtering, sacrifice, marriage, judgement, and blessing, all of which are mainly described in Leviticus, indicate the close link between MMT and Leviticus.

When MMT commands its readers to be pure and holy, it is influenced by the theme of holiness in Leviticus. In constructing this letter, the compiler of MMT respects the order of Leviticus and presents a wide range of cultic practices from Leviticus, with extensions and greater strictness, using Leviticus texts to persuade the audience to follow the laws correctly for their own protection. MMT uses Levitical texts to explain the place of slaughter, purity of hides and bones, and the slaughter of pregnant animals. Significantly, the author of B combines contradictory laws from Leviticus to produce a clearer law to help the audience understand the text. In B 64–72, MMT not only borrows the ideology of Leviticus but also follows its detailed process of purification.

Prohibitions regarding illegal mixture and marriage from Lev 21 are also a base text for B 75–82, with the purpose of protecting the priests and ensuring that the people are holy. Throughout, it appears the author of

MMT adapted words and expressions from Leviticus in order to describe the laws more clearly and precisely. Based upon all of this evidence, we can conclude that without Leviticus it would have been difficult for the author of MMT to compose section B.

In section C, though the author of MMT does not duplicate passages from Leviticus explicitly, the motif of blessing and cursing from Lev 26 as applied in C is implicit; the priestly encouragement to be separated from the majority, to become clean and remain pure, is obviously influenced by sections of Leviticus. As the survey in this chapter shows, parallels between MMT and Leviticus indicate the whole book of Leviticus prompts the construction of MMT in the order it is now found.

In chapter VII, I have attempted to show various uses of Leviticus in some other texts from Qumran. This chapter provides evidence that Leviticus significantly influences other scrolls in relation to sacrificial laws, purity laws, sexual laws, judgement, and covenant. Particular passages, ideology, or content from Leviticus become key factors in the compositions of other texts from Qumran.

As in the other texts from Qumran, Lev 26 is again a major source for composing scrolls. In the War Scroll, Apocryphon of Jeremiah, and 1QS, Lev 26 and its judgement and covenant are clearly found with identical expressions and ideology. Leviticus 26 lays a foundation for many other texts from Qumran, not only early or pre-sectarian texts but also later traditions contemporary with sectarian documents.

Priestly laws, purity laws, and sexual laws from Leviticus have been influential in both early or presectarian and later texts from the Qumran Caves. The Aramaic Levi Document uses the sacrificial process in Lev 1; the sacrificial law and time period for eating the fruits in the fifth year as found in Leviticus appear in the Genesis Apocryphon. In addition, purity laws, sexual laws, and notions of holiness from Lev 15, 18, 19, and 20 are found in these compositions. This research shows that the whole book of Leviticus influenced other texts from Qumran, not just for a certain era, but from early to later traditions with sectarian documents.

A compelling argument for my assertions regarding the prevalence of Leviticus in the scrolls is that apart from Deuteronomy, there are more allusions to Leviticus in the scrolls than from other books of the Torah. In addition, the frequent references to Lev 26 suggest that this chapter from Leviticus played a significant role.

Taken together, I believe that all of these chapters provide convincing evidence of the prevalence of Leviticus in the minds and practice of the compilers and authors of the Scrolls from the Qumran Caves, both those that reflect the communities that preceded the sectarian writings as well as the sectarian movement itself, part of which was responsible for gathering the scrolls together in the caves at and near Qumran.

To sum up my argument: the evidence of the influence and prevalence of Leviticus on the Dead Sea Scrolls is conclusive.

Bibliography

Abegg, Martin G., Jr. "The Calendar at Qumran." In *Judaism in Late Antiquity: Part Five, The Judaism of Qumran: A Systemic Reading of the Dead Sea Scrolls*, edited by Alan J. Avery-Peck et al., 145–72. HdO 56. Leiden: Brill, 2001.

———. "The Covenant of the Qumran Sectarians." In *The Concept of the Covenant in the Second Temple Period*, edited by Stanley E. Porter and Jacqueline C. R. de Roo, 81–97. JSJSup 71. Leiden: Brill, 2003.

Accordance Bible Software: Version 12.0.6. Altamonte Springs, FL: OakTree Software, 2017.

Aitken, James K., ed. *The T. & T. Clark Companion to the Septuagint*. London: T. & T. Clark, 2015.

Anderson, Jeff S. "Curses and Blessings: Social Control and Self Definition in the Dead Sea Scrolls." In vol. 1 of *The Dead Sea Scrolls in Context: Integrating the Dead Sea Scrolls in the Study of Ancient Texts, Languages, and Cultures*, edited by Armin Lange et al., 1:47–60. 2 vols. VTSup 140. Leiden: Brill, 2011.

Angel, Joseph L. *Otherworldly and Eschatological Priesthood in the Dead Sea Scrolls*. STDJ 86. Leiden: Brill, 2010.

———. "Damascus Document." In *Outside the Bible: Ancient Jewish Writings Related to Scripture*, edited by Louis H. Feldman et al., 3:2975–3035. 3 vols. Philadelphia: Jewish Publications Society, 2013.

Attridge, Harold, Torleif Elgvin, Józef T. Milik, Saul Olyan, John Strugnell, Emanuel Tov, James VanderKam, and Sidnie White. *Qumran Cave 4. VIII: Parabiblical Texts. Part 1*. DJD XIII. Oxford: Clarendon, 1994.

Avemarie, Friedrich. "'Tohorat Ha-Rabbim' and 'Mashqeh Ha-Rabbim': Jacob Licht Reconsidered." In *Legal Texts and Legal Issues: Proceedings of the Second Meeting of the International Organization for Qumran Studies Cambridge 1995: Published in Honour of Joseph M. Baumgarten*, edited by Moshe J. Bernstein et al., 215–29. STDJ 23. Leiden: Brill, 1997.

Baillet, Maurice, and Józef T. Milik. *Les 'Petites Grottes' de Qumran: Exploration de la falaise, Les grottes 2Q, 3Q, 5Q, 6Q, 7Q à 10Q; Le rouleau de cuivre*. DJDJ III. Oxford: Clarendon, 1962.

Bar-Asher Siegal, Elitzur A. "Who Separated from Whom and Why?: A Philological Study of 4QMMT." *RevQ* 98 (2011) 229–56.

Barthélemy, Dominique, and Józef T. Milik. *Qumran Cave 1*. DJD I. Oxford: Clarendon, 1995.

Baumgarten, Joseph M. *Qumran Cave 4. XIII: The Damascus Document (4Q266–273)*. DJD 18. Oxford: Clarendon, 1996.

———. *Studies in Qumran Law*. SJLA 24. Leiden: Brill, 1977.

———. "Tohorot." In *Qumran Cave 4. XXV: Halakhic Texts*, 79–122. DJD XXXV. Oxford: Clarendon, 1999.

———. "The Laws of the Damascus Document Between Bible and Mishnah." In *The Damascus Document: a Centennial of Discovery: Proceedings of the Third International Symposium of the Orion Center for the Study of the Dead Sea Scrolls and Associated Literature, 4–8 February, 1998*, edited by Joseph M. Baumgarten et al., 17–26. STDJ 34. Leiden: Brill, 2000.

———. "Some 'Qumranic' Observations on the Aramaic Levi Document." In *Sefer Moshe: The Moshe Weinfeld Jubilee Volume: Studies in the Bible and the Ancient Near East, Qumran, and Post-Biblical Judaism*, edited by Chaim Cohen et al., 393–401. Winona Lake, IN: Eisenbrauns, 2004.

Bautch, Richard J. *Glory and Power, Ritual and Relationship: The Sinai Covenant in the Postexilic Period*. New York: T. & T. Clark, 2009.

Beckwith, Roger T. "The Temple Scroll and Its Calendar: Their Character and Purpose." *RevQ* 69 (1997) 3–19.

Beek, Dionysia A. van. "A Temple Built of Words: Exploring Concepts of the Divine in the Damascus Document." In *Keter Shem Tov: Essays on the Dead Seas Scrolls in Memory of Alan Crown*, edited by Shani Tzoref and Ian Young, 319–31. PHSC 20. Piscataway, NJ: Gorgias, 2013.

Ben-Dov, Jonathan. "Tradition and Innovation in the Calendar of Jubilees." In *Enoch and the Mosaic Torah: The Evidence of Jubilees*, edited by Gabriele Boccaccini and Giovanni Ibba, 276–93. Grand Rapids: Eerdmans, 2009.

Berkovitz, Abraham J. "Some Temple Scroll Restoration." *RevQ* 99 (2012) 445–50.

Bergsma, John Sietze. *The Jubilee from Leviticus to Qumran: A History of Interpretation*. VTSup 115. Leiden: Brill, 2007.

Bernstein, Moshe J. "The Employment and Interpretation of Scripture in 4QMMT: Preliminary Observations." In *Reading 4QMMT: New Perspectives on Qumran Law and History*, edited by John Kampen and Moshe J. Bernstein, 29–51. SBLSym 2. Atlanta: Scholars, 1996.

———. "The Genesis Apocryphon and the Aramaic Targumin Revised: A View from Both Perspectives." *The Dead Sea Scrolls in Context: Integrating the Dead Sea Scrolls in the Study of Ancient Texts, Languages, and Cultures*, edited by Armin Lange et al., 2:651–71. VTSup 140. 2 vols. Leiden: Brill, 2011.

———. "The Genesis Apocryphon: Compositional and Interpretive Perspective." In *A Companion to Biblical Interpretation in Early Judaism*, edited by Matthias Henze, 157–75. Grand Rapid: Eerdmans, 2012.

———. *Reading and Re-Reading Scripture at Qumran*. STDJ 107/1. 2 vols. Leiden: Brill, 2013.

Bonani, Georges et al. "Radiocarbon Dating of Fourteen Dead Sea Scrolls." *Radiocarbon* 34 (1992) 843–49.

Brooke, George J. "The Amos–Numbers Midrash (CD 7:13b—8:1a) and the Messianic Document." *ZAW* 92 (1980) 397–404.

———. "Authority and the Authoritativeness of Scripture: Some Clues from the Dead Sea Scrolls." *RevQ* 100 (2012) 507–23.
———. "Biblical Interpretation at Qumran." In *The Bible and the Dead Sea Scrolls, Volume One: Scripture and the Scrolls: the Second Princeton Symposium on the Dead Sea Scrolls*, edited by James H. Charlesworth, 287–319. Waco, TX: Baylor University Press, 2006.
———."Biblical Interpretation in the Qumran Scrolls and the New Testament." In *The Dead Sea Scrolls: Fifty Years after Their Discovery: Proceedings of the Jerusalem Congress, July 20–25, 1997*, edited by Lawrence H. Schiffman et al., 60–73. Jerusalem: Israel Exploration Society, 2000.
———. "Exegetical Strategies in Jubilees 1–2: New Light from 4QJubileesa." In *Studies in the Book of Jubilees*, edited by Matthias Albani et al., 39–57. TSAJ 65. Tübingen: Mohr/Siebeck, 1997.
———. "The Explicit Presentation of Scripture in 4QMMT." In *Legal Texts and Legal Issues: Proceedings of the Second Meeting of the International Organization for Qumran Studies, Cambridge, 1995: Published in Honour of Joseph M. Baumgarten*, edited by Moshe J. Bernstein et al., 67–88. STDJ 23. Leiden: Brill, 1997.
———. "Jacob and His House in the Scrolls from Qumran." In *Rewriting and Interpreting the Hebrew Bible: The Biblical Patriarchs in the Light of the Dead Sea Scrolls*, edited by Devorah Dimant and Reinhard G. Kratz, 171–88. BZAW 439. Berlin: de Gruyter, 2013.
———. "The Messiah of Aaron in the Damascus Document." *RevQ* 15 (1991) 215–30.
———. "The Rewritten Law, Prophets and Psalms: Issues for Understanding the Text of the Bible." In *The Bible as Book: The Hebrew Bible and The Judaean Desert Discoveries*, edited by Edward D. Herbert and Emanuel Tov, 31–40. London: British Library & Oak Knoll Press, 2002.
———. "Scripture and Scriptural Tradition in Transmission: Light from the Dead Sea Scrolls." In *The Scrolls and Biblical Traditions: Proceedings of the Seventh Meeting of the IOQS in Helsinki*, edited by George J. Brooke et al., 1–17. STDJ 103. Leiden: Brill, 2012.
———. "The Ten Temples in the Dead Sea Scrolls." In *Temple and Worship in Biblical Israel*, edited by John Day, 417–34. LHBOTS 422. London: T. & T. Clark, 2005.
———. "Text, Timing, and Terror: Thematic Thoughts on the War Scroll in Conversation with the Writings of Martin G. Abegg, Jr." In *The War Scroll, Violence, War and Peace in the Dead Sea Scrolls and Related Literature: Essays in Honour of Martin G. Abegg on the Occasion of His 65th Birthday*, edited by Kipp Davis et al., 49–66. STDJ 115. Leiden: Brill, 2016.
———. "Zedekiah, Covenant, and the Scrolls from Qumran." In *On Prophets, Warriors, and Kings*, edited by George J. Brooke and Ariel Feldman, 95–109. BZAW 470. Berlin: de Gruyter, 2016.
Burgmann, Hans. "11QT: The Sadducean Torah." In *Temple Scroll Studies: Papers Presented at the International Symposium on the Temple Scroll, Manchester, December 1987*, edited by George J. Brooke, 257–63. JSPSup 7. Sheffield: JSOT Press, 1989.
Callaway, Phillip R. "Extending Divine Revelation: Micro-Compositional Strategies in the Temple Scroll." In *Temple Scroll Studies: Papers Presented at the International Symposium on the Temple Scroll, Manchester, December 1987*, edited by George J. Brooke, 149–62. JSPSup 7. Sheffield: JSOT Press, 1987.

———. *The Dead Sea Scrolls for a New Millennium*. Eugene, OR: Cascade Books, 2011.

Campbell, Jonathan G. *The Use of Scripture in the Damascus Document 1–8, 19–20*. BZAW 228. Berlin: de Gruyter, 1995.

Carmichael, Calum. *Illuminating Leviticus: A Study of Its Laws and Institutions in the Light of Biblical Narratives*. Baltimore: Johns Hopkins University Press, 2006.

Charlesworth, James H., ed. *The Dead Sea Scrolls: Hebrew, Aramaic, and Greek Texts with English Translations: Damascus Document II, Some Works of the Torah, and Related Documents*. PTSDSSP 3.Tübingen: Mohr/Siebeck, 1994.

Charlesworth, James H, and Craig A. Evans, eds. *The Pseudepigrapha and Early Biblical Interpretation*. JSPSup 14. Sheffield: JSOT Press, 1993.

Choi, Baesick. "The Exegetical Interpretation of Leviticus 19:1–18 and the Restoration of the Jewish Community in the Post-Exilic Period." M.A. thesis. Trinity Western University, 2013.

Collins, Antoinette. "The Temple Scroll: 'the Day of Blessing' or ' the Day of Creation'? Insights on Shekinah and Sabbath." In *Keter Shem Tov: Essays on the Dead Sea Scrolls in Memory of Alan Crown*, edited by Shani Tzoref and Ian Young, 361–74. PHSC 20. Piscataway, NJ: Gorgias Press, 2013.

Collins, John J. "The Genre of the Book of Jubilees." In *A Teacher for All Generations: Essays in Honour of James C. VanderKam*, edited by Eric F. Mason, 2:737–55. JSJSup 153. 2 vols. Leiden: Brill, 2012.

———. "Sectarian Consciousness in the Dead Sea Scrolls." In *Heavenly Tablets: Interpretation, Identity and Tradition in Ancient Judaism*, 177–92. JSJSup 119. Leiden: Brill, 2007.

———. *Scripture and Sectarianism: Essays on the Dead Sea Scrolls*. WUNT 332. Tübingen: Mohr/Siebeck, 2014.

Collins, Matthew A. *The Use of Sobriquets in the Qumran Dead Sea Scrolls*. LSTS 67. London: T. & T. Clark, 2009.

Crawford, Sidnie White. "The 'Rewritten' Bible at Qumran: A Look at Three Texts." In *The Bible and the Dead Sea Scrolls, Volume One: Scripture and the Scrolls: the Second Princeton Symposium on the Dead Sea Scrolls*, edited by James H. Charlesworth, 131–48. Waco, TX: Baylor University Press, 2006.

———. *Rewriting Scripture in Second Temple Times*. Grand Rapids: Eerdmans, 2008.

———. "The Use of the Pentateuch in the Temple Scroll and The Damascus Document." In *The Pentateuch as Torah: New Models for Understanding Its Promulgation and Acceptance*, edited by Gary N. Knoppers and Bernard M. Levinson, 301–18. Winona Lake, IN: Eisenbrauns, 2007.

Cross, Frank M. "The Development of Jewish Scripts." In *The Bible and the Ancient Near East: Essays in Honour of William Foxwell Albright*, edited by George Ernest Wright, 133–202. Garden City, NY: Doubleday, 1961.

———. "4QExod–Lev^{f}." In *Qumran Cave 4 VII Genesis to Numbers*, 133–44. DJD XIII. Oxford: Clarendon, 1994.

Davenport, Gene L. *The Eschatology of the Book of Jubilees*. StPB 20. Leiden: Brill, 1971.

Dávid, Nóra et al., eds. *The Hebrew Bible in Light of the Dead Sea Scrolls*. FRLANT 239. Göttingen: Vandenhoeck & Ruprecht, 2012.

Davies, Philip R. *The Damascus Covenant: An Interpretation of the "Damascus Document."* JSOTSup 25. Sheffield: JSOT Press, 1982.

———. "The Judaism(s) of the Damascus Document." In *The Damascus Document, a Centennial of Discovery: Proceedings of the Third International Symposium of the*

Orion Center for the Study of the Dead Sea Scrolls and Associated Literature, 4–8 February, 1998, edited by Joseph M. Baumgarten et al., 27–43. STDJ 34. Leiden: Brill, 2000.

———. "The Textual Growth of the Damascus Document Revisited." In *Is There a Text in This Cave?: Studies in the Textuality of the Dead Sea Scrolls in Honour of George J. Brooke*, edited by Ariel Feldman et al., 319–33. STDJ 119. Leiden: Brill, 2017.

Davis, Kipp. *The Cave 4 Apocryphon of Jeremiah and the Qumran Jeremianic Traditions: Prophetic Persona and the Construction of Community Identity*. STDJ 111. Leiden: Brill, 2014.

Debel, Hans. "Anchoring Revelations in the Authority of Sinai: A Comparison of the Rewriting of 'Scripture' in Jubilees and in the P Stratum of Exodus." *JSJ* 46 (2014) 471–91.

De Jonge, Marinus, and Johannes Tromp. "Jacob's Son Levi in the Old Testament Pseudepigrapha and Related Literature." In *Biblical Figures Outside the Bible*, edited by Michael E. Stone and Theodore A. Bergren, 203–36. Harrisburg, PA: Trinity, 1998.

De Troyer, Kristin. "From Leviticus to Joshua: The Old Greek in Light of Two Septuagint Manuscripts from the Schøyen Collection." *JAJ* 2 (2001) 29–78.

———. "The Legs and the Wings of the Grasshopper: A Case Study on Changes in the Masoretic Text and in the Old Greek Translation of the Book of Leviticus." In *Changes in Scripture: Rewriting and Interpreting Authoritative Traditions in the Second Temple Period*, edited by Hanne von Weissenberg et al., 153–63. BZAW 419. Berlin: de Gruyter, 2011.

Dimant, Devorah. "Between Qumran Sectarian and Non-Sectarian Texts: The Case of Belial and Mastema." In *The Dead Sea Scrolls and Contemporary Culture: Proceedings of the International Conference Held at the Israel Museum, Jerusalem (July 6–8, 2008)*, edited by Adolfo D. Roitman et al., 235–56. STDJ 93. Leiden: Brill, 2011.

———. *Qumran Cave 4. XXI: Parabiblical Texts, Part 4: Pseudo-Prophetic Texts*. DJD XXX. Oxford: Clarendon, 2001.

———. "Sectarian and Non-Sectarian Texts from Qumran: The Pertinence and Usage of a Taxonomy." *RevQ* 93 (2009) 7–18.

DiTommaso, Lorenzo. "Penitential Prayer and Apocalyptic Eschatology in Second Temple Judaism." In *Prayer and Poetry in the Dead Sea Scrolls and Related Literature: Essays in Honor of Eileen Schuller on the Occasion of Her 65th Birthday*, edited by Jeremy Penner et al., 115–33. STDJ 98. Leiden: Brill, 2012.

Doering, Lutz. *Ancient Jewish Letters and the Beginnings of Christian Epistolography*. WUNT 298. Tübingen: Mohr/Siebeck, 2012.

———. "The Concept of the Sabbath." In *Studies in the Book of Jubilees*, edited by Matthias Albani et al., 179–203. TSAJ 65. Tübingen: Mohr/Siebeck, 1997.

———. "Purity and Impurity in the Book of Jubilees." In *Enoch and the Mosaic Torah: The Evidence of Jubilees*, edited by Gabriele Boccaccini and Giovanni Ibba, 261–75. Grand Rapids: Eerdmans, 2009.

———. "The Reception of the Book of Exodus in the Book of Jubilees." In *The Book of Exodus: Composition, Reception, and Interpretation*, edited by Thomas B. Dozeman et al., 485–510. VTSup 164. Leiden: Brill, 2014.

Dongshin, Don Chang. *Phinehas, the Sons of Zadok, and Melchizedek: Priestly Covenant in Late Second Temple Texts*. LSTS 90. London: T. & T. Clark, 2013.

Duhaime, Jean. "War Scroll." In vol. 2 of *Outside the Bible: Ancient Jewish Writings Related to Scripture*, edited by Louis H. Feldman et al., 2:3116–51, 3 vols. Philadelphia: Jewish Publication Society of America, 2013.

Eisenman, Robert. "An Esoteric Relation Between Qumran's 'New Covenant in the Land of Damascus' and The New Testament 'Cup of The New Covenant in (His) Blood?'" *RevQ* 83 (2004) 439–56.

Elgvin, Torleif. "MS 4611. Mur/ḤevLev (Lev 26. 3–9, 33–37)." In *Gleanings from the Caves: Dead Sea Scrolls and Artefacts from the Schøyen Collection*, edited by Torleif Elgvin et al., 159–67. LSTS 71. London: T. & T. Clark, 2016.

Elior, Rachel. "From the Covenant of the Rainbow to the Covenant at Sinai, from the Pilgrimage to the Temple to the Vision of the Chariot, from Blessing of the First Fruits to the Priestly Blessing, and from the *Tiqqum leil Shavu'ot* to the Revelation of the *Shekhinah*." In *Crossing Boundaries in Early Judaism and Christianity: Ambiguities, Complexities, and Half-Forgotten Adversaries: Essays in Honour of Alan F. Segal*, edited by Kimberly B. Stratton and Andrea Leiber, 74–113. JSJSup 177. Leiden: Brill, 2016.

Elledge, Casey D. *The Statutes of the King: The Temple Scroll's Legislation on Kinship (11Q19 LVI 12—LIX 21)*. CahRB 56. Paris: Gabalda, 2004.

Endres, John C. *Biblical Interpretation in the Book of Jubilees*. CBQMS 18. Washington, DC: Catholic Biblical Association of America, 1987.

———. "Revising The Rebekah of the Book of Jubilees." In *A Teacher for All Generation: Essays in Honour of James C. VanderKam*, edited by Eric F. Mason et al., 2:765–82. JSJSup 153. 2 vols. Leiden: Brill, 2012.

Eshel, Hanan. "4QMMT and the History of the Hasmonean Period." In *Reading 4QMMT: New Perspective on Qumran Law and History*, edited by John Kampen and Moshe J. Bernstein, 53–65. SBLSym 2. Atlanta: SBL Press, 1996.

———. "The Damascus Document's 'Three Nets of Belial': A Reference to the Aramaic Levi Document." In *Heavenly Tablets: Interpretation, Identity and Tradition in Ancient Judaism*, edited by Lynn LiDonnici and Andrea Lieber, 243–55. JSJSup 119. Leiden: Brill, 2007.

———. *Exploring the Dead Sea Scrolls: Archaeology and Literature of the Qumran Caves*, edited by Shani Tzoref and Barnea Levi Selavan. JAJSup 18. Göttingen: Vandenhoeck & Ruprecht, 2015.

Eshel, Hanan, Yosi Baruchi, and Roi Porat. "Fragments of a Leviticus Scroll (ArugLev) Found in the Judean Desert in 2004." *DSD* 13 (2006) 55–60.

"Explore the Archive." Leon Levy Digital Library. http://www.deadseascrolls.org.il/explore-the-archive/manuscript/.

Evans, Craig A. "Covenant in the Qumran Literature." In *The Concept of the Covenant in the Second Temple Period*, edited by Stanley E. Porter and Jacqueline C. R. de Roo, 55–80. JSJSup 71. Leiden: Brill, 2003.

———. *Of Scribes and Sages: Early Jewish Interpretation and Transmission of Scripture*. Vol. 1 of *Ancient Versions and Traditions*. SSEJC 9. London: T. & T. Clark, 2004.

———. *Noncanonical Writings and New Testament Interpretation*. Peabody, MA: Hendrickson, 1992.

Evans, Craig A., and James A. Sanders, eds. *Early Christian Interpretation of the Scriptures of Israel: Investigations and Propopsals*. JSNTSup 148. Sheffield: Sheffield Academic, 1997.

———, eds. *The Function of Scripture in Early Jewish and Christian Tradition*. JSNTSup 154. Sheffield: Sheffield Academic, 1998.

Fabry, Heinz-Josef. "The Reception of the Book of Leviticus in Qumran." In *The Dead Sea Scrolls: Fifty Years after Their Discovery: Proceedings of the Jerusalem Congress, July 20–25, 1997*, edited by Lawrence H. Schiffman et al., 74–81. Jerusalem: Israel Exploration Society, 2000.

Falk, Daniel K. *The Parabiblical Texts: Strategies for Extending the Scriptures among the Dead Sea Scrolls*. LSTS 63. London: T. & T. Clark, 2007.

Faulkenberry Miller, John B. "4QLXXLev[a] and Proto-Septuagint Studies: Reassessing Qumran Evidence for the *Urtext* Theory." In *Qumran Studies: New Approaches New Questions*, edited by Michael Thomas Davis and Brent A. Strawn, 1–28. Grand Rapids: Eerdmans, 2007.

Feder, Yitzhaq. "The Polemic Regarding Skin Disease in 4QMMT." *DSD* 19 (2012) 55–70.

Fishbane, Michael. *Biblical Interpretation in Ancient Israel*. Oxford: Clarendon, 1985.

———. *The Garments of Torah: Essays in Biblical Hermeneutic*. Bloomington: Indiana University Press, 1989.

———. "Inner-Biblical Exegesis." In *Hebrew Bible/Old Testament: The History of Its Interpretation. Vol. 1 of From the Beginnings to the Middle Ages (Until 1300). Part 1 Antiquity*, edited by Magne Sæbø, 33–46. Göttingen: Vandenhoeck & Ruprecht, 1996.

———. *Text and Texture: Close Readings of Selected Biblical Texts*. New York: Schocken, 1979.

———. "Use, Authority and Interpretation of Mikra at Qumran." In *Mikra: Text, Translation, Reading and Interpretation of the Hebrew Bible in Ancient Judaism and Early Christianity*, edited by Martin Jan Mulder and Harry Sysling, 339–77. CRINT 1/1. Assen: Van Gorcum, 1988.

Fitzmyer, Joseph A. "Divorce among First-century Palestinian Jews." *ErIsr* 14 (1978) 106–10.

———. *The Genesis Apocryphon of Qumran Cave 1 (1Q20): A Commentary*. BibOr 18B. Roma: Pontifical Biblical Istitute Press, 2005.

———. *A Guide to the Dead Sea Scrolls and Related Literature*. Grand Rapids: Eerdmans, 2008.

Flint, Peter W. "The Book of Leviticus in the Dead Sea Scrolls." In *The Book of Leviticus: Composition and Reception*, edited by Rolf Rendtorff and Robert A. Kugler, 323–41. VTSup 93. Leiden: Brill, 2003.

Fraade, Steven D. "Interpretive Authority in the Studying Community at Qumran." *JJS* 44 (1993) 46–69.

———. *Legal Fictions: Studies of Law and Narrative in the Discursive Worlds of Ancient Jewish Sectarians and Sages*. JSJSup 147. Leiden: Brill, 2011.

———. "Rhetoric and Hermeneutics in Miqsat Ma‹Aśe Ha-Torah (4QMMT): The Case of the Blessings and Curses." *DSD* 10 (2003) 150–61.

———. "To Whom It May Concern: 4QMMT and Its Addressees(s)." *RevQ* 76 (2000) 507–26.

Freedman, David N. *Divine Commitment and Human Obligation: Poetry and Orthography*. Vol. 2 of *Divine Commitment and Human Obligation: Selected Writings of David Noel Freedman*, edited by John R. Huddlestun. Grand Rapids: Eerdmans, 1997.

Freedman, David. N, and Kenneth. A. Mathews. *The Paleo-Hebrew Leviticus Scroll (11QpaleoLev)*, plates 1–20. Winona Lake, IN: American Schools of Oriental Research, 1985.

Frevel, Christian. "Separate Yourself from the Gentiles (Jubilees 22:16): Intermarriage in the Book of Jubilees." In *Mixed Marriages: Intermarriage and Group Identity in the Second Temple Period*, edited by Christian Frevel. LHBOTS 547. New York: T. & T. Clark, 2011.

Frisch, Alexandria. "The Body in Qumran Literature: Flesh and Spirit, Purity and Impurity in the Dead Sea Scrolls." *DSD* 23 (2016) 155–82.

Ganzel, Tova, and Risa Levitt Kohn. "Ezekiel's Prophetic Message in Light of Leviticus 26." In *The Formation of the Pentateuch: Bridging the Academic Cultures of Europe, Israel, and North America*, edited by Jan. C. Gertz et al., 1075–84. FAT 111. Tübingen: Mohr/Siebeck, 2016.

García Martínez, Florentino. "Ancient Interpretations of Jewish Scriptures in Light of Dead Sea Scrolls." In *Textual Criticism and Dead Sea Scrolls: Studies in Honour of Julio Trebolle Barrera*, edited by Andrés Piquer Otero and Pablo A. Torijano Morales, 83–97. JSJSup 157. Leiden: Brill, 2012.

———. "Cave 11 in Context." In *The Dead Sea Scrolls: Texts and Context*, edited by Charlotte Hempel, 199–209. STDJ 90. Leiden: Brill, 2010.

———. "The Heavenly Tablets in the Book of Jubilees." In *Studies in the Book of Jubilees*, edited by Matthias Albani et al., 243–61. TSAJ 65. Tübingen: Mohr/Siebeck, 1997.

García Martínez, Florentino, and Eibert J. C. Tigchelaar. *The Dead Sea Scrolls Study Edition Vol. 1 (1Q1–4Q273)*. Leiden: Brill, 1999.

García Martínez., Florentino, Eibert J. C. Tigchelaar, and Adam S. van der Woude. *Qumran Cave 11: II 11Q2–18, 11Q20–31*. DJD XXIII. Oxford Clarendon, 1998.

Gilders, William K. "The Concept of Covenant in Jubilees." In *Enoch and the Mosaic Torah: The Evidence of Jubilees*, edited by Gabriele Boccaccini and Giovanni Ibba, 179–92. Grand Rapids: Eerdmans, 2009.

Gillihan, Yonder Moynihan. *Civic Ideology, Organization, and Law in the Rule Scrolls: A Comparative Study of the Covenanters' Sect and Contemporary Voluntary Associations in Political Context*. STDJ 97. Leiden: Brill, 2012.

Ginsburskaya, Mila. "Leviticus in the Light of the Dead Sea Scrolls: Atonement and Purification from Sin." In *The Dead Sea Scrolls in Context: Integrating the Dead Sea Scrolls in the Study of Ancient Texts, Languages, and Culture*, edited by Armin Lange et al., 1:263–77. 2 vols. VTSup 140. Leiden: Brill, 2011.

Grabbe, Lester L. " 4QMMT and Second Temple Jewish Society." In *Legal Texts and Legal Issues: Proceedings of the Second Meeting of the International Organization for Qumran Studies, Cambridge, 1995: Published in Honour of Joseph M. Baumgarten*, edited by Moshe J. Bernstein et al., 89–108. STDJ 23. Leiden: Brill, 1997.

———. "Jubilees and the Samaritan Tradition." In *Enoch and the Mosaic Torah: The Evidence of Jubilees*, edited by Gabriele Boccaccini and Giovanni Ibba, 145–59. Grand Rapids: Eerdmans, 2009.

Greenfield, Jonas C. et al. *The Aramaic Levi Document: Edition, Translation, Commentary*. SVTP 19. Leiden: Brill, 2004.

Grossman, Maxine L. "Reading for Gender in the Damascus Document." *DSD* 11 (2004) 212–39.

———. *Reading for History in the Damascus Document: A Methodological Study*. STDJ 45. Leiden: Brill, 2002.

Gruber, Mayer I. " Women in the Religious System of Qumran." In *Judaism in Late Antiquity*. Part 5 of *The Judaism of Qumran: A Systemic Reading of the Dead Sea Scrolls*, edited by Alan J. Avery-Peck, Jacob Neusner, and Bruce D. Chilton, 173–95. HdO 56. Leiden: Brill, 2001.

Guillaume, Philippe. *Land and Calendar: The Priestly Document from Genesis 1 to Joshua 18*. New York: T. & T. Clark: 2009.

Hanneken, Todd R. *The Supervision of the Apocalypses in the Book of Jubilees*. SBLStBL 34. Leiden: Brill, 2012.

Hanson, Richard S. "Paleo-Hebrew Scripts in the Hasmonean Age." *BASOR* 175 (1964) 26–42.

Harkins, Angela Kim. "The Emotional Re-Experiencing of the Hortatory Narratives Found in the Admonition of the Damascus Document." *DSD* 22 (2015) 285–308.

Harrington, Hannah K. "Holiness and Law in Dead Sea Scrolls." *DSD* 8 (2001) 124–35.

———. "Holiness in the Laws of 4QMMT." In *Legal Texts and Legal Issues: Proceedings of the Second Meeting of the International Organization for Qumran Studies, Cambridge, 1995: Published in Honour of Joseph M. Baumgarten*, edited by Moshe J. Bernstein et al., 109–28. STDJ 23. Leiden: Brill, 1997.

———. "How Does Intermarriage Defile the Sanctuary?" In *The Scrolls and Biblical Traditions: Proceedings of the Seventh Meeting of the IOQS in Helsinki*, edited by George J. Brooke et al., 177–95. STDJ 103. Leiden: Brill, 2012.

———. "Intermarriage in Qumran Texts: The Legacy of Ezra–Nehemiah." In *Mixed Marriages: Intermarriage and Group Identity in the Second Temple Period*, edited by Christian Frevel, 251–73. LHBOTS 547. New York: T. & T. Clark, 2011.

———. "Leniency in the Temple Scroll's Purity Law?" *Hen* 36 (2014) 35–49.

———. "The Rabbinic Reception of Leviticus." In *The Book of Leviticus: Composition and Reception*, edited by Rolf Rendtorff and Robert A. Kugler, 381–402. VTSup 93. Leiden: Brill, 2003.

Heger, Paul. "Qumran Exgesis, 'Rewritten Torah' or Interpretation?" *RevQ* 85 (2005) 61–87.

Hempel, Charlotte. *The Damascus Texts*. Companion to the Qumran Scrolls 1. Sheffield: Sheffield Academic, 2000.

———. "The Laws of the Damascus Document and 4QMMT." In *The Damascus Document a Centennial of Discovery: Proceedings of the Third International Symposium of the Orion Center for the Study of the Dead Sea Scrolls and Associated Literature*, edited by Joseph M. Baumgarten et al., 69–84. STDJ 34. Leiden: Brill, 2000.

———. *The Laws of the Damascus Document: Sources, Tradition and Redaction*. STDJ 29. Leiden: Brill, 1998.

———. "Reflection on Literacy, Textuality, and Community in the Qumran Dead Sea Scrolls." In *Is There a Text in This Cave?: Studies in the Textuality of the Dead Sea Scrolls in Honour of George J. Brooke*, edited by Ariel Feldman et al., 69–82. STDJ 119. Leiden: Brill, 2017.

Hengel, Martin et al. "The Polemical Character of 'On Kingship' in the Temple Scroll: An Attempt at Dating 11QTemple." *JJS* 37 (1986) 28–38.

Henshke, David. "'The Day after the Sabbath' (Lev 23:15): Traces and Origin of an Inter-Sectarian Polemic." *DSD* 15 (2008) 225–47.

Henze, Matthias. "Daniel and *Jubilees*." In *Enoch and the Mosaic Torah: The Evidence of Jubilees*, edited by Gabriele Boccaccini and Giovanni Ibba, 35–65. Grand Rapids: Eerdmans, 2009.

Himbaza, Innocent. "Textual Witnesses and Sacrifical Terminology in Leviticus 1–7." In *Sôfer Mahîr: Essays in Honour of Adrian Schenker Offered by Editors of Biblical Hebraica Quinta*, edited by Yohanan A.P. Goldman et al., 97–111. VTSup 110. Leiden: Brill, 2006.

Himmelfarb, Martha. "The Purity Laws of 4QD: Exgesis and Sectarianism." In *Things Revealed: Studies in Early Jewish and Christian Literature in Honour of Michael E. Stone*, edited by Esther G. Chazon et al., 155–69. JSJSup 89. Leiden: Brill, 2004.

———. *A Kingdom of Priests: Ancestry and Merit in Ancient Judaism*. Philadelphia: University of Pennsylvania Press, 2006.

———. *Between Temple and Torah: Essays on Priests, Scribes, and Visionaries in the Second Temple Period and Beyond*. TSAJ 151. Tübingen: Mohr/Siebeck, 2013.

Hogeterp, Albert L. A. "4QMMT and Paradigms of Second Temple Jewish Nomism." *DSD* 15 (2008) 359–79.

———. "Eschatological Identities in the Damascus Document." In *Defining Identities: We, You, and the Other in the Dead Sea Scrolls: Proceedings of the Fifth Meeting of the IOQS in Groningen*, edited by Florentino García Martínez and Mladen Popović, 111–30. STJD 70. Leiden: Brill, 2008.

———. "Relations to Gentiles in the Damascus Document and Biblical Tradition." In *The Scrolls and Biblical Traditions: Proceedings of the Seventh Meeting of the IOQS in Helsinki*, edited by George J. Brooke et al., 217–30. STDJ 103. Leiden: Brill, 2012.

Holtz, Gudrun. "Temple and Purification Rituals." In *The Scrolls and Biblical Traditions: Proceedings of the Seventh Meeting of the IOQS in Helsinki*, edited by George J. Brooke et al., 197–215. STDJ 103. Leiden: Brill, 2012.

Hultgren, Stephen. *From the Damascus Covenant to the Covenant of the Community: Literary, Historical, and Theological Studies in the Dead Sea Scrolls*. STDJ 66. Leiden: Brill, 2007.

———. "A New Literary Analysis of CD XIX–XX, Part 1: CD XIX:1–32a (with CD VII:b–VIII:18b): The Midrashim and the 'Princess of Judah.'" *RevQ* 84 (2004) 549–78.

Jacobs, Steven L. *The Biblical Masorah and the Temple Scroll: An Orthographical Inquiry*. New York: University Press of America, 2002.

Jamal-Dominique. "Patriarchs: Surveying the Analysis of Ida Fröhlich." Pages 239–52 in *With Wisdom as a Robe: Qumran and Other Jewish Studies in Honour of Ida Fröhlich*. Edited by Károly Dániel Dobos and Miklós Kőszeghy, Hebrew Bible Monographs 21. Sheffield: Sheffield Phoenix , 2009.

Japhet, Sarah. "The Prohibition of the Habitation of Women: The Temple Scroll's Attitude toward Sexual Impurity and Its Biblical Precedent." *JANES* 22 (1993) 69–87.

Jassen, Alex P. "Rule of the Community." In *Outside the Bible: Ancient Jewish Writings Related to Scripture*, edited by Louis H. Feldman et al., 2:2923–75. 3 vols. Philadelphia: Jewish Publication Society, 2013.

Justnes, Arstein. "The Lying Pen of Scribes: Manuscript Forgeries and Counterfeiting Scripture in the Twenty-First Century." Research Project Administered by the

University of Agder, Kristiansand, Norway. https://lyingpen.com/2016/08/11/a-list-of-70-unprovenanced-post-2002-dead-sea-scrolls-like-fragments/.

Kampen, John. "4QMMT and New Testament Studies." In *Reading 4QMMT: New Perspectives on Qumran Law and History*, edited by John Kampen and Moshe J. Bernstein, 129–44. SBLSym 2. Atlanta: SBL, 1996.

Kapfer, Hilary Evans. "Attitude toward the Temple as a Test Case." *DSD* 14 (2007) 152–77.

Keady, Jessica M. *Vulnerability and Valour: A Gendered Analysis of Everyday Life in the Dead Sea Scrolls Communities*. LSTS 91. London: Bloomsbury, 2017.

Kessler, John. "Patterns of Descriptive Curse Formulae in the Hebrew Bible, with Special Attention to Leviticus 26 and Amos 4:6–12." In *Formation of the Pentateuch: Bridging the Academic Cultures of Europe, Israel, and North America*, edited by Jan. C. Gertz et al., 943–84. FAT 111. Tübingen: Mohr/Siebeck, 2016.

Kister, Menahem. "The Development of the Early Recensions." *DSD* 14 (2007) 61–76.

Kratz, Reinhard G. "Law and Narrative in Deuteronomy and the Temple Scroll." In *The Reception of Biblical War Legislation in Narrative Contexts: Proceedings of the EABS Research Group 'Law and Narrative,'* edited by Christoph Berber and Harald Samuel, 109–21. BZAW 460. Berlin: de Gruyter, 2015.

———. "'The Place Which He Has Chosen': The Identification of the Cult Place of Deut 12 and Lev 17 in 4QMMT." In *Meghillot: Studies in the Dead Sea Scrolls V–VI. A Festschrift for Devorah Dimant*, edited by Moshe Bar-Asher and Emanuel Tov, 57–80. Jerusalem: Bialik Institute/Haifa University Press, 2007.

Kugel, James L. "Jubilees." In *Outside the Bible: Ancient Jewish Writings Related to Scripture*, edited by Louis H. Feldman et al., 1:272–465. 3 vols. Philadelphia: Jewish Publication Society, 2013.

———. "The Jubilees Apocalypse." *DSD* 1 (1994) 322–37.

———. *A Walk through Jubilees: Studies in the Book of Jubilees and the World of Its Creation*. JSJSup 156. Leiden: Brill, 2012.

Kugler, Robert A. "Priesthood at Qumran." In *The Dead Sea Scrolls after Fifty Years: A Comprehensive Assessment*, edited by Peter W. Flint and James C. VanderKam, 2:93–114. 2 vols. Leiden: Brill, 1999.

———. "Relexicalizing Leviticus in 4QMMT: The Beginning of Qumran Anti-Language?" In *The Social Sciences and Biblical Translation*, edited by Dietmar Neufeld, 129–40. Atlanta: Society of Biblical Literature, 2008.

———. "Rethinking the Notion of 'Scripture' in the Dead Sea Scrolls: Leviticus as a Test Case." In *The Book of Leviticus: Composition and Reception*, edited by Rolf Rendtorff and Robert A. Kugler, 342–57. VTSup 93. Leiden: Brill, 2003.

———. "Rewriting Rubrics: Sacrifice and the Religion of Qumran." In *Religion in the Dead Sea Scrolls*, edited by John J. Collins and Robert A. Kugler, 90–112. Grand Rapids: Eerdmans, 2000.

Kugler, Robert A., and Kyung S. Baek. *Leviticus at Qumran: Text and Interpretation*. VTSup 173. Leiden: Brill, 2017.

Kutz, Karl, Rebekah Josberger, Ruben Alvarado, Trevor Grant, Haley Kirkpatrick, Rebecca McMartin, Zachary Munoz, Alexander O'Leary, Clara Schinderwolf, Alyssa Schmid, Daniel Somboonsiri, Lynsey Stepan, and Chad Woodward. "Leviticus 23:24–28 (Inv. NCF. SCR. 004742)." In *Dead Sea Scrolls Fragments in the Museum Collection*, edited by Emanuel Tov et al., 110–24. Publication of Museum of the Bible 1. Leiden: Brill, 2016.

Lambert, David. "Last Testament in the Book of Jubilees." *DSD* 11 (2004) 82–107.

Lange, Armin. "The Dead Sea Scrolls and the Date of the Final Stage of the Pentateuch." In *On Stone and Scroll: Essays in Honour of Graham Ivor Davies*, edited by James K. Aitken et al., 289–304. BZAW 420. Berlin: de Gruyter, 2011.

———. *Handbuch der Textfunde vom Toten Meer: Die Handschriften biblischer Bücher von Qumran und den anderen Fundorten*. Tübingen: Mohr/Siebeck, 2009. **[K.C.]**

Lange, Armin, and Emanuel Tov, eds. *The Hebrew Bible: Pentateuch, Former and Latter Prophets*. Textual History of the Bible 1B. Leiden: Brill, 2017.

Lange, Armin, and Matthias Weigold. *Biblical Quotations and Allusions in Second Temple Jewish Literature*. JAJSup 5. Göttingen: Vandenhoeck & Ruprecht, 2011.

Langille, Tim. "Old Memories, New Identities: Traumatic Memory, Exile, and Identity Formation in the Damascus Document and Pesher Habakkuk." In *Memory and Identity in Ancient Judaism and Early Chritianity: A Conversation with Barry Schwartz*, edited by Tom Thatcher, 57–85. SBL 78. Atlanta: SBL Press, 2014.

Levine, Baruch A. "A Further Look at the *Mo'adim* of the Temple Scroll." In *Archaeology and History in Dead Sea Scrolls: The New York University Conference in Memory of Yigael Yadin*, edited by Lawrence H. Schiffman, 53–65. JSPSup 8. Sheffield: JSOT Press, 1990.

———. "Leviticus: Its Literary History and Location in Biblical Literature." In *The Book of Leviticus: Composition and Reception*, edited by Rolf Rendtorff and Robert A. Kugler, 11–23. VTSup 43. Leiden: Brill, 2003.

Levinson, Bernard M. "Refining the Reconstruction of Col. 2 of the Temple Scroll (11QTa): The Turn to Digital Mapping and Historical Syntax." *DSD* 23 (2016) 1–26.

Lichtenberger, Hermann. "Historiography in the Damascus Document." In *Yearbook 2006: History and Identity: How Israel's Later Authors Viewed Its Earlier History*, 231–37. DCLS. Berlin: de Gruyter, 2006.

Lied, Liv Ingebord. "Another Look at the Land of Damascus: The Spaces of the Damascus Document in the Light of Edward W. Soja's Thirdspace Approach." In *New Directions in Qumran Studies: Proceedings of the Bristol Colloquium on the Dead Sea Scrolls, 8–10 September 2003*, edited by Jonathan G. Campbell et al., 101–25. LSTS 52. London: T. & T. Clark, 2005.

Livneh, Atar. "Love Your Fellow as Yourself: The Interpretation of Leviticus 19:17–18 in the Book of Jubilees." *DSD* 18 (2011) 173–99.

———. "The Biblical Background of an Extra-Biblical Conflict Account." In *Old Testament Pseudepigrapha and the Scriptures*, edited by Eibert Tigchelaar, 123–35. BETL 270. Leuven: Peeters, 2014.

Loader, William. *The Dead Sea Scrolls on Sexuality: Attitudes towards Sexuality in Sectarian and Related Literature at Qumran*. Grand Rapids: Eerdmans, 2009.

Lyons, William J. "How have We Changed?." In *The Formation of the Pentateuch: Bridging the Academic Cultures of Europe, Israel, and North America*, edited by Jan. C. Gertz et al., 1055–73. FAT 111. Tübingen: Mohr/Siebeck, 2016.

Machiela, Daniel A. *The Dead Sea Genesis Apocryphon: A New Text and Translation with Introduction and Special Treatment of Columns 13–17*. STDJ 79. Leiden: Brill, 2009.

Maier, Johann. "Purity at Qumran: Cultic and Domestic." In *Judaism in Late Antiquity: Part Five, The Judaism of Qumran: A Systemic Reading of the Dead Sea Scrolls*, edited by Alan J. Avery-Peck et al., 91–124. HdO 56. Leiden: Brill, 2001.

———. *Die Qumran-Essener: Die Texte vom Toten Meer.* Vol. 3: *Einführung, Zeitrechnung, Register und Bibliographie.* Uni-Taschenbücher 1916. Munich: Reinhardt, 1996.

———. *The Temple Scroll: An Introduction, Translation and Commentary.* JSOTSup 34. Sheffield: University of Sheffield, 1985.

Markl, Dominik. "Sinai: The Origin of Holiness and Revelation in Exodus, Deuteronomy, the Temple Scroll, and Jubilees." In *Holy Places in Biblical and Extrabiblical Traditions: Proceedings of the Bonn-Leiden-Oxford Colloquium on Biblical Studies*, edited by Jochen Flebbe, 23–43. BBB 179. Bonn: Bonn University Press, 2016.

Mathews, Kenneth. A. "The Leviticus Scroll (11QpaleoLev) and the Text of the Hebrew Bible." *CBQ* 48 (1986) 171–207.

———. "The Paleo-Hebrew Leviticus Scroll from Qumran." *BA* (March 1987) 45–54.

McLean, Mark D. "The Use and Development of Paleo-Hebrew in the Hellenistic and Roman Period." PhD diss., Harvard University, 1982.

McNamara, Martin. *Targum and Testament: Revisited Aramaic Paraphrases of the Hebrew Bible.* 2nd ed. Grand Rapids: Eerdmans, 2010.

Metso, Sarianna. "The Character of Leviticus Tradition at Qumran." In *In the Footsteps of Sherlock Holmes: Studies in the Biblical Text in Honour of Anneli Aejmelaeus*, edited by Kristin De Troyer et al., 645–57. CBET 72. Leuven: Peeters, 2014.

———. "Evidence from the Qumran Scrolls for the Scribal Transmission of Leviticus." In *Editing the Bible: Assessing the Task Past and Present*, edited by John S. Kloppenborg and Judith H. Newman, 67–79. Resources for Biblical Studies 69. Atlanta: SBL, 2012.

———. "Qumran Community Structure and Terminology as Theological Statement." In *The Bible and the Dead Sea Scrolls: The Dead Sea Scrolls and the Qumran Community*, edited by James H. Charlesworth, 3:283–300. Waco, TX: Baylor University Press, 2006.

———. *The Serekh Texts.* LSTS 62. London: T. & T. Clark, 2007.

———. "Shifts in Convenantal Discourse in Second Temple Judaism." In *Scripture in Transition: Essays on Septuagint, Hebrew Bible, and Dead Sea Scrolls in Honour of Raija Sollamo*, edited by Anssi Voitila and Jutta Jokiranta, 497–512. JSJSup 126. Leiden: Brill, 2008.

———. "The Textual Traditions of the Qumran Community Rule." In *Legal Texts and Legal Issues: Proceedings of the Second Meeting of the International Organization for Qumran Studies Cambridge 1995: Published in Honour of Joseph M. Baumgarten*, edited by Moshe Bernstein et al., 141–47. STDJ 23. Leiden: Brill, 1997.

Metso, Sarianna, and Eugene Ulrich. "The Old Greek Translation of Leviticus." In *The Book of Leviticus: Composition and Reception*, edited by Rolf Rendtorff and Robert A. Kugler, 381–402. VTSup 93. Leiden: Brill, 2003.

Milgrom, Jacob. "HR in Leviticus and Elsewhere in the Torah." In *The Book of Leviticus: Composition and Reception*, edited by Rolf Rendtorff and Robert A. Kugler, 24–40. VTSup 43. Leiden: Brill, 2003.

———. *Leviticus 1–16.* AB 3. New York: Doubleday, 1991.

———. *Leviticus 17–22.* AB 3A New York: Doubleday, 1991.

———. "The Qumran Cult: Its Exegetical Principles." In *Temple Scroll Studies: Papers Presented at the International Symposium on the Temple Scroll Manchester, December 1987*, edited by George J. Brooke, 165–80. JSPSup 7. Sheffield: JSOT Press, 1987.

———. "'Sabbath' and 'Temple City' in the Temple Scroll." *BASOR* 232 (1978) 25–27.

———. "The Scriptural Foundation and Deviations in the Laws of Purity of the Temple Scroll." 83–100 in *Archaeology and History in the Dead Sea Scrolls*. Edited by Lawrence H. Schiffman. JSPSP 8. Sheffield: JSOT Press, 1990.

———. "Studies in the Temple Scroll." *JBL* 97 (1978) 501–23.

Milik, Józef T. *The Books of Enoch: Aramaic Fragments of Qumran Cave 4*. Oxford: Clarendon, 1976.

Milik, Józef T., and Roland de Vaux, *Qumrân Grotte 4: II (4Q.128–4Q.157): Part I: Archeologie. Part II: Tefillin, Mezuzot et Targums*. DJD VI. Oxford: Clarendon, 1977.

Miller, Marvin Lloyd. *Performances of Ancient Jewish Letters: From Elephantine to MMT*. JAJSup 20. Göttingen: Vandenhoeck & Ruprecht, 2015.

Monger, Matthew Phillip. "The Transmission of Jubilees: Reevaluating the Textual Basis." In *New Vistas on Early Judaism and Christianity: From Enoch to Montreal and Back*, edited by Lorenzo DiTommaso and Gerbern S. Oegema, 153–71. Jewish and Christian Text 22. London: T. & T. Clark, 2016.

Mulder, Martin Jan. "The Transmission of the Biblical Text." In *Mikra: Text, Translation, Reading and Interpretation of the Hebrew Bible in Ancient Judaism and Early Christianity*, edited by Martin Jan Mulder and Harry Sysling, 87–125. CRINT 1/1 Assen: Van Gorcum, 1988.

Najman, Hindy. "Interpretation as Primordial Writing: Jubilees and Its Authority Conferring Strategies." *JSJ* 30 (1999) 379–410.

———. *Past Renewals: Interpretive Authority, Renewed Revelation and the Quest for Perfection in Jewish Antiquity*. JSJSup 53. Leiden: Brill, 2010.

———. *Seconding Sinai: The Development of Mosaic Discourse in Second Temple Judaism*. JSJSup 77. Leiden: Brill, 2003.

Naudé, Jacobus A. "Holiness in the Dead Sea Scrolls." In *The Dead Sea Scrolls after Fifty Years: A Comprehensive Assessment*, edited by Peter W. Flint and James C. VanderKam, 2:171–99. 2 vols. Leiden: Brill, 1999.

Nitzan, Bilhah. "Repentance in the Dead Sea Scrolls." In *The Dead Sea Scrolls after Fifty Years: A Comprehensive Assessment*, edited by Peter W. Flint and James C. VanderKam, 2:145–70. 2 vols. Leiden: Brill, 1999.

Norton, Jonathan D. H. "Composite Quotations in the Damascus Document." In *Composite Citations in Antiquity: Jewish, Graeco-Roman, and Early Christian Uses*, edited by Sean A. Adams and Seth M. Ehorn, 92–118. LNTS 525. London: T. & T. Clark, 2016.

Olyan, Saul M. "Defects, Holiness, and Pollution in Biblical Cultic Texts." In vol. 2 of *Sibyls, Scripture, and Scrolls: John Collins at Seventy*, edited by Joel Baden et al., 1018–28. JSJSup 175. 2 vols. Leiden: Brill, 2016.

Pakkala, Juha. "The Temple Scroll as Evidence for Editorial Processes of the Pentateuch." In *Crossing Imaginary Boundaries*, edited by Mika S. Pajunen and Hanna Tervanotko, 101–27. Helsinki: Finnish Exegetical Society, 2015.

Pérez Fernández, Miguel. "4QMMT: Redactional Study." *RevQ* 70 (1997) 191–205.

Peters, Dorothy M., and Esther Eshel. "Cutting Off and Cutting Down Shechem: Levi and His Sword in the Rylands Genizah Fragment of the Aramaic Levi Document." In *The War Scroll, Violence, War and Peace in the Dead Sea Scrolls and Related Literature: Essays in Honour of Martin G. Abegg on the Occasion of His 65th Birthday*, edited by Kipp Davis et al., 237–59. STDJ 115. Leiden: Brill, 2016.

Peters, Marvin K. H., ed. *XIV Congress of the International Organization for Septuagint and Cognate Studies. Helsinki: Septuagint Cognate Studies, 2010*. StBL 59. Atlanta: SBL, 2013.

Petersen, Anders Klostergaard. "Rewritten Bible as a Borderline Phenomenon—Genre, Textual Strategy, or Canonical Anachronism?" In *Flores Florentino: Dead Sea Scrolls and Other Early Jewish Studies in Honour of Florentino García Martínez*, edited by Anthony Hilhorst et al., 285–306. JSJSup 12. Leiden: Brill, 2007.

Pfann, Stephen J. "Cryptic Texts." In *Qumran Cave 4: XXVI Cryptic Texts*, 515–701. DJD XXXVI. Oxford: Clarendon, 2000.

———. "Historical Implications of the Early Second Century Dating of the 4Q249–250 Cryptic A Corpus." In *Things Revealed: Studies in Early Jewish and Christian Literature in Honour of Michael E. Stone*, edited by Esther G. Chazon et al., 172–86. JSJSup 89. Leiden: Brill, 2004.

Qimron, Elisha. *The Dead Sea Scrolls: The Hebrew Writings*. Vol. 2. Jerusalem: Yad Ben-Zvi, 2013. [Heb.]

———. "Toward a New Edition of the Genesis Apocryphon." *JSP* 10 (1992) 11–18.

Qimron, Elisha, and John Strugnell. *Qumran Cave 4. V. Miqṣat Maʿaśe Ha-Torah*. DJD X. Oxford: Clarendon, 1994.

———."An Unpublished Halakhic Letter from Qumran." In *Biblical Archaeology Today: Proceedings of International Congress on Biblical Archaeology, Jerusalem, April 1984*, 400–407. Jerusalem: Israel Exploration Society, 1985.

Rabin, Chaim. *The Zadokite Documents I. The Admonition II. The Laws*. Oxford: Clarendon, 1958.

Regev, Eyal. *Sectarianism in Qumran: A Cross-Cultural Perspective*. RelSoc 45. Berlin: de Gruyter, 2007.

Reinhartz, Adele. "We, You, They: Boundary Language in 4QMMT and the New Testament Epistles." In *Text, Thought, and Practice in Qumran and Early Christianity: Proceedings of the Ninth International Symposium of the Orion Center for the Study of the Dead Sea Scrolls and Associated Literature, Jointly Sponsored by the Hebrew University Center for the Study of Christianity 11–13 January, 2004*, edited by Ruth A. Clements and Daniel R. Schwartz, 89–105. STDJ 84. Leiden: Brill, 2009.

Riska, Magnus. *The House of the Lord: A Study of the Temple Scroll Columns 29:3b–47:18*. Helsinki: Finnish Exegetical Society, 2007.

Rooke, Deborah W. "The Blasphemer (Leviticus 24): Gender, Identity and Boundary Construction." In *Text, Time and Temple: Literary, Historical and Ritual Studies in Leviticus*, edited by Francis Landy et al., 153–69. HBM 64. Sheffield: Sheffield Phoenix, 2015.

Rothstein, David. "The Laws of Immolation and Second Tithe in 11QTa: A Reassessment." *DSD* 14 (2007) 334–53.

Ruiten, Jacques T. A. G. M. van. "The Covenant of Noah in *Jubilees* 6.1–38." In *The Concept of the Covenant in the Second Temple Period*, edited by Stanley E. Porter and Jacqueline C. R. De Roo, 168–90. JSJSup 71. Leiden: Brill, 2003.

———. "Divine Sonship in the Book of Jubilees." In *The Divine Father: Religious and Philosophical Concepts of Divine Parenthood in Antiquity*, edited by Felix Albrecht and Reinhard Feldmeier, 85–105. TBN 18. Leiden: Brill, 2014.

———. "Land and Covenant in *Jubilees* 14." In *The Land of Israel in Bible, History, and Theology: Studies in Honour of Ed Noort*, edited by Jacques van Ruiten and J. Cornelis de Vos, 259–76. VTSup 124. Leiden: Brill, 2009.

Ruzer, Serge. *Mapping the New Testament: Early Christian Writings as a Witness for Jewish Biblical Exgesis*. Jewish and Christian Perspectives 13. Leiden: Brill, 2007.

Samely, Alexander. "Observations on the Structure and Literary Fabric of the Temple Scroll." In *The Temple in Text and Tradition: A Festschrift in Honour of Robert Hayward*, edited by R. Timothy McLay, 233–77. LSTS 83. London: Bloomsbury, 2015.

Sanders, James A. *Torah and Canon*. 2nd ed. Eugene, OR: Cascade Books, 2005.

Schattner-Rieser, Ursula. "Levi in the Third Sky: On the 'Ascent to Heaven' Legends Within Their Near Eastern Context and Józef T. Milik's Unpublished Version of the Aramaic Levi Document." In *The Dead Sea Scrolls in Context: Integrating the Dead Sea Scrolls in the Study of Ancient Texts, Languages, and Cultures*, edited by. Armin Lange et al., 2:801–19. VTSup 140. 2 vols. Leiden: Brill, 2011.

Schiffman, Lawrence H. "The Book of Jubilees and the Temple Scroll." In *Enoch and the Mosaic Torah: The Evidence of Jubilees,* edited by Gabriele Boccaccini and Giovanni Ibba, 99–115. Grand Rapids: Eerdmans, 2009.

———. *The Courtyards of the House of the Lord: Studies on the Temple Scroll*. Edited by Florentino García Martínez. STDJ 75. Leiden: Brill, 2008.

———. "The *Milluim* Ceremony in the Temple Scroll." In *New Qumran Texts and Studies: Proceedings of the First Meeting of the International Organization for Qumran Studies*, edited by George J. Brooke with Florentino García Martínez, 255–72. STDJ 15. Leiden: Brill, 1994.

———. "The Patriarchs and Halakhah in the Dead Sea Scrolls." In *Rewriting and Interpreting the Hebrew Bible: The Biblical Patriarchs in the Light of the Dead Sea Scrolls*, edited by Devorah Dimant and Reinhard G. Kratz, 251–62. BZAW 439. Berlin: de Gruyter, 2013.

———. "The Place of 4QMMT in the Corpus of Qumran Manuscripts." In *Reading 4QMMT: New Perspectives on Qumran Law and History*, edited by John Kampen and Moshe J. Bernstein, 81–98. SBLSym 2. Atlanta: SBL, 1996.

———. *Qumran and Jerusalem: Studies in the Dead Sea Scrolls and the History of Judaism*. Grand Rapids: Eerdmans, 2010.

———. *Reclaiming the Dead Sea Scrolls*. Philadelphia: Jewish Publication Society, 1994.

———. "The Relationship of the Zadokite Fragments to the Temple Scroll." In *The Damascus Document a Centennial of Discovery: Proceedings of the Third International Symposium of the Orion Center for the Study of the Dead Sea Scrolls and Associated Literature, 4–8 February, 1998*, edited by Joseph M. Baumgarten et al., 133–45. STDJ 34. Leiden: Brill, 2000.

———. "Sacrifical Halakhah in the Fragments of the Aramaic Levi Document from Qumran, The Cairo Genizah, and Mt. Athos Monastery." In *Reworking the Bible: Apocryphal and Related Texts at Qumran: Proceedings of a Joint Symposium by Orion Center for the Study of the Dead Sea Scrolls and Associated Literature and the Hebrew University Institute for Advanced Studies Research Group on Qumran, 15–17 January, 2002*, edited by Esther G. Chazon et al., 177–202. STDJ 58. Leiden: Brill, 2005.

———. *Sectarian Law in the Dead Sea Scrolls: Courts, Testimony, and the Penal Code*. BJS 33. Chico, CA: Scholars, 1983.

———. "The Temple Scroll." In *ABD* 6:348–50.

———. "Temple Scroll." In *Outside the Bible: Ancient Jewish Writings Related to Scripture*, edited by Louis H. Feldman et al., 3:3036–107. 3 vols. Philadelphia: Jewish Publication Society, 2013.

———. "The Temple Scroll (11Q19): Paper Presented at the Society of Biblical Literature International Meeting, St Andrews, July 7–11, 2013." *Hen* 36 (2014) 6–20.

———. "The Unfinished Scroll: A Reconstruction of the End of the Temple Scroll." *DSD* 15 (2008) 67–78.

Scott, James M. "The Chronologies of the Apocalypse of Weeks and the Book of Jubilees." In *Enoch and the Mosaic Torah: The Evidence of Jubilees*, edited by Gabriele Boccaccini and Giovanni Ibba, 67–81. Grand Rapids: Eerdmans, 2009.

Segal, Michael et al. "An Early Leviticus Scroll from En-Gedi: Preliminary Publication." *Textus* 26 (2016) 1–30.

Segal, Michael. *The Book of Jubilees: Rewritten Bible, Redaction, Ideology and Theology*. JSJSup 117. Leiden: Brill, 2007.

———. "The Composition of Jubilees." 22–35 in *Enoch and the Mosaic Torah: The Evidence of Jubilees*, edited by Gabriele Boccaccini and Giovanni Ibba. Grand Rapids: Eerdmans, 2009.

———. "Legal and Narrative Passage in Jubilees." In *Reworking the Bible: Apocryphal and Related Texts at Qumran Proceedings of a Joint Symposium by the Orion Center for the Study of the Dead Sea Scrolls and Associated Literature and the Hebrew University Institute for Advanced Studies Research Group on Qumran*, edited by Esther G. Chazon et al., 203–28. STDJ 58. Leiden: Brill, 2005.

Sharp, Carolyn J. "Phinehan Zeal Rhetorical Strategy Study." *RevQ* 70 (1997) 208–22.

Shemesh, Aharon and Cana Werman. "Halakhah at Qumran: Genre and Authority." *DSD* 10 (2003) 104–29.

Shemesh, Aharon. "4Q265 and the Authoritative Status of Jubilees at Qumran." In *Enoch and the Mosaic Torah: The Evidence of Jubilees*, edited by Gabriele Boccaccini and Giovanni Ibba, 247–60. Grand Rapids: Eerdmans, 2009.

———."Qumran Polemic on Marital Law: CD 4:20–5:11 and Its Social Background." In *The Damascus Document a Centennial of Discovery: Proceedings of the Third International Symposium of the Orion Center for the Study of the Dead Sea Scrolls and Associated Literature, 4–8 February, 1998*, edited by Joseph M. Baumgarten et al., 147–75. STDJ 34. Leiden: Brill, 2000.

———. "The Scriptural Background of the Penal Code in the Rule of the Community and Damascus Document." *DSD* 15 (2008) 191–224.

Siegel, Jonathan. P. "The Employment of Paleo-Hebrew Characters for the Divine Names at Qumran in the Light of Tannaitic Sources." *HUCA* 42 (1971) 159–72.

Skehan, Patrick W. et al. *Qumran Cave 4. IV: Palaeo-Hebrew and Greek Biblical Manuscripts*. DJD IX. Oxford: Clarendon, 1992.

Stackert, Jeffrey. "How the Priestly Sabbaths Work: Innovation in Pentateuchal Priestly Ritual." In *Ritual Innovation in the Hebrew Bible and Early Judaism*, edited by Nathan MacDonald, 79–111. BZAW 468. Berlin: de Gruyter, 2016.

Steudel, Annette. "4Q448—The Lost Beginning of MMT?" In *From 4QMMT to Resurrection: Mélanges qumraniens en hommage à Émile Puech*, edited by Florentino García Martínez et al., 247–64. STDJ 61. Leiden: Brill, 2006.

———. "The Damascus Document (D) as a Rewriting of the Community Rule(s)." *RevQ* 100 (2012) 605–20.

Stökl Ben Ezra, Daniel. "Further Reflections Caves 1 and 11: A Response to Florentino García Martínez." In *The Dead Sea Scrolls: Texts and Context*, edited by Charlotte Hempel, 211–23. STDJ 90. Leiden: Brill, 2010.

Stone, Michael E. and Esther Eshel. "Aramaic Levi Document." In *Outside the Bible: Ancient Jewish Writings Related to Scripture*, edited by Louis H. Feldman et al., 2:1490–506. 3 vols. Philadelphia: Jewish Publication Society, 2013.

Stone, Michael E. "Enoch, Aramaic Levi and Sectarian Origins." *JSJ* 19 (1988) 159–70.

Stone, Michael E. and Jonas C. Greenfield. "Aramaic Levi Document." In *Qumran Cave 4. XVII: Parabiblical Texts, Part 3*, 1–72. DJD XXII. Oxford: Clarendon, 1996.

Strugnell, John et al. *Qumran Cave 4, XXIV Sapiential Texts, Part 2 4QInstruction (Mûsār Lĕ Mēvîn): 4Q415 ff.* DJD XXXIV. Oxford: Clarendon, 1999.

Stuckenbruck, Loren T. "Pseudepigraphy and First Person Discourse in the Dead Sea Documents: From the Aramaic Texts to Writings of the Yaḥad." In *The Dead Sea Scrolls and Contemporary Culture: Proceedings of the International Conference Held at the Israel Museum*, edited by Adolfo D. Roitman et al., 295–326. STDJ 93. Leiden: Brill, 2011.

Stuckenbruck, Loren, and David N. Freedman. "The Fragments of a Targum to Leviticus in Qumran Cave 4 (4Q156): A Linguistic Comparsion and Assessment." In *Targum and Scripture: Studies in Aramaic Translations and Interpretation in Memory of Ernest G. Clarke*, edited by Paul V. M. Flesher, 79–95. Studies in the Aramaic Interpretation of Scripture 2. Leiden: Brill, 2002.

Swanson, Dwight D. "A Covenant Just Like Jacob's: The Covenant of 11QT 29 and Jeremiah's New Covenant." In *New Qumran Texts and Studies: Proceedings of the First Meeting of the International Organization for Qumran Studies, Paris 1992*, edited by George J. Brooke with Florentino García Martínez, 273–86. STDJ 15. Leiden: Brill, 1994.

———. *The Temple Scroll and The Bible: The Methodology of 11QT.* STDJ 14. Leiden: Brill, 1995.

Talmon, Shemaryahu. *Masada VI: Yigael Yadin Excavations 1963–1965 Final Reports Hebrew Fragments from Masada.* Jerusalem: Israel Exploration Society, 1999.

The Hebrew and Aramaic Lexicon of the Old Testament. Ludwig Koehler, Walter Baumgartner, and Johann J. Stamm. Translated and edited under the supervision of Mervyn E. J. Richardson. 4 vols. Leiden: Brill, 1994–1999.

Tigchelaar, Eibert. "The Cave 4 Damascus Document Manuscripts." In *The Bible as Book: The Hebrew Bible and the Judaean Desert Discoveries*, edited by Edward D. Herbert and Emanuel Tov, 93–109. London: British Library & Oak Knoll, 2002.

———. "A Partial Reedition of 4Q26a (4QLeviticus^{e}): A New Fragment and a Reinterpretation." *DSD* 21 (2014) 234–39.

———. "A Provisonal List of Unprovenanced, Twenty-First Century, Dead Sea Scrolls-like Fragments." *DSD* 24 (2017) 173–88.

Tov, Emanuel "4QLev^{c}." In *Qumran Cave 4: VII Genesis to Numbers*, 189–201. DJD XII. Oxford: Clarendon, 1994.

———. "4QLev^{d}." In *Qumran Cave 4: VII Genesis to Numbers*, 193–98. DJD XII. Oxford: Clarendon, 1994.

———. "4QLev^{e}." In *Qumran Cave 4: VII Genesis to Numbers*, 197–201. DJD XII. Oxford: Clarendon, 1994.

———. "4QLev[g]." In *Qumran Cave 4: VII Genesis to Numbers*, 203–4. DJD XII. Oxford: Clarendon, 1994.

———. "The Biblical Texts from the Judean Desert: An Overview and Analysis of all the Published Texts." In *The Bible as Book: the Hebrew Bible and The Judean Desert Discoveries*, edited by Edward D. Hebert and Emanuel Tov, 139-66. London: British Library & Oak Knoll, 2002.

———. "The Dimensions of the Qumran Scrolls." *DSD* 5 (1998) 69–91.

———. *Hebrew Bible, Greek Bible, and Qumran: Collected Essays.* TSAJ 121. Tübingen: Mohr/Siebeck, 2008.

———. "Rewritten Bible Compositions and Biblical Manuscripts, with Special Attention to the Samaritan Pentateuch." *DSD* 5 (1998) 334–54.

———. *Scribal Practices and Approaches Reflected in the Texts Found in the Judean Desert.* STDJ 54. Leiden: Brill, 2004.

———. "The Scribes of the Texts Found in the Judean Desert." In *The Quest for Context and Meaning: Studies in Biblical Intertextuality in Honor of James A. Sanders*, edited by Craig A. Evans and Shemaryahu Talmon, 131–52. BibIntSer 28. Leiden: Brill, 1997.

———. *Textual Criticism of the Hebrew Bible.* 3rd ed. Minneapolis: Fortress, 2012.

———. *Textual Criticism of the Hebrew Bible, Qumran, Septuagint: Collected Essays, Volume* 3. 3 vols. Leiden: Brill, 2015.

Tov, Emanuel, and Sidnie White. "Reworked Pentateuch." In *Qumran Cave 4. VIII: Parabiblical Texts. Part 1*, edited by James VanderKam, 187–352. DJD XIII. Oxford: Clarendon, 1994.

Tromp, Johannes. "Damascus Document IV 10–12." In *Flores Florentino: Dead Sea Scrolls and Other Early Jewish Studies in Honour of Florentino García Martínez*, edited by Anthony Hilhorst et al., 225–37. JSJSup 122. Leiden: Brill, 2007.

Tzoref, Shani. "Covenantal Election in 4Q252 and Jubilees' Heavenly Tablets." *DSD* 18 (2011) 74–89.

———. "The Use of Scripture in the Community Rule." In *A Companion to Biblical Interpretation in Early Judaism*, edited by Matthias Henze, 203–33. Grand Rapids: Eerdmans, 2012.

Ulrich, Eugene. "4QLev-Num[a]." In *Qumran Cave 4 VII Genesis to Numbers*, 153–76. DJD XII. Oxford: Clarendon, 1994.

———. "4QLev[b]." In *Qumran Cave 4: VII Genesis to Numbers*, 177–87. DJD XII. Oxford: Clarendon, 1994.

———. *The Dead Sea Scrolls and the Developmental Composition of the Bible.* VTSup 169. Leiden: Brill, 2015.

———. "The Evolutionary Growth of the Pentateuch in the Second Temple Period." In *Pentateuchal Traditions in the Late Second Temple Period: Proceedings of the International Workshop in Tokyo, August 28–31, 2007*, edited by Akio Moriya and Gohei Hata, 39–56. Leiden: Brill, 2012.

———."An Index of the Passages in the Biblical Manuscripts from the Judean Desert (Genesis–Kings)." *DSD* 1 (1994) 113–29.

———. "A Revised Edition of the '1QpaleoLev-Num[a]' and '1QpaleoLev[b]?' Fragments." *RDQ* 22 (2006) 341–47.

VanderKam, James C. *The Book of Jubilees.* Guides to the Apocrypha and Pseudepigrapha. Sheffield: Sheffield Academic, 2001.

———. "The Calendar, 4Q327, and 4Q394." In *Legal Texts and Legal Issues: Proceedings of the Second Meeting of the International Organization for Qumran Studies, Cambridge, 1995: Published in Honour of Joseph M. Baumgarten*, edited by Moshe J. Bernstein et al., 179–94. STDJ 23. Leiden: Brill, 1997.

———. "The End of the Matter? Jubilees 50:6–13 and the Unity of the Book." In *Heavenly Tablets: Interpretation, Identity and Tradition in Ancient Judaism*, edited by Lynn LiDonnici and Andrea Lieber, 267–87. JSJSup 119. Leiden: Brill, 2007.

———. "Exegesis of Pentateuchal Legislation in Jubilees and Related Texts Found at Qumran." In *Pentateuchal Tradition in the Late Second Temple Period: Proceedings of the International Workshop in Tokyo, August 28–31, 2007*, edited by Akio Moriya and Gohei Hata, 177–200. JSJSup 158. Leiden: Brill, 2012.

———. *From Revelation to Canon: Studies in the Hebrew Bible and Second Temple Literature*. JSJSup 62. Leiden: Brill, 2000.

———. "Genesis 1 in Jubilees 2." *DSD* 1 (1994) 300–21.

———. "The Manuscript Tradition of Jubilees." In *Enoch and the Mosaic Torah: The Evidence of Jubilees*, edited by Gabriele Boccaccini and Giovanni Ibba, 3–21. Grand Rapids: Eerdmans, 2009.

———. "Moses Trumping Moses: Making the Book of Jubilees." In *Dead Sea Scrolls: Transmission of Traditions and Production of Texts*, edited by Sarianna Metso et al., 25–44. STDJ 92. Leiden: Brill, 2010.

———. "The Origins and Purposes of the Book of Jubilees." In *Studies in the Book of Jubilees*, edited by Matthias Albani et al., 3–24. TSAJ 65. Tübingen: Mohr/Siebeck, 1997.

———. "The Pre-History of the Qumran Community with a Reassessment of CD 1:5–11." In *The Dead Sea Scrolls and Contemporary Culture: Proceedings of the International Conference held at the Israel Museum, Jerusalem (July 6–8, 2008)*, edited by Adolfo D. Roitman et al., 59–76. STDJ 93. Leiden: Brill, 2011.

———. "The Temple Scroll and The Book of Jubilees." In *Temple Scroll Studies: Papers Presented at the International Symposium on the Temple Scroll, Manchester, December 1987*, edited by George J. Brooke, 211–36. JSPSup 7. Sheffield: JSOT Press, 1987.

———. *Textual and Historical Studies in the Book of Jubilees*. HSM 14. Missoula, MT: Scholars, 1977.

Vermes, Geza. *Scripture and Tradition in Judaism: Haggadic Studies*. 2nd ed. StTB 4 Leiden: Brill, 1973.

Wacholder, Ben Zion. *The Dawn of Qumran: The Sectarian Torah and the Teacher of Righteousness*. HUCM 8. Cincinnati: Hebrew Union College, 1983.

———. *The New Damascus Document: The Midrash on the Eschatological Torah of the Dead Sea Scrolls: Reconstruction, Translation and Commentary*. STDJ 56. Leiden: Brill, 2007.

Wassen, Cecilia. *Women in the Damascus Document*. AcBib 21. Atlanta: Society of Biblical Literature, 2005.

Watts, James W. "The Historical and Literary Contexts of the Sin and Guilt Offerings." In *Text, Time and Temple: Literary, Historical and Ritual Studies in Leviticus*, edited by Francis Landy et al., 85–93. HBM 64. Sheffield: Sheffield Phoenix, 2015.

Weissenberg, Hanne von. *4QMMT: Reevaluating the Text, the Function, and the Meaning of the Epilogue*. STDJ 82. Leiden: Brill, 2009.

———. "The Centrality of the Temple in 4QMMT." In *The Dead Sea Scrolls: Texts and Context*, edited by Charlotte Hempel, 293–305. STDJ 90. Leiden: Brill, 2010.

Wellhausen, Julius. *Prolegomena to the History of Israel*. Translated by John S. Black and Allan Menzies. Edinburgh: T. & T. Clark, 1885.

Wentling, Judith L. "11QT Eschatological Temple and the Qumran Community." *RevQ* 53 (1989) 61–74.

Werman, Cana. "CD XI:17: Apart from Your Sabbaths." In *The Damascus Document a Centennial of Discovery: Proceedings of the Third International Symposium of the Orion Center for the Study of the Dead Sea Scrolls and Associated Literature, 4–8 Feburary, 1998*, edited by Joseph M. Baumgarten et al., 201–12. STDJ 34. Leiden: Brill, 2000.

Werrett, Ian C. "The Reconstruction of 4QMMT." In *Northern Lights on the Dead Sea Scrolls: Proceedings of the Nordic Qumran Network 2003–2006*, edited by Anders Klostergaard Petersen et al., 206–16. STDJ 80. Leiden: Brill, 2009.

———. *Ritual Purity and the Dead Sea Scrolls*. STDJ 72. Leiden: Brill, 2007.

Wevers, William J. *Notes on the Greek Text of Leviticus*. Septuagint and Cognate Studies Series 44. Atlanta: Scholars, 1997.

Weyde, Karl William. *The Appointed Festivals of YHWH*. FAT 2. Tübingen: Mohr/Siebeck, 2004.

Wilkinson, Robert J. *Tetragrammaton: Western Christians and the Hebrew Name of God: From the Beginnings to the Seventeenth Century*. Studies in the History of Christian Tradition 179. Leiden: Brill, 2015.

Wilson, Andrew M., and Lawrence M. Wills. "Literary Sources of the Temple Scroll." *HTR* 75 (1982) 275–88.

Wintermute, O. S. "Jubilees: A New Translation and Introduction." in vol. 2 of *The Old Testament Pseudepigrapha*, edited by James H. Charlesworth, 2:35–142. Garden City, NY: Doubleday, 1985.

Wise, Michael O. "The Concept of a New Covenant in the Teacher Hymns from Qumran (1QHA X–XVII)." 99–128 in *The Concept of the Covenant in the Second Temple Period*, edited by Stanley E. Porter and Jacqueline C. R. de Roo. JSJSup 71. Leiden: Brill, 2003.

———. "The Covenant of Temple Scroll XXIX." *RevQ* 53 (1989) 56–57.

———. *A Critical Study of the Temple Scroll from Qumran Cave 11*. SAOC 49. Chicago: The Oriental Institute, 1990.

Wise, Michael O. et al. *The Dead Sea Scrolls: A New Translation*. San Francisco: HarperSanFrancisco, 2005.

Wright, N. Tom. "Justification and Eschatology in Paul and Qumran: Romans and 4QMMT." In *History and Exegesis: New Testament Essays in Honour of Dr. E. Earle Ellis for His 80th Birthday*, edited by Sang-Won (Aaron) Son, 104–32. London: T. & T. Clark, 2006.

Yadin, Azzan. "4QMMT, Rabbi Ishmael, and the Origins of Legal Midrash." *DSD* 10 (2003) 130–49.

Yadin, Yigael, ed. *The Temple Scroll*. 3 vols. Jerusalem: Israel Exploration Society, 1983.

———. *The Temple Scroll: The Hidden Law of the Dead Sea Sect*. London: Weidenfeld and Nicolson, 1985.

Young, Ian. "The Stabilization of the Biblical Text in the light of Qumran and Masada: A Challenge for Conventional Qumran Chronology?" *DSD* 9 (2002) 364–90.

Zahn, Molly M. "Genre and Rewritten Scripture: A Reassessment." *JBL* 131 (2012) 271–88.

———. "Identifying Reuse of Scripture in the Temple Scroll: Some Methodological Reflections." In *A Teacher for All Generation: Essays in Honour of James C. VanderKam*, edited by Eric F. Mason, et al., 1:341–58. JSJSup 153. Leiden: Brill, 2012.

———. *Rethinking Rewritten Scripture: Composition and Exegesis in the 4QReworked Pentateuch Manuscripts*. STDJ 95. Leiden: Brill, 2011.

Zeitlin, Solomon. *The Book of Jubilees: Its Character and Its Significance*. Philadelphia: Dropsie College for Hebrew and Cognate Learning, 1939.

Index of Ancient Documents

OLD TESTAMENT

Genesis

Exodus

Leviticus

Leviticus (*continued*)

Leviticus *(continued)*

Leviticus (*continued*)

Leviticus (*continued*)

Numbers

Deuteronomy

PSEUDEPIGRAPHA (OLD TESTAMENT)

1 Enoch

Jubilees

DEAD SEA SCROLLS

1Q3 (palaeoLev)

1Q3 (palaeoLev–Num[a])

1Q3 (palaeoLev–Num[b])

1Q8

1Q20 (Genesis Apocryphon)

11Q13 (Melch)

11Q19 (T[a])

11Q20 (T^{b})

ALD (Aramaic Levi Document)

APU 2, DSS F.152 [Levi]

ArugLev

Damascus Document

Damascus Document (CD) Cairo Genizah copies

Damascus Document (CD) Cairo Genizah copies *(continued)*

Damascus Document (D)

Dearing Fragment DSS F.162 [Lev2]

Mas 1a (MasLev[a])

Mas 1b (MasLev[b])

MMT (*Ma'ase Ha-Torah*)

www.ingramcontent.com/pod-product-compliance
Lightning Source LLC
Chambersburg PA
CBHW051640230426
43669CB00013B/2378
* 9 7 8 1 5 3 2 6 9 2 2 2 2 *